EISENSTEIN AT WORK

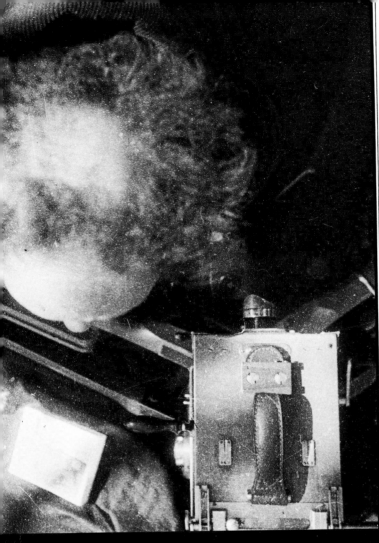

EISENSTEIN AT WORK

BY JAY LEYDA & ZINA VOYNOW
INTRODUCTION BY TED PERRY

PANTHEON BOOKS / THE MUSEUM OF MODERN ART: NEW YORK

This book is dedicated to Naum Kleiman, scholar and friend.

Library of Congress Cataloging in Publication Data

Leyda, Jay, 1910-
Eisenstein at work.

Bibliography: p.
Includes index.
1. Eisenstein, Sergei, 1898-1948. I. Voynow, Zina. II. Title.
PN1998.A3E556   1982   791.43'0233'0924   82-47874
ISBN 0-394-41262-1
ISBN 0-394-74812-3 (pbk.)   AACR2

Grateful acknowledgment is made to the following for permission to reprint previously published material:

The Dreiser Trust: Excerpt from *An American Tragedy* by Theodore Dreiser. Reprinted by permission of The Dreiser Trust, Harold J. Dies, Trustee.

Holt, Rinehart & Winston and Peter Viertel: Excerpt from *The Kindness of Strangers* by Salka Viertel. Copyright © 1969 by Salka Viertel. Reprinted by permission of Holt, Rinehart & Winston, Publishers, and Peter Viertel.

Selznick Properties, Ltd.: Excerpt from *Memo from David O. Selznick.* Courtesy of Selznick Properties, Ltd.

Authors' Note: Translations of notes that Eisenstein made in languages other than English appear in boxes beneath the drawings to which they apply.

CONTENTS

INTRODUCTION

THE HIROSHIGE WOODCUT (TOP) THAT INSPIRED EISENSTEIN'S SKETCH OF THE PROFILE OF IVAN THE TERRIBLE

Sergei Mikhailovich Eisenstein (1898–1948), the Soviet film artist, is best known for the motion pictures he completed: *Strike* (1925), *Battleship Potemkin* (1925), *October* (1927), *Old and New (The General Line,* 1929), *Alexander Nevsky* (1938), *Ivan the Terrible, Parts I and II* (1944, 1958). Few people know that Eisenstein was also a brilliant aesthetician and film theorist. His essays, collected in such English-language volumes as *Film Form, The Film Sense, Notes of a Film Director,* and *Film Essays,* are seminal works for the history of film and in the development of any film aesthetic. Even fewer people are familiar with Eisenstein's work as theater and opera director, as scene designer, as graphic artist, and finally as teacher.

The six completed films are only the most visible products of a rich life which embraced scores of other projects in film and theater, and extensive work as an aesthetician, pictorialist, and teacher. *Eisenstein at Work* demonstrates not only the diversity of Eisenstein's life but also its coherence. The work of the graphic artist complemented the visual sense of the filmmaker. Film teaching, film-making and the writing of film theory were all really the same task. The films depended upon the theoretical writing, and the essays were derived from the films. The teaching was made possible by the essay writing and the film-making. The most effective films taught the audience while the most successful teaching stimulated the most vital films. Because Eisenstein's work must be viewed in its entirety, no part can be understood without understanding the whole. The arrangement of the various elements into one fully realized composition is the achievement of *Eisenstein at Work.*

The numerous drawings done by the Soviet film-maker provide a convincing argument for the existence of separate but related careers. He began sketching at a very early age, filling notebook after notebook with unusually perceptive and skilled drawings which commented, often satirically, upon the human experience. In later years, as theorist and creator, Eisenstein continually sought a way to transmute his abstract concerns into perceptible form. To think through an idea, to give it discernible form, was to sketch it. Abstractions were encountered, grappled with, and rendered as visual ideas. To portray the cruelty of Ivan the Terrible, Eisenstein sketched a face which drew its inspiration from a savage bird portrayed in a Hiroshige woodcut.

As the Hiroshige woodcut suggests, many visual artists influenced Eisenstein. In a more general way his drawings implicitly reveal the broad range of his investigative, acquisitive impulses, and in a more specific way point to the artists who most impressed him. Daumier and El Greco were often acknowledged as direct influences. One can also see easily the presence of Jacques Callot, Goya, Piranesi, Gauguin, Michelangelo, and many others. There is an organic connection between the films, Eisenstein's drawings, and the work of sun-

THE SCENE FROM _IVAN THE TERRIBLE_ THAT WAS INSPIRED BY A PASSAGE IN THE AUTOBIOGRAPHY OF MARK TWAIN.

dry visual artists. To discover these sources through the drawings is to understand the visual style and structure of the films.

The drawings done in 1930–1932, while Eisenstein was in Mexico working on the ill-fated Mexican film, reveal the influence of pre-Columbian and Mayan artists, along with such contemporary muralists and painters as Diego Rivera, José Clemente Orozco, José Posada, David Siqueiros, and Jean Charlot. Each of the four episodes in _Qué Viva México!_ was to honor the visual inspiration of a particular painter. The Prologue was dedicated to Siqueiros and the Epilogue to Posada. Goya was to be celebrated in one novella and Orozco in another.

Just as the drawings provide us with a clue to the visual inspirations for Eisenstein's own work, so also can we discern a multitude of literary sources. Speaking, reading, and writing in at least four languages, Eisenstein was extraordinarily well-informed. His letters were filled with requests for more and more books, and he hounded his friends with pleas for specific titles which he could not find in the Soviet Union. More than one visitor to his home expressed admiration for his library. He boasted to one artist that he had everything published on Daumier. Often when a new project was offered to him he could begin his planning almost immediately, using his own books. More than once Eisenstein drew upon his literary knowledge. That a scene from _Ivan the Terrible_ should have as its antecedent a passage in the autobiography of Mark Twain, quoted below, demonstrates quite clearly the extensiveness of Eisenstein's literary resources.

The shooting down of poor old Smarr in the main street at noonday supplied me with some more dreams; and in them I always saw again the grotesque closing picture—the great family Bible spread open on the profane old man's breast by some thoughtful idiot and rising and sinking to the labored breathings and adding the torture of its leaden weight to the dying struggles . . . an anvil would have been in better taste there than the Bible, less open to sarcastic criticism and swifter in its atrocious work. In my nightmares I gasped and struggled for breath under the crush of that vast book for many a night. [*]

Eisenstein cited the powerful effect upon him of a story by Edgar Allan Poe, in which the author described looking out of a window and seeing a giant prehistoric monster pulling itself to a mountaintop, only to discover that this supposed monster was a tiny insect battling its way up a windowpane. It was, as Eisenstein explained in recalling the story, the kind of composition in depth which the camera could effectively capture.

Detective novels were of compelling interest to Eisenstein. He even planned a book on the works of "detection and deduction." In Will Durant's _Story of Philosophy_, Eisenstein found the inspiration for a film on Giordano Bruno. The study of Japanese culture provided new insights for his theoretical investigations. Characters in the Japanese language could be combined in order to create concepts: "From separate hieroglyphs has been fused—the ideogram. By the combination of two 'depictables' is achieved the representation of something that is graphically undepictable."[†]

After Joyce the great influence upon Eisenstein was Freud's study of Da Vinci. Through that work Eisenstein came to an understanding of the reasons for his investigative nature, of the organic relationship between his pursuits of theory and practice, and of the effect of his father's treatment of him as a young man.

Eisenstein at Work reveals how the Soviet film-maker's drawings, knowledge of graphic artists, and voracious reading were all necessary elements in his working process. Eisenstein's personal life also played an important role in the realization of his ideas. The visit which he made to Paris in 1906 furnished material for years to come. Specific sequences in _October_ were based upon a Méliès film, _400 Farces du Diable,_ and the wax figures at the Musée Grévin. The drapery he saw around Napoleon's tomb appeared in the drawings for _War and Peace_ in 1942.

The trip to Europe and America in the years 1929 through 1932 provided Eisenstein with direct, personal contacts among the most notable artists of his age. His appointment books cite meetings with Joyce, Cocteau, Max Ernst, Marinetti, Guilbert, and many others. Nor were his early engineering studies wasted, since these provided Eisenstein with

[*]Mark Twain, _Autobiography of Mark Twain,_ ed. Charles Neider, New York, Harper & Row, 1959, p. 41.
[†]Sergei Eisenstein, _Film Form,_ New York, Harcourt, Brace & Co., 1949, p. 30.

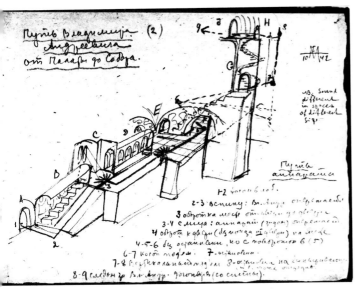

EISENSTEIN'S INTRICATE SKETCH FOR A SCENE FROM <u>IVAN THE TERRIBLE</u>.

an understanding and appreciation of the need for systematic planning. He developed intricate, detailed blueprints for each project, as his scripts and sketches testify.

Cruelty was a fact fundamental to Eisenstein's own personal life and to his films. He remembered quite vividly the pain he felt when his mother once denied that he was her son. The truly malevolent figure was the father, however, who persecuted the boy during his early years.

A French film which Eisenstein saw at an early age provided the most pervasive image of cruelty. A farmer had some prisoners working on his farm, and one of the prisoners, a sergeant, fell in love with the farmer's wife. The farmer had the man branded on the shoulder. Every time that Eisenstein had a cruel idea for a film, or for anything else, he would see the smoke rising from the prisoner's flesh. As Eisenstein said:

> In my childhood it gave me nightmares. It used to come to me at night. Sometimes I became the sergeant, sometimes the branding iron. I would grab hold of his shoulder. Sometimes it seemed to be my own shoulder. At other times it was someone else's. I no longer knew who was branding whom. For years on end, blond side-whiskers (the sergeant was fair) or black ones . . . evoked this scene from me. Until the time when . . . the ocean of cruelty in my own films swamped the impressions produced by this "fateful" film, to which, nonetheless, the cruelties were in certain respects indebted.*

The element of cruelty in Eisenstein's films was a complex working out of his own personal relationships with cruel and autocratic authoritarian figures. His father was one such person, but he also labored against the hatred and jealousy of his fellow film workers. The head of the Soviet film industry was for many years Eisenstein's enemy, blocking projects before they began, halting those already in progress, withdrawing prints from circulation, and ordering extensive editing of

some completed films. In 1930, while in Hollywood, Eisenstein was rejected by the very people who invited him to America and promised to produce his films. Jesse Lasky, then head of Paramount, showed no interest in Eisenstein's proposal to adapt Blaise Cendrars's *L'Or* (*Sutter's Gold*) or in his desire to do an original subject, *The Glass House*. After months of work on an adaptation of Dreiser's *An American Tragedy*, Lasky let their agreement lapse. The Upton Sinclairs agreed to be his new benefactors, and with their support he left for Mexico. After spending all of 1931 and part of 1932 filming *Qué Viva México!* Eisenstein was thwarted in his attempts to finish the film, one of the most important of his entire career. The unedited footage was to be shipped to him in the Soviet Union, but that never happened. He held the Sinclairs responsible for its demise and for preventing him from editing the footage which was shot.

Ivan the Terrible was the most complicated working out of this theme of cruelty, dealing as it does with the despotic figure of the Tsar. Cruelty is common, however, throughout all of Eisenstein's films. Horrible killings occur repeatedly. In *Strike* workers are murdered like oxen in a slaughterhouse and children are thrown from a rooftop. In *Battleship Potemkin* children and adults are massacred on the steps of Odessa. There is a vivid scene of barbarism in *Alexander Nevsky* when men and children are thrown into a fire. *Ivan the Terrible* contains repeated scenes of people being stabbed and poisoned. A father murders his own child in *Bezhin Meadow.* The tower of Timur in *Ferghana Canal* is constructed with tortured human bodies.

As his drawings indicate, Eisenstein became obsessed with cruelty and death during the time he spent in Mexico. Hundreds of sketches were devoted to the beheading of John the Baptist, the slaying of King Duncan in *Macbeth*, and the matador's ritualistic murder of the bull. The strain of his relationship with the Sinclairs may have motivated some of these drawings, but the predominant source of inspiration was Eisenstein's encounter with a primitive world where even death was celebrated, as in the Day of the Dead observances which fascinated him.

There is nothing unique about an artist drawing upon literary and artistic sources and his own personal experience. In Eisenstein's case, however, this natural process was magnified because of his insatiable appetite for information and experience. This particular artist, drawing upon his resources, happened to be a person of intense curiosity, a student of literature, the arts, language, politics, and science. Every subject compelled his interest. Other artists built upon their own resources, but because of his extraordinary, investigative mind Eisenstein surpassed them in the quantity of information and experience at his disposal. It was this same brilliant, acquisitive mind which animated and orchestrated the multiple careers of Eisenstein.

---

*Yon Barna, *Eisenstein*, Bloomington, Indiana University Press, 1973, p. 27.

Nowhere is the multifaceted nature of Eisenstein's career more obvious than in his devotion to theoretical investigation. In 1923 during his theatrical career, Eisenstein had published an essay entitled "The Montage of Attractions," based on his experiences in staging Ostrovsky's *The Wise Man* (1923). That same process, writing theoretical statements about a work in progress, continued during his film career. His first published book, *The Film Sense* (1942), brought together essays on which he had been working for years. As early as 1928 he began a project to produce a thorough analysis of his own films and the general aesthetic they contained. In 1946, just two years before his death, he had completed three-fourths of this book, *On Direction.*

The theoretical statements made by Eisenstein were an important part of his work, providing the means to articulate the problems posed and solutions found in his films. The films illustrated the subtle arguments in the written critiques. The films and the essays clarified and completed one another. Because of this reciprocity it is misleading to consider Eisenstein only as a film-maker or only as a film theorist. He was both; the theorist and creator were symbiotically joined. If there was a dominant mode, it was the theoretical.

> I make use of all available scientific data; I discuss with myself problems of programme and principle; I make calculations and draw inferences. I "dissect music" in the course of its progress, and sometimes anticipating its progress, with the result that its elements are buried in my drawers among heaps of material relating to principle. I stop writing the scenario and instead plunge into research work, filling pages and pages with it. I don't know which is more useful, but abandoning creative work for scientific analysis is what I am often guilty of. Very often I settle a particular problem of principle only to lose all interest in its practical application. *

Theory and practice were propelled toward one another in still another way. Eisenstein was also a teacher. During his early years in the theater, he taught the directing workshop for the Proletcult. In 1928 he began teaching at the State Cinema Technicum (GTK). While traveling through Europe and the United States, 1929–1930, he lectured extensively at such institutions as the Sorbonne, Cambridge, Yale, Harvard, and Columbia. The year 1932 found him appointed the head of the Department of Direction at the All-Union State Cinema Institute (GIK). His students worked with him on a number of projects. Exercises were elaborations upon the aesthetic issues he was confronting in his writings and in his films. The classroom was a laboratory of research, theory, and practice, reaching back into old publications, lectures, and films, and going forward to new enterprises.

Eisenstein's accomplishment consisted not only in the films but also in the teaching and the theoretical publications. *Ei-*

senstein at Work reveals the complicated interaction between the various components of Eisenstein's career, each part informing the others and coming together to create a whole. It is now more obvious how Eisenstein toiled, how he selected and distilled ideas into scripts, how he went about selecting people and locations, and what he hoped to achieve. This fascinating history is enhanced by an account of the various unfinished tasks on which Eisenstein labored. As examples of the kinds of ideas which attracted him and as illustrations of his working process, they provide us with important links in our understanding of Eisenstein's intellectual and artistic growth.

Some unrealized projects are of course common to any artist's career, but Eisenstein yet again exceeded the norm. *An American Tragedy* and *Qué Viva México!* were particular disappointments. When he returned from Mexico to the Soviet Union in 1932 he tried unsuccessfully to produce a motion picture on the history of Moscow, using some of the same strategies which he had planned for the Mexican film. His enemies were also successful in halting the *Bezhin Meadow* project, on which he had worked from 1935 to 1937. The signing of the German-Soviet Non-Aggression Pact in 1939 meant that his *Alexander Nevsky*, a completed film which depicted barbarous Germans, was withdrawn from circulation. The film then in progress, *Ferghana Canal*, was also halted. The one positive result of the pact for Eisenstein was that he was asked to stage *Die Walküre* for the Bolshoi Theater. With his usual enthusiasm he threw all of his energies into this new endeavor, attracted by Wagner's theories about an opera which would synthetically unite literature and legend, myth and music, color and sound, spectacle and spectator. Paul Robeson agreed to star in a film entitled *Black Majesty*, based on the novel by John Vandercook with some sequences taken from Vinogradov's novel *The Black Consul.* This labor was halted for lack of official interest. A film about Pushkin's life, *The Love of a Poet*, was extensively planned but never made; it would have been the first motion picture in which Eisenstein dealt with romantic love and with color. His sketches and notes for the Pushkin project depict a unique approach to the role of color in the cinema. The last years before his death in 1948 were filled with frustration. Part II of *Ivan the Terrible* was attacked and he had to mutilate it by removing the offending sections. He was prevented from editing Part III and the footage was subsequently destroyed.

In detailing a number of these unrealized efforts, *Eisenstein at Work* reveals not only the enthusiasm and erudition with which he approached each new challenge but also the formal issues with which he grappled. There is also a clear record of an indefatigable spirit who persevered in spite of many obstacles and disappointments.

Eisenstein had several professions and yet only one. To say

---

*Sergei Eisenstein, *Notes of a Film Director*, Moscow, 1959, p. 108.

that his life was polyphonic, a simultaneous combination of many parts, is to state one of the formal concerns which animated his work. As theorist, film-maker, and teacher, Eisenstein's multifaceted career was a mirror of the polyphonic construction he admired.

His interest in polyphony was evident very early when, in 1915, Eisenstein entered the Institute of Civil Engineering in Petrograd. In the course on bridge building he was fascinated by the task of assembling a pontoon bridge since it represented a unique orchestration of human efforts within the context of specific time and space coordinates.

Later when he was on duty during the Civil War he actually saw such a pontoon bridge being built across the Neva.

> The young recruits, like a throng of ants swarming along symmetrically laid-out paths, worked with precision and disciplined movements, endlessly assembling the bridge, which edged forward hungrily across the river. Somewhere in the midst of the ants, I, too was moving about . . . Everything fused into an amazing contrapuntal orchestration in all its varied harmonies and the bridge grew longer and longer . . . Men scrambled about. The minute hand raced round . . . hell, how splendid it all was! As it crept forward over the immeasurably vast breadth of the Neva, the pontoon bridge opened up to me for the first time the fascination of a passion that never left me! The irresistible force of its impression on me is easily explained; it impinged upon my consciousness at exactly the moment when my passion for art was beginning to take a step forward. *

The building of the pontoon bridge became a seminal image in Eisenstein's aesthetic. Something specific had been created out of the complex movements of men and material. Many things happening simultaneously with one effect, that was the polyphonic construction which fascinated him. For the rest of his life he sought to replicate such an event. It was the image of order and harmony for Eisenstein.

Almost all of Eisenstein's early work in the theater involved the use of simultaneous attractions. In his adaptation and staging of Jack London's *The Mexican* (1921), the action occurred in a parallel course on two planes. The audience, he thought, was thereby exposed to a more complicated emotional shock. The production he did with Yutkevich, a parody of *The Veil of Columbine* (1922), included a tightrope act during a scene seemingly unrelated to it. In the introduction to Ostrovsky's *The Wise Man* (*Enough Simplicity in Every Sage*, 1923), as a way of emphasizing the duality of Glumov's character, Eisenstein had him playing on two planes at once, leaping from one to the other and carrying over parts of dialogue from one scene to the next. As it changed context, the dialogue took on new significance and meaning.

The obvious awkwardness of having such events follow one another in rapid succession points up the reason why Eisenstein became convinced that it was not the theater but the cinema which most effectively could represent this notion of simultaneity, multiple attractions, or polyphony. The physical basis of the film-viewing experience was, after all, a complete expression of this idea raised to the level of dialectical materialism. The eye saw two discordant film frames and out of these synthesized motion. If film so accurately replicated, on the physical level, the materialist activity, then surely the medium lent itself to elaborating more complicated aspects of the materialist process. The eye could see two discordant attractions and out of these synthesize some meaning not contained in either attraction. Collateral stimuli within a shot, between two shots, or within a single image could be resolved by the viewer into a new experience. Counterpoint of sound and image would produce new understanding. The dialectic method, Eisenstein observed, "was the ne plus ultra of philosophy and the method of film, which was the ne plus ultra in today's stage of the development of art." If the medium lent itself to articulation of the materialist process, then surely it could be used to demonstrate historical materialism. While editing *October* in 1927, Eisenstein became so convinced of the possibility of this intellectual cinema, the film of ideas, that he began making plans to film Marx's *Das Kapital*. Simultaneity, montage, polyphony, fugue were all terms which Eisenstein used in his description of the elements at work in a materialist cinema.

Eisenstein thought of his film *Battleship Potemkin* as polyphonic. One sequence in particular had as its compositional strategy three elements: mist, water, and silhouettes. The events throughout the film were intended to be developed simultaneously on an epic plane, a dramatic plane, and a lyric plane.

The *Bezhin Meadow* project explored polyphonic construction. In Eisenstein's words:

> On the editing table this episode will be handled in the same way a composer works on a fugue in four voices. The material we are filming here is only one of the voices. Most of it will be used for rear-projection and transparencies when the second voice will be worked out—with figures and close-ups in the foreground. That is why the Armavir compositions are incomplete; spaces are being left for the second motif of the image. The third and fourth voices (or motifs) are in sound—sound and speech. †

Alexander Nevsky was considered by Eisenstein to be a fugue on the theme of patriotism.

In one scene in *Ivan the Terrible*, Eisenstein called for three voice lines to be woven into a polyphonic tapestry of sound and image. Ivan's overt actions and his consciously articu-

---

*Barna, *Eisenstein*, p. 59.

†Jay Leyda, *Kino*, New York, Macmillan Co., 1973, p. 330.

lated thoughts constituted one voice. The second voice consisted of his interior monologue, which was communicated by the song which the monk intoned. Present-day affairs, as spoken by Malyuta, were the third voice. In this case, as in all others involving simultaneity, it was in and through the collision of the individual voices, or stimuli, that the viewer created the meaning of the sequence.

Eisenstein's rough cutting notes for the "Maguey" section of *Qué Viva México!* call for three elements to be intercut: the dawn hymn of the peons, the formal meeting of Sebastián and María, and, throughout, the pulque industry of the hacienda.

A more complex form of polyphony was overtonal montage, a term which Eisenstein obviously derived from music. The simpler form of montage had been the arrangement of shots based upon their dominant element, often in conflict. Overtonal montage brought together pieces of film with primary and secondary stimuli which formed a more complex unity and acted directly, in a physiological way, on the spectator's senses. In *Old and New*, Eisenstein described the religious procession as being linked "not merely through one indication—movement, or light values, or stage in the exposition of the plot, or the like—but through a *simultaneous advance* of a multiple series of lines, each maintaining an independent compositional course and each contributing to the total compositional course of the sequence."* After detailing the seven separate lines, voices, or themes, Eisenstein noted that "the general course of the montage was an uninterrupted interweaving of these diverse themes into one unified movement. Each montage-piece had a double responsibility—to build the *total line* as well as to continue the movement within *each of the contributory themes.*"†

A different plan for polyphonic construction occurred in Mexico, where Eisenstein decided that the Mexican film would present the history of successive civilizations, not in vertical, chronological sequences, but on a horizontal plane. Various stages of Mexican culture would be unfolded as coexisting in a geographical context. Mexican history would be unraveled from the prehistoric days to the Spanish conquest, feudalism, and the Civil War, to the present day and finally projected forward to the country's future.

The unrealized project entitled *Moscow* which Eisenstein pursued after his return from Mexico was conceived as an account of Moscow's history through four centuries. A Muscovite working family would serve as the thread through the epochs; the history of Moscow would be told in and through the story of this one family. If completed, *Moscow* would have provided the means for realizing the ideas he had for portraying Mex-

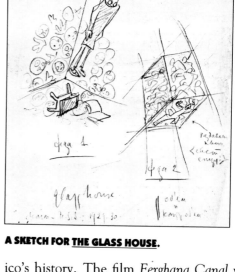

A SKETCH FOR THE GLASS HOUSE.

ico's history. The film *Ferghana Canal* would also have followed a similar pattern, tracing the history of Asia from antiquity to the present-day collective farms of Uzbekistan.

One of the clearest examples of how polyphony could serve as the generative idea for an entire film occurs in the notes and sketches which Eisenstein made for a never-realized enterprise entitled *The Glass House*. The undertaking drew its inspiration from a number of different sources: the visit to the new glass wonder which was the Berlin Hessler Hotel, some knowledge of Zamyatin's novel entitled *We*, and Frank Lloyd Wright's plans for a glass skyscraper. As early as 1926 and as late as 1947 Eisenstein made notes and sketches for the project. He was fascinated with the visual possibilities of seeing multiple actions in different parts of a glass house where opaque objects, such as rugs, would interrupt the line of sight and serve as compositional devices. Of utmost interest was the possibility that the same shot, or scene, could contain not only an action but also people, on the other side of the glass walls, seeing and reacting to the action. Eisenstein's term for such a film, stereoscopic, referred not only to the three-dimensional quality of the image but also, and more importantly, to the simultaneous interplay of the subjective and the objective. Instead of a shot of an event alternating with a shot of people's reaction, the objective event and the subjective reaction would take place within the same image.

No wonder Eisenstein would write on February 15, 1928, "on Saturday received *Ulysses*, the Bible of the new cinema." Eisenstein's fascination with Joyce and with his novel *Ulysses* centered around "his dual-level method of writing: unfolding the display of events simultaneously with the particular manner in which these events pass through the consciousness and feelings and the associations of one of his chief characters."‡

*Sergei Eisenstein, *The Film Sense*, New York, Harcourt, Brace & Co., 1942, 1947, p. 75.

†*Ibid.*, p. 76.

‡Eisenstein, *Film Form*, pp. 184–85.

Eisenstein's pursuit of a counterpoint between sound and image were based upon his awe of the way in which Joyce concurrently presented both objective and then subjective renderings. The counterpoint is evident in some of his plans for the "audiovisual polyphony" in *Bezhin Meadow*:

> In the scene, Stepok and his mother's corpse, distinctly:
>
> The boy's crying—by acting in shot. "The indifference of nature"—by the composition of the shot.
>
> The mother's death—music in the shot. This is the correct polyphonic scheme. It would be vulgar to do it this way:
> Cry with acting
> Crying with the composition of the shot
> Crying with the music.

It is misleading, however, to think that for Eisenstein polyphony was merely the simultaneous presentation of discordant events, or the concurrent presentation of objective events and the subjective responses to them. The concern with polyphony as a formal issue was not as it might seem merely a concern with an organizational principle. He was not interested in polyphony as a structural device but rather in the effect that polyphony had upon the viewer. The presentation of multiple stimuli, simultaneously and organically interrelated, provided the dialectical poles for the viewer to use in synthesizing his response to the film. Eisenstein's materialist conception required that the spectator be drawn into a creative act when experiencing the work. The viewer was not dominated by the author; the response to the film was developed in harmony with the author's purpose. Polyphonic construction, or montage in all of its meanings, became the formal device for overcoming the representational nature of the intransigent shots, making it possible for the viewer to create new thoughts and feelings.

To wrest meaning from a most uncooperative world was at the very heart of Eisenstein's aesthetic and his life. No understanding of the Soviet film artist can be complete which does not recognize the passion with which he sought to assert himself and the multiplicity of layers upon which he lived and worked simultaneously. The achievement of *Eisenstein at Work* is to clarify vividly that these various levels existed— teacher, theorist, creator—and to demonstrate categorically that any understanding must be based upon a grasp of all the particulars and how they interacted. Each film, drawing, lecture, essay stands alone and yet is also a part of a larger complex of activity, consisting not only of the completed efforts but also the unrealized projects, the plans, and the hopes. Going beyond any one endeavor, Eisenstein's achievement is the consuming aspiration which gave purpose and unity to his life. That he sought to achieve so much, with such genius, is the legacy of Sergei Mikhailovich Eisenstein.

Ted Perry / New York, 1980

RIGA & PETROGRAD

Following the triumphant release of his film *Alexander Nevsky* in 1938, Sergei Eisenstein received an invitation to join the Soviet Academy of Arts. The *curriculum vitae* which he prepared for this occasion, shown here in part, moves from his birth in Riga in 1898 until the document ends in 1938. In the chronology which follows here, excerpts from this document are italicized; other dates of interest have been added. See also the chronology at the end of the book.

Biography of S. M. Eisenstein.

1898 *Born in the city of Riga.*
[January 10; revised calendar, January 22.]
Son of a civil engineer. [Mikhail Osipovich Eisenstein; mother, Julia Ivanovna (née Konetskaya).]

1906 Visits Paris with his parents, sees Napoleon's tomb, the Botanical Garden, the waxworks of the Musée Grévin, and his first film, Méliès's *400 Farces du Diable.* (Left, below.)

1908 Learns English and French in addition to his German and Russian. In his father's library, reads *Les Misérables,* other novels by Hugo, Zola's cycle of *Les Rougon-Macquart,* and discovers Daumier's lithographs in a picture book of the Paris Commune. Enters the first class of the Riga city secondary school.
Organizes and leads a children's theater group with an enthusiastic ten-year-old named Maxim Strauch, whose family (von Strauch) lived in Moscow and summered on the Baltic Coast, and with other children of summer resort families. The group imitates performances seen in the Riga theater and even ventures into original works.
Becomes interested in drawing. A friend of his father suggests that the animal world might be easier to draw for his illustrated stories than human subjects. (The sequence on the following pages may have been drawn prior to his mother's departure for St. Petersburg in 1909.)

1909 His mother moves to St. Petersburg. He stays in Riga with his father. On a visit to his mother sees his first circus, returning as often as possible.

1910 Stages two acts of Hebbel's tragedy, *Die Nibelungen.*

1912 Attends the Riga performances of the touring Nezlobin Theater, sees Gozzi's *Princess Turandot.*

1913 Fills notebooks with "In the World of Animals," a series of satirical observations.

1914 Spends the summer in Staraya Russa with his mother, sees the religious procession for the opening of a new church.

1915 [May] *Completed secondary schooling in Riga and entered the Institute of Civil Engineering in Petrograd.* [September]

1916 Sees Meyerhold's production of Calderón's *Steadfast Prince* and Yevreinov's vaudeville theater. Studies history of the "theater of masks."

1917 *Mobilized and transferred to the Ensigns' Engineering School in Petrograd.*

1917 Feb. The Imperial Government overthrown. Sees Meyerhold's new production of Lermontov's *Masquerade;* sells his first political cartoons to the journal *Satirikon* and the Petrograd *Gazette;* buys Lukovsky's *History of the Ancient Theater.*

1917 Mar. Joins city militia and is called up for military service.

ABOVE: A SCENE FROM GEORGES MÉLIÈS'S 400 FARCES DU DIABLE, THE FIRST FILM SEEN BY EISENSTEIN, AT AGE EIGHT.

LEFT: SERYOZHA AT AGE SEVEN OR EIGHT.

PRECEDING PAGE: EISENSTEIN EDITING STRIKE.

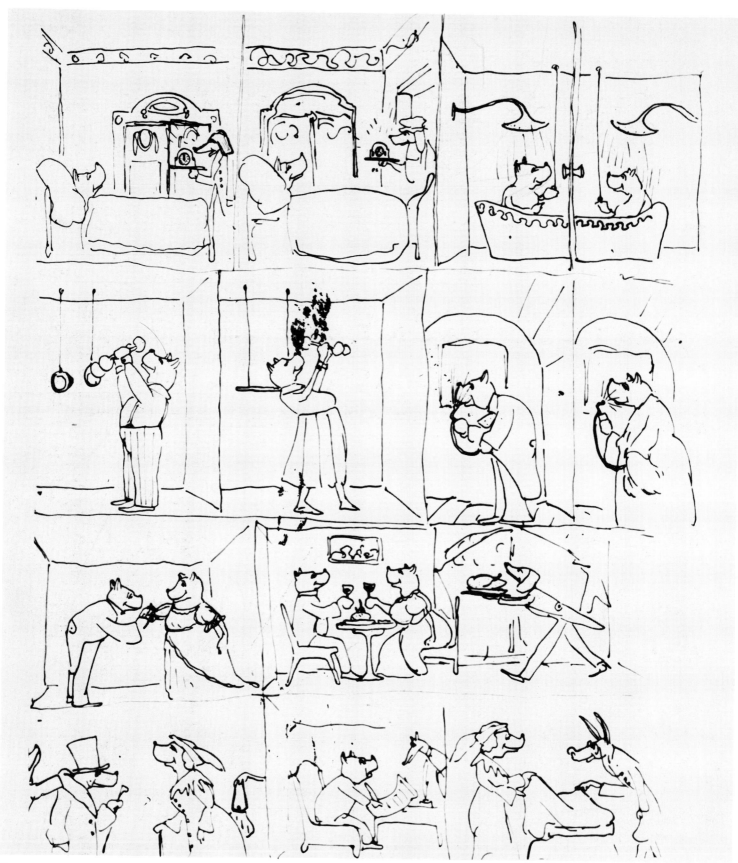

"A DAY IN THE LIFE OF A BOURGEOIS FAMILY."

1917 Jul. Participates in the demonstrations on Nevsky
Prospect.
1917 Aug. His section of the Ensigns' school is ordered to the
Front.

[Left] Papa wakes up. Mama wakes up in her separate bedroom.
They take showers. They exercise. Papa leaves for his office.
Mama shops for cloth.
[Right] Papa receives messages. Callers visit papa. Papa and
mama meet and take a carriage. They eat dinner. Indulge in
sports. Visit an art gallery. Go to the theater. Go home very tired.

1918 Jan. *After the Engineering School closes, returns to the Institute.*

1918 Feb. *Volunteers for construction of military defenses in Gatchina (for the defense of Petrograd).*

1918-1920 July *In defense construction, serving as draftsman, technician and adjutant to the chief of works, Gatchina, Vozhega (the Archangel Front), Dvinsk, Polotsk (the Western Front).*

FRONT-LINE THEATER

Polotsk-Smolensk-Minsk. Transferred to the Political Direction for the Western Front [PUZAP] to serve as designer for the front-line theater troupe. Decoration of agit-trains [mobile propaganda units].

Eisenstein's archives contain a large number of dated theater designs for his work with army theaters between 1917 and 1920. Although some of these designs may not have been realized in production, taken together they indicate the intensity of his theatrical studies even while he was moving from front to front.

1917 Sept. *La putta onorata* (Goldoni)

1917 Nov. *Les Millions de Pierrot* (pantomime by Eisenstein)

1917 *Hamlet* (Shakespeare)
First Die and Then You Can Be Honored (a translated vaudeville)
Dawn of the Red Alarm (Eisenstein)
Evolution of a Witch (Eisenstein)
Die Weber (Hauptmann)
Schluck und Jau (Hauptmann)

1917-1918 *Achilliade*
La donna serpenta, L'Augellin belverde,
L'Amore delle tre melarancie (Gozzi)

1918 Feb. *Les Fourberies de Scapin* (Molière)

1918 26 June *Birds, Clouds, Lysistrata* (Aristophanes)

July *The Slipper, or The Career of Prince Donkeysky* (farce begun by Eisenstein)

1919 June *Queen Theodora* (miracle-play or by Sardou?)

1919 June-1920 Jan. *Les douze heures de Colombine* (a "Grand Colombino-Arlequinade" by Eisenstein)

1919 July-1920 Aug. *La Princesse Maleine* (Maeterlinck)

1919 Summer *Red Truth, or, Red and Poor* (A. Vermishev)

1919 Oct. *Brand* (Ibsen)

1919 Nov. *The Two Gossips* (*Los Habladores,* by Cervantes?)
Woman for Sale (Thomas Hardy?)

1919 Dec. *Miracle of St. Nicholas* (*Le Jeu de saint Nicholas,* by Jean Bodel*)

1919 Miracle-play, *Notre-Dame* (one of several entitled *Un Miracle de Nostre-Dame*)
Bartholomew Fair (Jonson)

1919 *Volpone* (Jonson)

1919 *Peer Gynt* (Ibsen)

1919 *Erik XIV* (Strindberg)

---

*In L. -J. -N. Monmerqué, ed., *Théâtre Français au Moyen Age,* Paris, 1879. This appears to have been Eisenstein's chief source for medieval theater. The following title is also in this collection.

ABOVE: THE BIRDS (ARISTOPHANES).
LEFT: EISENSTEIN ON THE TRAIN CARRYING THE FRONT-LINE THEATER.

1919 Morality-play about Lazarus (*Moral a six personnages, c'est a scavoir, le Lazare, Marte seur de Lazare, Iacob serviteur de Lazare, Marye Madalaine et ses deux Seurs**)

1919? *Elga* (Hauptmann)

1919? *The King's Barber* (Lunacharsky)

1919? *A Play about George the Brave* (Rozanov?)

end of 1919 *Nymphs of the Ancient Gardens*

1919-1920? *Dubrovsky* (Napravnik's opera based on Pushkin's story)
Mysteria-Bouffe (Mayakovsky)

1919-1921 *Comedy of Power-Queen Isabella* (Eisenstein)

1920 Jan.-Feb. (repeat) *The Double* (Averchenko) (Eisenstein played the central role in this)

1920 8 Jan. (repeat 6 Feb.) *The Mirror* (Sluchaini)

1920 21 Jan. (*The Hacienda of*) *Donna Manuela*

1920 9-12 Feb. (repeat) *The Lawsuit* and *The Gamblers* (Gogol)

1920 Feb.-Mar. *Marat* (A. Amnuel, pseud. of N. Nikolayev)

1920 10 Mar.-1921 23 Sept. *Les Contes d'Hoffmann* (Offenbach)

1920 11 Mar.—16 June *Authentic Comedy about the Lustful Witch Tortellini, the Black Goat, the Just Judge, etc.* (Peregrinus Tiss, pseud. of Eisenstein)

1920 Apr. *Georges Dandin* (Molière)
Le Quatorze Juillet (Rolland)

1920 end of Apr. *Persian Stories* (from *Apollon*)

1920 May *The Wreck of the Good Hope* (Heijermans)
Wedding of the Banker Campozzi

---

*In *Recueil de Farces, Moralités, Sermons Joyeux*, No. 41, Paris, 1837; mentioned in Monmerqué, *Théâtre Français au Moyen Age*, p. xii.

1920 May-June *Comedy Without a Title—Cordelia* (Eisenstein)
The Haunted House (Plautus) and *The Eunuch* (Terence)
Jean et Madelein (Octave Mirbeau)
The Seminarist (Adapted by Eisenstein from Nikolai Pomialovsky)
Vanka, the Butler, and Page Jean (Sologub)
King John (John Bale or Shakespeare?)

1920 July-Sept. Morality-play, *The Builder of Cologne Cathedral*

1920 July-Oct. *König Harlekin* (Rudolph Lothar)

1920 Sept. *Comedy of a Page Who Stole the Young Princess's Heart*

1920 Oct. (repeated) *Marriage* (Gogol)

Oct. 1920 *Les Héritiers Rabourdin* (Zola)
Une Vieille Maîtresse (Barbey d'Aureville)

1920 *L'Avocat Patelin* (D. A. Brueys and Jean Palaprat)

1920 *Aglavaine et Sélysette* (Maeterlinck)

1920 *Tartuffe* (Molière)

1920 *The First Distiller* (Tolstoy, adapted by Eisenstein)

1920 *Vasilisa Melentyeva* (A. Ostrovsky)

1920 Two operas: *Demon* (Rubinstein) and *Yevgeni Onegin* (Chaikovsky)

1920 *King Henry IV* (Shakespeare)

1920 *King Richard III* (Shakespeare)

1920 *The School for Scandal* (Sheridan)

1920 *Amusing Interlude of Two Cavaliers in Love with the Same Girl* (Eisenstein)

1920 *The Victory of Mademoiselle Tamarina*

ABOVE AND RIGHT: BARTHOLOMEW FAIR.

ABOVE: EISENSTEIN'S EMBLEM FOR THE FRONT-LINE THEATER.

**BELOW: DESIGN FOR THE SECOND AND THIRD
SCENES OF GOGOL'S <u>MARRIAGE</u>.**

1920 *Miracle-play of an Emperor Who Murdered His Nephew
(Moralité . . . d'ung Empereur qui tua son nepveu*)*

1920 *Twelfth Night (Shakespeare)*

1920 *Savva (Andreyev)*

1920 *Los Intereses Creados (Benavente)*

1920 *Pot Bouille? (Zola)*

1920 Oct. *Commandeered by PUZAP to go to Moscow to study
Japanese language at the General Staff Academy (for the Eastern
Front). At the same time given the direction of the design
department of the Central Workers Theater of the All-Russian
Proletcult.*

1920 *In December leave the [General Staff] Academy to devote myself
solely to the Proletcult Theater.*

1921 Mar. *Begin working [at Proletcult] as codirector and designer.
First collaboration in the theater (with V. S. Smishlayev): "The
Mexican," adapted from Jack London. (I also take part in the
staging). [Starts workshop in direction (among his students:
Strauch, Alexandrov, Glizer).]*

1921 Apr. Design and direction collaboration on *King Hunger* by
Andreyev. At the last rehearsal of *Mysteria-Bouffe* (second
version) Eisenstein meets Meyerhold and Mayakovsky.

1921 May Opening performances of *The Mexican.*

1921 Spring *Apply and enroll [with Yutkevich] in the State Advanced
Directorial Workshop, under supervision of V. S. Meyerhold.*

---

*In Edouard Fournier, ed., *Le Théâtre Français avant la Renaissance*, Paris, 1872.

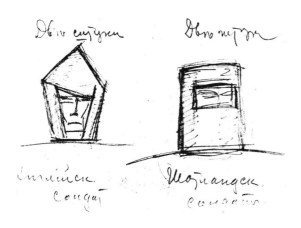

Eisenstein's work (chiefly as designer) in various Moscow theaters

Most of our information on Eisenstein's work in the theater comes from the period when, as a demobilized soldier, he arrived in Moscow and joined the Proletcult Theater. This period, from the work on *The Mexican* to the staging of *Gas-Masks*, frames most of his later references to his theater experience.

1921 Jan. *The Yellow Jacket* (George Hazleton)
Dawn of the Proletcult (V. Ignatov)

1921 Mar. *The Mexican* (Jack London, dramatized by B. Arvatov, V. Smishlayev, and Eisenstein)

1921 Apr.-July *King Hunger* (Andreyev)

1921 Oct. *Lena* [Goldfields] (V. Pletnyov)

1921 Nov.-1922 Apr. *Lady Macbeth* (finally shown as *Macbeth*)

1921 22 Dec. Meyerhold assigns a project to Eisenstein: *Puss-in-Boots* by Ludwig Tieck.

1921 *An Improved Relation with Horses* (Vladimir Mass)

1921 *Honest Harlequin* (for marionette theater)

1921-1922 *Le Comte de Monte Cristo* (Dumas)

1921-1922 *Meister Martin der Küfner und seine Gesellen* (Hoffmann)

1922 Jan. *Melodramatic Sketch* (Vladimir Mass)

1922 Feb. *Masks* (pantomime to Debussy's "Menestrels")

1922 May *The Veil of Columbine* (Eisenstein and Yutkevich, to music by Dohnanyi)*

1922 Sept.-Oct. *Patatra, or, The Break* (V. Pletnyov)

1922 *Precipice* (V. Pletnyov)

1922 *Child-Thieves* (*Les deux orphelines*, by Adolphe d'Ennery)

1922 *The Merchant of Venice* (Shakespeare)

1922 *The Phenomenal Tragedy of Phetra* (Foregger's parody of Tairov's production of Racine's *Phèdre*)

1922 *Heartbreak House* (Shaw), Meyerhold's commission, rehearsed but not performed

1922 *The Treaty of Ghent* (Vladimir Mass)

---

*A typescript has survived for an elaborate three-act satirical pantomime, *The Columbian Girl's Garter*, signed by Eisenstein and Yutkevich and dedicated to the "patriarch" Meyerhold.

LEFT: SKETCHES OF HELMETS FOR <u>MACBETH</u>. THE SOLDIER AT LEFT IS ENGLISH, THE SOLDIER AT RIGHT, SCOTTISH.

ABOVE: THE HELMETS FOR <u>MACBETH</u> REAPPEARED IN 1938 ON THE TEUTONIC KNIGHTS OF <u>ALEXANDER NEVSKY</u>.

MEYERHOLD'S ASSIGNMENT TO EISENSTEIN.

"Confidentially: my plan for staging: the [false] audience faces us as do the conductor of the orchestra and the prompter; beneath the stage: the playwright, technicians, and workers, Return immediately."

ABOVE AND BELOW: EARLY SKETCHES FOR <u>PUSS-IN-BOOTS</u>.

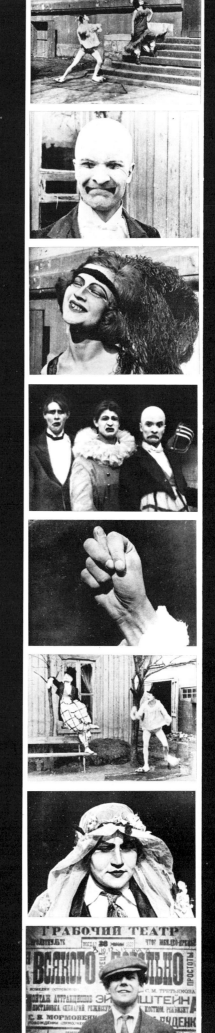

PROLETCULT: FROM SAGE TO STRIKE

1922 *Works as an apprentice on V. Meyerhold's production of "The Death of Tarelkin."*

1922 Autumn *Appointed director in Proletcult's Touring Theater. Leaves V. Meyerhold's theater. Proletcult Theater is given permanent quarters.*

1922-1923 Winter Attends Kuleshov's Film Workshop for three months.

1923 Mar. *I show my first independent production, "Enough Simplicity in Every Sage" [by Ostrovsky] (as director and designer, collaborating with S. M. Tretyakov on treatment of text).*

THE CONCLUSION OF EISENSTEIN'S FIRST SHOOTING SCRIPT.

> Yanukova / Yanukova (long shot) / Baby / Head of Strauch / Strauch (long shot) / Mashenka (close-up) / Legs / Mashenka and Glumov (close-up) / Check paid to organization (long shot) / Thumb / Trio [Pyriev, Antonov, Strauch] / Thumb / Trio / Grisha [Alexandrov] / I bow

ABOVE: EDITING STRIKE.
LEFT: SHOTS FROM EISENSTEIN'S FIRST FILM, USED IN THE STAGING OF ENOUGH SIMPLICITY IN EVERY SAGE.

ENOUGH SIMPLICITY IN EVERY SAGE

A feature of this circus-like satirical production was a short film interlude shown twice at each performance—at its place in the "story" and at the conclusion. For "Glumov's Diary," the untrained Proletcult group was given Dziga Vertov as advisor and Lemberg as cameraman. But, as Eisenstein observed, "after watching us take our first two or three shots, Vertov gave us up as a hopeless case and left us to our own fate." Lemberg also left, being replaced by Frantzisson. The filming was completed in a single day, and, as Proletcult had been warned about wasting precious raw film, each shot was filmed exactly as it was to be cut—nothing was left over from the 120 meters that were shot!

1923 Mar. Works with Esfir Shub on recutting of the two parts of Lang's *Dr. Mabuse* to a single film, *Gilded Putrefaction*, for Soviet distribution.

1923 Publication of Eisenstein's first theoretical manifesto, "The Montage of Attractions," based on the experience of *Sage*. In *Lef*, No. 3, 1923.

1923 22 Apr. *Rabochaya Gazeta* reports on Proletcult Workshop: ". . . physical training, embracing sport, boxing, light athletics, collective games, fencing, and bio-mechanics. Next it includes special voice training, and beyond this there is education in the history of the class struggle. Training is carried on from ten in the morning till nine at night. The head of the training workshop is Eisenstein."

1923 7 Nov. *Premiere of the production of S. M. Tretyakov's* [agit-guignole] *"Do You Hear, Moscow?"*

1924 Jan. *Premiere of the production of S. M. Tretyakov's "Gas-Masks".* [Feb. 29; staged in the Moscow Gas Works]

SCENES FROM **ENOUGH SIMPLICITY IN EVERY SAGE.**
TOP LEFT: TWO OF THE CLOWNS, MIKHAIL YURTSEV (ABOVE) AND M. ESKIN (BELOW). **TOP RIGHT:** OPENING SCENE. GERMANY (LEFT); FRANCE (RIGHT). **CENTER:** "HURRAH! THE BRIDE IS IN MY POCKET," READS THE SIGN ON THE MANNEQUIN OF GLUMOV.

OPPOSITE PAGE: EISENSTEIN (AT TOP) REHEARSING GAS-MASKS IN THE MOSCOW GAS FACTORY.

ABOVE: "THE FIGHT FOR THE FACTORY WHISTLE," THE MOST DIFFICULT
SCENE OF STRIKE. TISSE FACES OUT FROM CAMERA; EISENSTEIN IN SMOCK;
TWO EXHAUSTED ACTORS AT LEFT.

STRIKE

1924 Apr. Proposes to the First Studio of Goskino a cycle of
seven films for Proletcult showing the Russian revolutionary
movement before 1917, under the general title "Towards
Dictatorship of the Proletariat": *Geneva-Russia;
Underground; May Day; 1905; Strike; Prison Riots and
Escapes; October.*

". . . of the seven parts of 'Towards Dictatorship,' which is
impersonal throughout, only two have a mass character.
That is why one of these two, *Strike*, which is *fifth* in order of
the series, was chosen to be filmed *first*." The strike in one
factory is made a synthesis of many such clashes between the
workers and the owners, who are supported by the police
and their provocateurs. Script work on the cycle—by Valeri
Pletnyov, E. I. Kravchunovsky, Grigori Alexandrov, with
advice from Esfir Shub—was concentrated on the shooting
script of *Strike*. Boris Mikhin, head of the First Studio,
introduces Eisenstein to Edward Tisse, a Latvian
cameraman who had distinguished himself in newsreel work
during the Civil War.

1924 Spring *I begin my first film production, "Strike" (in
collaboration with Proletcult).*

1924 Dec. [actually Feb. 1, 1925]. *Public release of "Strike."*

At this point the Proletcult film group worked no further on
their "Dictatorship" cycle. It was the "Eisenstein group" that
prepared, instead, a film based on Isaac Babel's *First Cavalry
Army* stories, to be produced at Sevzapkino. In this interval of
desk work Alexander Belenson approached Eisenstein for information on the theories and methods at the base of *Strike's*
effectiveness, for a book he was preparing, *Cinema Today*, the
other film-makers being Kuleshov and Vertov. The most
quoted passage in Belenson's book (published by himself at
the OGPU print shop, in an edition of 10,000) is the montage
list for the bloody conclusion of *Strike*. Though Eisenstein
himself wrote disparagingly (" . . . see the book, *Cinema Today*, where, rather disheveled and illegible, my approach to
the construction of film works is described."), it appears now
that Eisenstein actually wrote, unbeknownst to his contemporaries, two manuscripts (in his hand and in the first person),
which have been found in the Eisenstein archive (The following translation is by Elizabeth Henderson).

THE MONTAGE OF FILM ATTRACTIONS

These thoughts do not aspire to be manifestoes; rather they represent an attempt at least to come to some understanding of our complex craft.

If we regard film as a means of producing an emotional impact on the masses (and even the Kino-eye people, who want, whatever the cost, to withdraw film from the category of Art, have made up their minds on this), then it follows that we must secure it in the impact category. In seeking ways to build the cinema we must make extensive use of the experience and latest accomplishments in those arts that set themselves similar tasks. First of all, of course, is the theater, which shares with the cinema the same *basic* material—*the audience*—and the same goal—*influencing this audience in the desired direction* through a series of calculated pressures on its psyche. I consider it unnecessary to expand on the meaningfulness of this sort of unitary ("agit") approach to cinema and theater, since it is quite self-evident and well-grounded from the perspective of social need (the class struggle) as well as from the very nature of these arts and the growing force of their formal peculiarities: a series of blows to the consciousness and feelings of the audience. Finally, only an ultimate striving of this sort can serve to justify entertainments that give the audience *real* satisfaction (physical and moral) as a result of *fictive* cooperation with what is shown (through motor imitation of the actions by the perceiver and through psychological "empathizing"). Without this phenomenon, which, by the way, alone causes the attractiveness of the theater, the circus, and the cinema, we would be able to overcome thoroughly the force of internalized social mores at a more intensive pace, and sport-clubs would count among their membership a larger number of those who depend on the physical development of their natures.

Thus the cinema, like the theater, is meaningful only as "one of the forms of pressure." Their means differ but they share a basic device, the montage of attractions. My work in the theater with Proletcult has confirmed this, and I am now applying it to the cinema. This is the path that liberates the film from the fictional plotting of the scenario and that, for the first time, takes film material both thematically and formally into structural account. Furthermore, the attraction approach provides criticism with a method for evaluating the objective expertise of theater or film pieces, replacing the printed exposition of personal impressions and sympathies mixed in with quotes from the usual political lecture popular at the given moment. An attraction (N.B.: See details in "The Montage of Attractions") in our understanding is any demonstrable fact (action, object, phenomenon, conscious combination, etc.) known and tested as a calculated effect on the attention and emotions of the audience. In combination with similar facts, it possesses the characteristic of concentrating the emotions of the audience in one direction or another, as dictated by the production's goal. From this point of view a film cannot be a simple show or demonstration of events; rather it must be a tendentious selection and juxtaposition, free from narrowly fictional tasks, molding the audience in accordance with its goal. (About *Kino-Pravda*: *Kino-Pravda* does not follow this path. Attractions are not calculated in its construction. It "grabs" you with the attraction of its themes and, in a purely superficial way, with its formal mastery in the montage of separate pieces, which hides under short metrage its "sexless," superficially epic "statement of facts".) The extensive use of all available means of influence does not make the cinema of attractions a cinema of finished style but a cinema of useful class action. It is class cinema because of its formal method, as the calculation of attractions is conceivable only for an audience whose homogeneous composition is known in advance. The method of the montage of attractions (the juxtaposition of facts) is even more applicable to the cinema than to the theater. I would call the cinema "the art of juxtapositions," because it does not show facts; instead, it shows conventional (photo) reflections (as opposed to "real actions" in the theater, when theater is using the technique we affirm); and, for the exposition of even the simplest phenomena, the cinema must juxtapose (by consecutive, separate means) the elements that compose these phenomena. Montage (in the technical, cinematic meaning of the word) is basic to the cinema: it is deeply grounded in the conventions of the cinema and in corresponding perceptions of cinema.

If in the theater an effect is achieved primarily by the physiological perception of an actual fact in process (for example, a murder), in the cinema the effect is produced by the juxtaposition and accumulation of associations in the psyche of the audience, which are needed for the film's task. These associations are aroused by the separate elements (montage pieces) of the analyzed fact. Only in the aggregate do these produce a tangential effect similar to and often stronger than the effect of the fact itself. (N.B.: Direct animal-spectator action through motor-imitative acts, which are similar to real acts, but differ from the pale shadows on the screen. I have tested such methods of theater action in my staging of *Do You Hear, Moscow?*) For example let us take a murder: the grabbing of a throat, eyes bulging out, the thrust of a knife, victim closes eyes, blood splatters on a wall, the victim falls to the floor, a hand wipes off the knife—each piece is chosen for "the provocation" of associations.

In the montage of associations an analogous process occurs—in fact, what is juxtaposed is not phenomena but chains of associations connected with the given phenomena for the given audience (N.B.: Understood in time (in sequence), which here plays not only the role of a sad technical condition, but also that of a condition necessary for the thorough inculcation of the association.) It is perfectly obvious that, for a worker and for a former policeman, the chain of associations released by seeing a meeting broken up and the corresponding emotional effect, in juxtaposition to the material which frames this scene, will be somewhat different. I have had occasion to test the correctness of this position quite definitively on one example, where, because of the failure to observe what I would call this law, the comic effect of a well-tried device fell flat. I have in mind the place in *The Adventures of Mister West in the Land of the Bolsheviks* where a huge truck pulls a tiny sled with Mr. West's briefcase. This [reverse] construction can be found among the variations of any clown act—from a tiny top hat to huge boots. Although the appearance of such a combination in the circus arena is enough to cause laughter, when the whole combination was shown on the screen in one shot the effect was very weak (even though it occurred while the truck drove through the gates, so that there was a short pause—as long as the cord from the truck to the sled). And, if in life a real truck is perceived immediately in all its immensity and compared to a real briefcase in all its insignificance, and it is enough to see them side by side, the cinema demands that the "reflection" of the truck be given first for a stretch of time sufficient to arouse the appropriate associations, before the incongruously light freight is seen.

I recall the construction of an analogous moment in a Chaplin film [*The Bank*, 1915] where a considerable length of film is spent on an endlessly complicated opening of the locks on a huge safe (N.B.: With the preliminary showing of several bank interiors), and only after this (and I believe even from a different angle) do we see the brushes, rags, and pail hidden inside the safe. The Americans also use this feature brilliantly for characterization—I remember the way Griffith "introduced" the "Musketeer," the gang-leader in *Intolerance*: a wall of his room is shown completely covered with pictures of nude women, and then he himself appears. How much stronger and more filmic this is than, for example, the presentation of the workhouse inspector in *Oliver Twist* [1922 ?] in a scene where he hurries two cripples; that is, he is revealed through an action (a purely theatrical device for sketching character through action) and not by arousing the necessary associations. From what has been said, it is clear that the center of gravity of effectiveness in the cinema is not opposed to the theater in direct *physiological* effects, although purely *physical* effectiveness can be attained sometimes (in a chase, with the montage of two pieces with opposing movements across the shot). It seems that no one has either studied or evaluated the purely physiological effect of montage irregularity and rhythm, even as used simply for narrative illustration (the story tempo that corresponds with what is being told). The montage of attractions and its device of juxtaposition should not be confused with the usual montage parallelism used in stating a theme nor with the similar storytelling principle used in Kino-Pravda, where first you have to try to guess what is going on and then you get intellectually involved with the theme.

Closer to the montage of attractions (though sufficiently compromised, it is true, in *Palace and Fortress* [1924], where the device is so naively laid bare) is the device of simple contrasting juxtapositions that often definitely produces a strong emotional effect (chained legs and the little feet of a ballerina, an example from *Palace and Fortress*). We must point out however that any *calculation of the juxtapositions* was completely ignored in the construction of the shots intended for this sequence—their construction does not aid association but disrupts it, and the juxtaposition does not enter the consciousness of the audience visually but as literature. For example, Nechayev, seen from the waist up, his back to the camera, beats on a barred door, and the prison warden, in a long shot, somewhere in a corner near a window, holds a canary in a cage. The chaining of the legs is horizontal—the ballerina's points are shot about four times larger, vertical, etc.

What is new in the montage of attractions is the juxtaposition of subjects with an emphasis on thematic effect. I refer now to the first version of the montage resolution in the finale of my film *Strike*—the massacre. For the finale, I adopted the associational juxtaposition of the massacre with a slaughterhouse. I did so, on the one hand, to avoid overacting in "the dying bit" by extras from the labor exchange and, more important in such a serious scene, to avoid falseness, which the screen does not tolerate and which is unavoidable with the most brilliant "dying," and, on the other hand, to squeeze out the maximum effect of bloody horror. The massacre is given only in "establishing" long and middle shots of 1,500 workers falling over a cliff, the crowd running, rifle shots, etc. And all close-ups are from the demonstration of the real horrors of a slaughterhouse where cattle are butchered and skinned. One of the montage variants was composed approximately as follows:

1. The head of a bull, the butcher's knife takes aim and moves upward out of the frame.
2. Close-up. The hand holding the knife strikes beyond the lower frame line.
3. Long shot. 1,500 persons roll down a slope—shown from the side.
4. Fifty persons raise themselves from the ground and stretch their arms forward.
5. Face of a soldier taking aim.
6. Middle-shot. A volley of gunfire.
7. The shuddering body of the bull (head outside the frame) falls over.
8. Close-up. The bull's legs jerk convulsively. A hoof beats in a pool of blood.
9. Close-up. The bolts of a rifle.
10. The bull's head is fastened with rope to a bench.
11. One thousand persons rush past the camera.
12. From behind bushes, a line of soldiers appears.
13. Close-up. The bull's head dies under unseen blows (the eyes glaze).
14. A volley, in a longer shot, seen from behind the soldiers' backs.
15. Middle-shot. The bull's legs are bound together in the Jewish custom/tradition (the cattle are butchered in a prone position).
16. Closer shot. People fall off a cliff.
17. The bull's throat is cut, blood pours out.
18. Middle close-up. People rise into the frame with arms outstretched.
19. The butcher moves past the camera (panning) carrying his bloody rope.
20. The crowd runs to a fence, breaks through it, beyond the fence is an ambush (in two or three frames).
21. Arms fall into the frame.
22. The head of the bull is severed from the trunk.
23. A volley.
24. The crowd rolls down the slope into the water.
25. A volley.
26. Close-up. Teeth are knocked out by the shot.
27. The soldier's feet walk away from the camera.
28. Blood flows into the water, coloring it.
29. Close-up. Blood gushes from the throat of the bull.
30. Hands pour blood out of a basin into a pail.
31. Dissolve from a platform with pails of blood . . . in motion towards a processing plant.
32. The dead bull's tongue is pulled through the slit throat (one of the slaughterhouse customs, probably so that the teeth will not damage it during convulsions).
33. The soldiers' feet walk away from the camera (a longer shot).
34. The skin is stripped off the bull's head.
35. Fifteen hundred dead bodies at the foot of the cliff.
36. Two dead skinned bulls' heads.
37. A human hand lying in a pool of blood.
38. Close-up. Filling the entire screen. The eye of the dead bull.

THE END.

The downfall of most of our Russian films is caused by makers who do not know how to construct schemas of attractions consciously; only from time to time do they fumblingly bump into successful combinations. An inexhaustible source of material for the study of these devices (on the purely formal, without content, level) is the American detective film and, to an even greater extent, the American comedy film (the device in its pure form). Griffith's films, if we saw them and did not know them merely from descriptions, would teach us a great deal about this kind of montage used with a social purpose alien to us. It does not follow, however, that we should "transplant" America, although in all areas the study of technical devices at first takes the form of imitation. What does follow is that we must train ourselves to select attractions from our own materials.

Thus, we are gradually coming to one of the most critical problems of today—the scenario. The first thing we must remember is that there is, or rather should be, no other cinema but agit-cinema. The device of agitation by using the spectacle consists in the creation of new chains of conditioned reflexes by associating selected phenomena with the unconditioned reflexes they evoke (through appropriate devices). (If you want to evoke sympathy for the hero, you surround him with kittens, which unconditionally enjoy general sympathy. Not one of our films yet has failed to show white [guard] officers engaged in revolting drunkenness, etc.) Keeping in mind this basic situation, we should treat with great care the question of fiction films; they have such a strong influence that we must not ignore them. I think that the attack against the very idea of fiction films has been provoked by the prevailing low level of scenarios as well as the technology of the performers. More on the latter further on. As to scenarios, with our approach we can conceive of making something different from the cozy little stories and romances with an intrigue, which for the most part (and not without reason) scare people away from such films. As an example of this kind of construction, I offer here the project for treating historical revolutionary material that I presented, which was accepted after long debates with the advocates of "rightist" everyday-life films (who dream of adapting for the screen either the life of some conspirator or notorious provocateur or an invented story based on real materials). (Apropos, historical, revolutionary material has been absolutely ignored by the cinema "seekers" and given over to the disposal and abuse of the right-wing directors: see *Andrei Kozhukov, Stepan Khalturin, Palace and Fortress!*)

Basic to my approach to this theme was to give an account of and to show the *technology of the underground* and to give *an outline of its production methods* in separate characteristic examples. How to sew boots—how the October Revolution was made. Our audience, trained to take an interest in production, is not at all interested in—and *should not be interested* in—the emotions of an actor made up to look like Beideman, or in the tears of his fiancée. What is interesting is the conditions of the Petropavlovsky prison—presented not through the personal sufferings of the hero but through the direct exposition of its methods . . . .

[The section omitted here deals mainly with the actors' tasks, quoting several works on human muscles and muscular control, including Eisenstein's own Proletcult brochure on expressive movement (A portion of this projected brochure was translated (as "Expressive Movement") by Alma Law for *Millennium Film Journal*, No. 3, Winter/Spring 1979); Lipps's *Das Wissen vom fremden "Ich"*; Duchenne's *Physiology of Motion* (1885); the propositions of Rudolph Bode (1921), as translated by Tretyakov, Heuppe (1899); Klages' *Ausdrucksbewegung und Gestaltungskraft* (1923); Nothnagel's *Topische Diagnostik der Gehirnkrankheiten* (1879); Behhügel, Krukenberg's *Vom Gesichtsausdruck des Menschen* (1923); and Vsevolodsky's *History of Theatrical Education in Russia.*]

An example of the ideal form of the verbal-rhythmic effect of movement (constructed on the basis of matching a sound schema as we match the schema of an expressive task) is the performer in a jazz band. His mastery of movement lies in an amazing use of a process of neutralizing the inertia of a big movement into a series of pantomimic and percussive movements and their combination with fine new motor elements. If this process were to be replaced by a combination of continually renewing innervations of the limbs (that is, if the jazz musician were not a good dancer), without regard for the rhythmic vibrations of the body, his exaggerated movements, ceasing to fit into an organic schema, would have the effect of pathological contortions (precisely because of their lack of an organic origin). This one example should be sufficient to confirm the rule of the preservation of inertia, the rule that determines how convincing a motor process is when the preservation of motor inertia renders it a unified action. Let us take as an example of this use of inertia the eccentrics of Fatty's [Arbuckle] film group. They use this device in such a way that, to each complex of complicated movement—liquidated under the conditions of one scene or another—they unfailingly lend a completely ungrounded, purely motor ending—always a brilliant little stunt because of their skill. In mechanical terms this is the device for discharging the accumulated supply of inertia going through an entire complex of movement. I will not go into the details of their method. I will only point out that for this kind of work what basically is demanded from the performer is the healthy organic rhythm of his normal physical functions, without which it is impossible either to master this system or to perceive it rhythmically from a clear screen. This is so despite the fact that, in the theater, the success of emotional infectiousness can be stronger because of the nervous imbalance that accompanies, or rather conditions, this precisely in a performer. (This has been tested on two of my actors—it was curiously difficult to find two or three "unsmeared" frames in a row at any tempo of their filmed movement, so imbalanced was the nervous foundation of their rhythm.) The question of fixation, which is so decisive for the screen, here follows as a natural consequence since, regardless of the outcome of any conflict depicted that conflict passes through a moment of equalization; that is, a state of rest. If there is too great a disproportion of forces, there can be no fixation and no expressive movement, for it becomes either an act or state of rest, depending upon which tendency dominates.

In this way we can realize a montage (assemblage) of movements that in themselves are purely organic. I would call them elements of working movement. The arrangement thus assembled involves the audience in imitation to a maximum degree and, through the emotional effect that this produces, in the appropriate psychic reworking. Moreover, this montage of movements as a whole also produces (though it is possible to construct it without this) the visual effect of the emotion supposedly experienced.

As we see, in the mechanics of their implementation the devices for processing the audience are no different from other forms of industrial movement and produce, first and foremost, the same kind of *real physical work* on their material—the audience.

With this approach to the work of the performer the question no longer arises of the "shamefulness" of acting (an association that has taken root thanks to the truly shameful devices of the emotional-experience school of acting). There will be no difference in the way a shoemaker sewing a boot or a terrorist throwing a bomb (re-enacted) is perceived on the screen because, proceeding from the identical materialist bases of their work, both of them first of all process the audience by means of their actions, the shoemaker playing (of course not intentionally but through the proper presentation by the assembler) on pride in well-organized production (more precisely, on illusory building together) and the terrorist, on the feeling of class hatred (more precisely, on its illusory implementation). In both cases emotional effect is basic. I think that this kind of movement, apart from its direct effectiveness, which I have demonstrated in the theater both in its tragic and comic aspects, would be the most photogenic. For a definition of what is photogenic one might paraphrase Schopenhauer's good old definition of the "beautiful." An idea expressed completely is photogenic; that is, an object is photogenic when it most fully answers to the idea of the purpose instilled in it. (N.B.: A definition that fully suits Delluc's observation that photogenic faces are those which in the first place possess "character," which for a face is the same thing we are saying about movements.) An automobile is more photogenic than a cart because its structure more fully corresponds to its purpose of transportation, etc. That the objects and costumes of earlier epochs are not photogenic (as noted, for example, by Delluc in the article translated in the journal *Veshch,* No. 3) can be explained, I believe, by the way they were designed. Taking costumes as an example, their design did not take the form of a search for normal clothing and special uniforms suitable for various kinds of production; that is, the forms most closely corresponding to the purposes for which they were intended—the "idea." Rather, design followed from purely accidental motivation, such as, say, the fashion of red-yellow combinations, the so called "cardinal sur la paille," in honor of the Cardinal de Rohan, imprisoned in the Bastille in connection with the affair of the "Queen's Necklace." Or lace headdresses "à la fontanges," in connection with the piquant episode of Louis XIV and Mlle de Fontanges who lost her lace pantaloons and saved the situation by quickly adding them to her already elaborate headdress. The search for functional forms of costume, the approach which makes possible photogenic dress, is characteristic only in recent times (noted, it seems, for the first time, by the Japanese General Staff). Consequently only contemporary costumes are photogenic. Work uniforms provide the richest material; for example, a deep-sea diver's costume. In the given case, the most photogenic movements are those that correspond most logically and organically to the phases of the flow of some action. Aside from theoretical probability, a practical indication that precisely this kind of movement is most photogenic is the example of animals, which are very photogenic and whose movements are structured strictly according to these laws; their automatic nature is not infringed upon by the interference of the rational principle (Bode). Labor processes which also flow in accordance with these laws have similarly been shown to be photogenic.

There remains for us to add to the system we have been elaborating one more circumstance that formally is more critical for the cinema than for the theater. For the cinema "the organization of the surface" (of the screen) is an extremely serious problem: the organization of the space encompassed by the frame is closely related to

graphic art; the flow of this surface and the continual juxtaposition of the surface thus organized in movement (the montage succession of frames) is specifically cinematic. I believe that in the matter of establishing consecutively necessary (in the form of a correctly constructed superstructure to movement) spatial correctives little remains to be added to Kuleshov's "axial system" that seems to elucidate this question comprehensively. Its one basic mistake lies in the fact that its inventors consider it the primary approach to movement in general, which results in its divorce from the mechanical and dynamic bases of movement—we do not have a smooth process of movement but an alternation of disconnected "positions" (poses). The motor results of this lead to grimacing instead of mimicry, to movement outside the energetic purpose of material work, to their own sort of mechanical doll. This undermines confidence in their extraordinarily valuable devices for the spatial organization of material on the screen. In this case only the personal taste of the director can serve as a criterion for staging, playing havoc with rhythmic schemas of peaceful scenes and resulting in chaos in the motor organization of fights and other energetically saturated places that demand, first of all, organization in subordination to the power and mechanical schemas, only after which they can be subjected to some sort of external shaping. This kind of approach inevitably must and does lead to stylization.

The attraction approach to the construction of all elements, from the film as a whole to the slightest movement of the performer, does not affirm personal taste or the search for a finished style for Soviet cinema; rather it affirms a method for handling montage, for influences useful to our class, and for the clear realization of utilitarian goals for the cinema in the Soviet Republic.

[signed] S. Eisenstein, Moscow, October 1924

THE YEAR 1905

1925 *Begin to work exclusively in films. Receive assignment from the Jubilee Committee of the USSR to produce "The Year 1905." Scenario by [Nina] Agadzhanova and myself.*

[The hectic months of 1925 are described by Eisenstein in these letters to his mother.]

1925 14 Apr. I begin to be eager for work again. *Konarmiya* [*First Cavalry Army*] has been temporarily shelved. In connection with this I have left Sevzapkino and in a few days I'll sign a year's contract at Goskino. . . . It will probably be at Goskino that I'll film *The Year 1905*—terribly interesting material. . . .

1925 3 May I'm about to go mad with work. I think I'll be traveling a lot this summer—to the south where I'll film a mutiny in the fleet. . . .

1925 2 July I'm making *1905*. Will start to film in a few days. July—in the country (outside Moscow–farms–and in the Tambov district). August, September (and perhaps October) in the south (Odessa and Sevastopol). The film is to be ready in a year (we're to give it in in August 1926). At

THE FIRST SCENES FOR 1905. LEFT: AN UNDERTAKERS' STRIKE. IN THE BOTTOM PICTURE, EISENSTEIN IS IN WHITE TROUSERS; IN FRONT OF HIM IS ALEXANDER LEVITSKY, THE EARLIEST CAMERAMAN FOR 1905. ABOVE: A PRINTERS' STRIKE. ALEXANDER LYOVSHIN AND MIKHAIL GOMOROV IN STRIPED SHIRTS. THE STRIKE AT MOSCOW'S SYTIN PRINT SHOP WAS ACTUALLY STAGED IN ODESSA. THE CAMERAMAN WAS YEVGENI SLAVINSKY.

the same time I'll be making *Benya Krik*, a scenario by Babel. (Do you remember reading those "Odessa Tales" in *Lef?*) Both very interesting. But the work is hellish . . . .

The first sequence taken for *1905* was shot in July 1925. The assistant Lyovshin had accidentally noticed some stored funeral equipment in a Moscow courtyard; when the planned first sequence could not be filmed on the first day, the group improvised a strike of undertakers' employees. The baroque and eccentric theater methods of *Strike* were still in control.

BATTLESHIP POTEMKIN

Alexander Lyovshin, one of Eisenstein's five assistants, tells of the working routine in Odessa:

After each day's filming, we rehearsed the next day's scenes before dinner. Alexandrov stayed near the camera, Strauch watched over the foreground, and the mass scenes were divided up among Antonov, Gomorov, and me, each being in charge of a hundred people. Antonov's group was to walk or run from one point to another, Gomorov's to move across them, and mine to move at an angle established by the camera's position that day. Each of us, representing our hundred, walked or ran through the rehearsed *mise-en-scène* while Eisenstein made corrections in the shooting script. Although 75 percent of the shooting script was ready in advance, most of the remainder was determined in these rehearsals. We were then ready to solve the balance during the next day's work. Our "Five" would now know what their tasks would be during the actual shooting.

1925 Dec. *Release of "Battleship Potemkin."*

1926 Jan. Eisenstein and Tretyakov plan *Zhung-kuo,* a film on the Chinese revolution.

1926 Mar.-Apr. *I* [and Tisse] *sent by Soyuzkino to Berlin to become acquainted with Western cinematography.*

Eisenstein and Tisse visit the UFA studio, meeting Murnau and Jannings working on *Faust.* They discuss the *Metropolis* plans with Lang, Rittau, Freund, and Thea von Harbou, with particular interest in the various uses of the moving camera.

The success of *Potemkin* encouraged its German distributor to move it into a larger cinema and to commission Edmund Meisel to compose a score for the theater orchestra. By the time of Eisenstein's arrival, Meisel had reached the last reel. Eisenstein's advice to him: "The music for this reel should be rhythm, rhythm, and, before all else, rhythm."

ABOVE: WORKING AT NIGHT ON THE POTEMKIN SCRIPT. LONDON HOTEL, ODESSA. THE DECISION HAS BEEN MADE TO JETTISON ALL OF THE 1905 SCRIPT EXCEPT THE POTEMKIN MUTINY. FROM LEFT, GRIGORI ALEXANDROV, YAKOV BLIOKH (PRODUCTION MANAGER), EISENSTEIN.
LEFT: PARS PRO TOTO [A PART FOR THE WHOLE]. THE PINCE-NEZ REPRESENTING THE DOCTOR IN POTEMKIN.
OPPOSITE PAGE: EISENSTEIN AND LYOVSHIN DURING THE RECONSTRUCTION OF POTEMKIN'S QUARTERDECK ON THE DISMANTLED TWELVE APOSTLES.

ABOVE: THIS SCENE OF ESCAPE THROUGH A FLOWER-SELLER'S DISPLAY—ONE OF EISENSTEIN'S LAST ECHOES OF THE ECCENTRIC THEATER—WAS NOT USED IN THE FINAL CUTTING.

BELOW: SHOOTING PLAN FOR THE BEGINNING OF REEL 4.*

ABOVE: THE CREW AT WORK OVER THE ODESSA STEPS. TISSE AND ALEXANDROV AT CAMERAS; EISENSTEIN WITH MEGAPHONE; LYOVSHIN AND GOMOROV ON LADDER; MAX STRAUCH SEATED BELOW.

BELOW: THE LADY SEEMS TO STEP ON THE WOUNDED CHILD, PLAYED BY ABRAM GLAUBERMAN. AT CAMERA, TISSE, WITH TWO REFLECTORS IN REAR; EISENSTEIN IN DARK GLASSES ON STEPS.

Potemkin. <u>Sailboats</u>
On two planes two leading themes, alternating and accompanying:
[Left column] Theme of sailboats / Crescendo, second theme enters, columns / Columns forced forward, sails in accompaniment / Arch materializes as sculptural group (sails in view—emotion)
[Right column] 2 persons / 3 [persons] in foreground; birth of "background" theme / Theme quickly comes to foreground and from static line into dynamics of struggle

*Post facto? This undated editing sketch may not have been made while *Potemkin* was in production. Possibly it belongs to Eisenstein's later analysis of *Potemkin;* it could be the draft for a series of frames drawn for an essay written in 1934.

THE GENERAL LINE BEGINS

1926 June Eisenstein and Alexandrov complete the scenario for *The General Line,* about Soviet agriculture policy and the links between the factory cities and the countryside.

1926 July Fairbanks and Pickford visit Moscow, are shown *Potemkin,* and invite Eisenstein to work at United Artists.

1926 Aug.-Sept. Eisenstein's group films old peasant huts and the death of the bull for *The General Line.*

1926 Oct. The team films in Rostov and Baku.

1926 Dec. Marfa's dream is filmed on the Mugan Steppe.

ABOVE: THE GENERAL LINE. EISENSTEIN BOOSTING TISSE FOR A HIGH SHOT (PROLETCULT-TYPE ACROBATICS ARE STILL USEFUL). THREE CAMERAS ARE USED TO FILM A HARD-TO-REPEAT SHOT.

BELOW: FILMING THE PROLOGUE FOR THE FIRST VERSION, 1926–1927. AT CAMERA, TISSE AND EISENSTEIN. ALEXANDROV'S REAL LEG IS ADDED TO THE MARBLE ONE.

TOP: FILMING THE REPAIR OF THE TRACTOR. FROM LEFT, GOMOROV, ALEXANDROV, TISSE (BEHIND CAMERA).

ABOVE: MARFA (FAR RIGHT) OBLIGED TO PLOW WITH HER COW. EISENSTEIN, STANDING, WITH DARK GLASSES: TISSE, BAREFOOT, SITTING ON MEGAPHONE.

A CLOSE-UP, USING TISSE'S REFLECTORS. EISENSTEIN STANDING, LEFT; GOMOROV AT CAMERA.

TOP: THE RELIGIOUS PROCESSION FILMED NEAR LENINGRAD. EISENSTEIN BEARING THE LARGE CROSS; GOMOROV WITH MEGAPHONE; TISSE IN CORK HELMET; STRAUCH DIRECTLY IN FRONT OF THE MOVING CAMERA TROLLEY, CONTROLLING ITS SPEED.

BOTTOM LEFT: FILMING MARFA AS SHE BEGS THE KULAK FOR THE LOAN OF A HORSE FOR HER PLOWING.

BOTTOM RIGHT: THE SHOT AS IT APPEARED IN THE FILM, SHOWING TISSE AND EISENSTEIN'S CONTINUING EXPLORATION OF "DEPTH OF FIELD" FOR DYNAMIC AND DRAMATIC PURPOSES.

ABOVE: EISENSTEIN SHOWING AN ACTRESS HOW TO DRINK TEA ELEGANTLY WHILE SITTING ON A HARROW.

ABOVE: THE BOOKKEEPER IS NOT QUITE SO DWARFED BY HIS BOOKS AS HE IS IN THE SKETCH BELOW.

BELOW: IN THE FILM ITSELF, THE BUREAUCRACY SEQUENCE BECAME LESS FANTASTIC THAN SKETCHED—THE CASHIER NO LONGER A ROOSTER, THE ABACUS BACKGROUND DELETED.

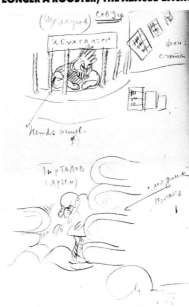

OCTOBER

IN FILMING THE WINTER PALACE I DID NOT OMIT CERTAIN EPISODES OF MY OWN BIOGRAPHY.

1927 *Commissioned by the Jubilee Committee for the Tenth Anniversary of the October Revolution to make a film (with Comrade Alexandrov), "October"—by 7 November 1927.*

In the summer of 1926, the Eisenstein group was assigned the 1917 anniversary film. They hoped that the shooting of *The General Line* could be finished first. However, as they began their research for *October* during the month in Mugan (shooting the tractor parade there), they recognized that the first film could not be concluded at the same time that *October* was to begin. Regretfully *The General Line* was put aside, unfinished. Signed by Eisenstein and Alexandrov, the *October* scenario was written in two parts, the first extending from the February Revolution to the taking of the Winter Palace and the opening of the Second Congress of Soviets, the second including the consolidation of power and episodes of the Civil War.* One of the first problems to arise after the acceptance of the scenario was "How is Lenin to be depicted?" The following documents are passages from the production diary that Maxim Strauch kept during the making of *October*:

> *31 January. We read aloud the shooting script, taken from the literary treatment. All satisfied. Eisenstein threw out the scenes of sabotage and consolidation of power as being superfluous after the capture of the Winter Palace. Actually, these could be the prologue to the new [second] film.*
>
> *Edward [Tisse] himself petitioned for the visa and license to get a new camera. They were quick to give him the license. Shvedchikov was furious. [He said] "Fine, now I know our workers can do dirty tricks, to undermine us." Edward became offensive. Eisenstein had to go over to patch up the incident.*
>
> *8 March. [At the commission for the October anniversary] they got to the reading of our October scenario. Podvoisky was taking notes so energetically that I got scared. I sent a note to Eisenstein: "It looks as though we'll have to spend an evening with Podvoisky, discussing things." The reading ended. Pelshe had listened to the whole scenario, with his face in his hands. Now he shook Eisenstein's hand and spoke to him—I found this quite moving.*
>
> *Knorin said: "This places a great responsibility on you. (Podvoisky interrupted, "This will be tougher than Potemkin!") The party is showing great confidence in you."*
>
> *Podvoisky agreed to go to Leningrad with Eisenstein to look at locations. Then added: "You know how stubborn I am, you'd better not argue with me! Better listen to me, and then later don't do it. But make a note of everything I say so that I have the impression I'm being listened to." Leaving, he yelled across the hall: "Eisenstein! Be prepared!"*
>
> *28 March. Can't find witnesses to the pulling down of Alexander III's monument. Finally located the architect Osipov, who was in charge of its destruction. Pieces of it are still stored in the cellars of the church of Christ Savior. So there we went! Padlocked and inscribed: "People's Commission to Preserve Monuments of Art." Dust. Wires rusted. Had to saw our way*

ABOVE: REHEARSING THE ATTACK ON THE WINTER PALACE. FROM RIGHT, NILSEN, GOMOROV, EISENSTEIN, ALEXANDROV.

OPPOSITE PAGE: AT THE HERMITAGE ENTRANCE. POINTING, ALEXANDROV; AT RIGHT, NILSEN, TISSE, EISENSTEIN; BELOW, ILYA TRAUBERG.

---

*This unrealized Part II is translated in *Eisenstein: Three Films*, New York, Harper & Row, 1974.

TOP: OCTOBER: THE FIRST SHOT. MARCH 13, 1927. AT LEFT, TISSE PLAYS A GERMAN OFFICER IN THE FRATERNIZING SCENE (DETAIL ABOVE). ALEXANDROV, BEHIND CAMERA; BEHIND HIM, EISENSTEIN; VLADIMIR NILSEN ASSISTING, CAMERA FRONT.

BELOW: FILMING THE QUEUE AT THE BREAD SHOP. APRIL 15, 1927.

through. Wandering along catacombs. Dust. 200 pieces of the monument. They couldn't drag it all here. Left eagle on the street. Found Alexander's head in another cellar. They had torn down the monument with "prehistoric" methods—ropes and clubs.

The entire crew participated, to some degree, in the vital process of finding the right faces—American film producers call this type-casting—but it was Strauch who had the chief responsibility for bringing his results (every possible person was photographed) to Eisenstein for final decisions.

12 April. Still hunting our Kerensky and Chkheidze. Even advertised in newspapers.

14 April. Tomorrow we're filming the hunger queue at the bread shop. But no gaunt faces! We even went to the TB clinics. We must have thin children. There aren't any! Whenever we find a thin child, his expression is too happy—the inside shows!—no sad eyes. I was at the labor pool—women's section. So we'll wrap up the women's faces, hide them in shawls.

Yesterday a very good officer type refused to come to the filming. I went to him first thing this morning. I even wore a new necktie and clean collar and horn-rimmed glasses. It worked—O the power of horn-rimmed glasses and pince-nez!

Schedule for night filmings of the attack on the Winter Palace:

	Stationed at the Admiralty & Nevsky	Stationed at the Arch	Stationed at Pevchesky & Millionaya
12 June	600 sailors 300 soldiers 100 workers	300 sailors 100 soldiers 700 workers	100 workers 100 soldiers 250 workers 250 soldiers
13 June	300 sailors 100 soldiers 100 workers	200 sailors 100 workers 500 workers	200 soldiers 200 workers
14 June	300 workers 75 women-defenders	300 soldiers 200 sailors	100 junkers

June 15, 16, 17, 18. On these dates, fewer "typages" were summoned for closer shots and close-ups.

In December 1927 two Harvard graduates, Alfred H. Barr, Jr., and Jere Abbott, arrived in Moscow for a visit. Both kept diaries. Barr met Eisenstein for the first time at Tretyakov's apartment on December 28, where Barr and Abbott were promised a screening in a fortnight of "parts of his two new films," *October* and *The General Line*. "Both were intended for the October celebration but were delayed." This and the following are excerpts from Alfred Barr's diary.

14 January. . . . with [May O'Callaghan] to the Russkino to see Eisenstein. He was extremely affable—humorous in talk, almost a clown in appearance. He studied (we learned later from Tretyakov) architecture at Riga, was an official artist during the war, worked with Meyerhold for a year, spent two years in the Proletcult and 1924 in the Kino. Potemkin was his second film.

We saw four reels of October—his revolutionary film which was supposed to be finished three months ago—and may be ready by February. His mastery of cutting and camera placement was clearly shown, especially in the July riot scenes. We didn't see the storming of the winter palace, which is the high point of the film. Certain faults appeared—he seemed to yield to the temptation of the fine shot—viz. the drawbridge scene [inserted:] the strangling scene. At times too the tempo was too fast. The film seemed, however, a magnificent accomplishment.

After October we saw his reconstructed film—the Generalnaya Linya, intended to show the differences between old and new methods of farming, cattle raising, dairying, etc. The parts were still uncut and gave us an excellent idea of Eisenstein's raw material—procession of Eikons—praying in fields—reaping with sickles—wind—rain—airplane propellor. We asked whether much of the excellence of Eisenstein's films did not develop in the cutting rather than in the shooting. He laughed and answered that the critics wrote of his filming as "always carefully premeditated," having a sense of humor. He hopes to come to America after The General Line is finished—perhaps in June.

2 February? To Eisenstein's to see about stills for articles on October and The General Line. Found him very weary. "Will you go on a vacation after October is finished?" "No, I'll probably die." We found out through Diego [Rivera] why October has been so delayed [not confided to diary].

15 February. After dinner (4:30) to Eisenstein's apartment. He received us with his customary comical remarks and pseudo-foot-in-the-grave manner. After we had gone thru a vast pile of stills from October and Generalnaya Linya (of which he generously gave us several dozen), we looked at his books on Daumier and the history of the theater—a very fine library with some scarce volumes. He reads all important European languages—and talks four of them. Daumier is his great hobby.

1928 14 Mar. Released for distribution the final version of "October," my scenario with Comrade Alexandrov.

ABOVE: THE CLIMAX OF THE OPENED BRIDGE.
BELOW: THE FIRST FILM SEEN BY EISENSTEIN, IN PARIS, 1906 —MÉLIÈS'S 400 FARCES DU DIABLE.

DAYLIGHT REHEARSAL (ABOVE) FOR NIGHT ATTACK ON THE WINTER PALACE (BELOW).

RIGHT: EISENSTEIN SEATED WITH MEGAPHONE.

OPPOSITE PAGE: FROM RIGHT, GOMOROV, EISENSTEIN, ALEXANDROV, NILSEN.

ABOVE: FILMING FROM THE SURFACE OF THE NEVA.

BELOW: A SCENE INSPIRED BY EISENSTEIN'S MEMORY OF HIS VISIT IN 1906 TO THE MUSÉE GRÉVIN, PARIS. ONE OF THE WAX TABLEAUX THERE SHOWED THE VENGEFUL CRUELTY OF THE PARISIAN CITIZENS TOWARD THE COMMUNARDS.

BOTTOM: EISENSTEIN HIMSELF POSING THE SCENE.

LEFT: EISENSTEIN DIRECTING NIKANDROV IN LENIN'S GESTURE FOR THE LAST SCENE OF OCTOBER.

Investigations

"ON SATURDAY RECEIVED ULYSSES, THE BIBLE OF THE NEW CINEMA."—FEBRUARY 15, 1928

The year 1928 is a high point in the history of Eisenstein's experiments. *October,* filmed in 1927, had provided a primary vehicle for the historical and "intellectual" cinema at which he had aimed since the beginning, exampled by such sequences as Kerensky's ascent to power and dictatorship and the parade of god-figures set off by Kornilov's banner "In the Name of God and Country."

While completing the lengthy process of the montage of *October* at the beginning of 1928, Eisenstein, through his experiments in the filming of abstract ideas, was led to hope that Marx's *Das Kapital* might be filmed. Notes that he made for this project, jotted down while in the cutting room, extend through March 1928, the month of *October's* general release.* Throughout 1928 he made public references to the filming of *Das Kapital* and finally, on December 16, 1928, felt obliged to explain these to his friend Léon Moussinac:

> The "proclamation" that I'm going to make a movie on Marx's *Das Kapital* is not a publicity stunt. I believe that the films of the future will be found going in this direction (or else they'll be filming things like *The Idea of Christianity* from the bourgeois point of view!). In any case, they [films] will have to do with philosophy. It is true that I won't get to this for another year, or year and a half, since the field is absolutely untouched. *Tabula rasa.* And it will be necessary to do a lot of sketching before trying to treat such an enormous theme without compromising it.†

In the same letter to Moussinac, Eisenstein suggests that the material for this new form will also be radically changed:

> I think I am ready to overturn my entire system. Thematically as well as formally. I think that we shall find the key to pure cinematography on the "other side" of the acted film—that is, in the film as newsreel, as well as in the film as itself. And, most amusing of all, this cinematography will be genetically ideological, for its substance will be the screening of . . . *Begriff* [concept, idea].

*Notes for *Kapital,* translated in *October,* no. 7.
†Léon Moussinac, *Sergei Eisenstein,* New York, 1970.

THE ONLY PICTORIAL RESEARCH IN EISENSTEIN'S ARCHIVE FOR KAPITAL WAS A PICTURE POSTCARD OF THE AGHA KHAN.

> On deity: Agha Khan—irreplaceable material—cynicism of shamanism carried to the extreme. God—a graduate of Oxford University. Playing rugby and ping-pong and accepting the prayers of the faithful. And in the background, adding machines click away in "divine" bookkeeping, entering sacrifices and donations. Best exposure of the theme of clergy and cult.

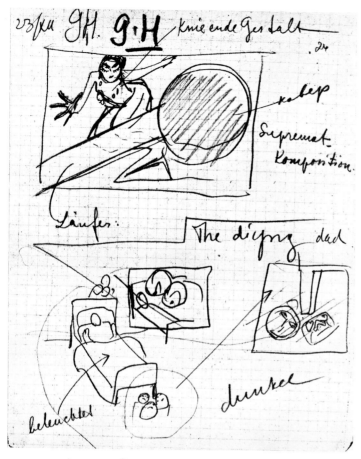

Another Project: The Glass House

When Eisenstein returned from Leningrad to Moscow to work on the cutting of *October*, ideas for *The Glass House* kept coming to mind.

> Today I've been thinking over—the American film that will have to be done with Sinclair. "Glass House" (invented in Berlin, Hotel Hessler, No. 73, mid-April 1926)—a glass skyscraper. A look at America through walls. Ironic, like [Anatole] France. Treatment to parody the material of real America—America seen through Hollywood clichés. Reality to be an element of parody, as if Hollywood clichés were factual element. Only Upton can help this.
>
> Explain to [Albert Rhys] Williams with his attitude of bourgeois gentility towards American conditions.
>
> And perhaps later it could be accepted by the Douglas Fairbanks Corporation [of United Artists]. Their definite invitation, dated 16 Dec. 1926, came yesterday. *January 13, 1927.*
>
> Take the most ordinary actions and change the point of view.
>
> Take the most traditional types and psychological collisions and change the point of view. For the first—polishing floors—rolling up carpets—cleaning and placing furniture.
>
> Do it as farce, as grotesque, as nightmarish tragedy.

Loneliness while constantly being "among people" and being seen from all sides.

Coldness of things. The cold of glass par excellence . . . That's where all the attempts to seek new points of view will be explored. For camera angles as well as for treatment.

Introduce a series of episodes with typically American "stars" playing various characters—and "kill" them with reality—real men.

Sergei Vasiliyev congratulated me on the idea of "G.H." How did he hear about this project? It was invented in Berlin. Hotel Hessler on Kantstrasse. Under influence of architectural experiments with glass. *September 17, 1927.*

All, all, all attention to "Glass House"!

1) Kummer [sorrow, despair]: Mantegna—from below
2) A white ball on the ground floor and a dismal zigzagging black figure on the floor above. Over their white circling.
3) Despair of man (from below) throwing himself on the floor. Rolling on the floor. In the six or eight floors above him, from the top floor to his room, lights are being turned on. Montage of the lighted floors. Final view of the gloomy heartlessness of the building. A nightmare of smooth glass.
4) Transitions from floor to floor—"diaphragmented" [dissolving?]—to a scene shot through the floor—a carpet rolls out and out step the characters on an upper floor, etc.
5) Prologue—a symphony in glass (non-objective). All forms. Glass hair and threads reach out. Surfaces, edges, objects, a glass automobile (saw in some magazine), house.
6) Unexpected characteristics —elegant, but then a close-up, a shoe-sole, sign of hopelessness.
7) "Floating" effect of heavy objects—light obliterates glass as a material substance and makes only solid objects visible.

Nudité.

8) On the contrary, the "play" of everything that is glass. At a different psychological moment.
9) Indifference to each other is established by showing that the characters do not see each other through the glass doors and walls because they do not *look*—a developed "non-seeing." Against this background one person goes crazy, because he alone *pays attention* and looks. All live *as though there are real walls,* each for himself. In tragic moments they see their neighbors. Lavish dinner in well-lit salon, while nearby are dark, hungry "cells" where people seem to be at the same table—but hungering. Well-fed ones do *not* look. Same theme as farce—pull a curtain over the wall. Contrasting a completely intimate mood, ignoring the "neighbors." There may be ideas for comedy here such as occurred in the ruined areas of Odessa or the administrative offices in Yalta and Sevastopol doing business in the open air after the earthquake.

10) Doors should be made of solid material. Strong symbol of convention. Generally accepted morality, relationships, established traditions, etc.

11) Major line can be built on the gradual growth of "seeing" by the inhabitants. They begin to see each other, to look at and pay attention to each other, and in a capitalist sphere this leads to chaotic hatred, violence and catastrophe. Explosion of passions until the house is in ruins. Introduce the thought that in itself technology is neutral and great—but that it can be used for mercenary ends.

Suddenly they realize that these walls can be "used." The psychopath makes them see this. A series of crimes take place. Blackmail attempts by one who spied on a cheating wife. The blackmailer should be a white-haired, very respectable lady. Spying on neighbor's documents, affairs, break-up of families, etc. Examples to be selected, not from these stereotypes, but from those most characteristic of the American way of life. Rampage of the "moral" police, private and official . . . (Hatred) In one of the rooms the furniture is set on fire, a mother with child and others watch it burn—watching through the glass—final scenes—during the atmosphere of crime. Society woman perishes in fire. She was set on fire by others . . .

Suicide in a single room with light on. He sees no one, but all eyes are on him. Watching with bated breath . . . . *September 18, 1927.*

During the hanging or the burning—the walls, floor, and ceiling seem made of faces. Especially effective—the floor and the ceiling. He walks on one and hangs from the other . . . . *November 16, 1927.* [See 1947 drawing, p. 42.]

Shadow of figures embracing, seen on frosted glass of door (more precisely on a door made of frosted glass). All else is transparent; he sees only the shadows on door and doesn't see them through the transparent glass. This is for an episode during the early part, before the transparency of glass is perceived . . . . Associative material for G.H.: "But the Emperor Has No Clothes!" *January 4, 1928.*

In the cutting room of *October* ideas for the filming of *Capital* took the place of notes for *The Glass House*, though this project was by no means forgotten. On December 23, 1928, in the turmoil of revising *The General Line*, Eisenstein formulated an outline in six "acts" for *The Glass House*—in Russian, French, and English (for by this time the group's trip abroad was being discussed):

Prologue. History of glass from ancient times through foolish uses of glass.

1) Unconsciousness (a curiosity for the public).
2) Jesus. Consciousness. Shame.
3) Shame—speculation.
4) Speculation—conflicts.
5) Tragedy—catastrophes.
6) *Epilogue.* The wrecked house.

Alternating with frame compositions. Perhaps for the premiere worth trying a monster screen—four times the usual screen size?

Why not???

Sometime between the completion of *October* and the resumption of *The General Line*, Eisenstein squeezed in a rest in Gagri, where his new copy of *Ulysses* received a thorough study, making it as significant in his development as was Freud's study of Leonardo da Vinci.

The jointly signed "Statement on the Sound-Film,"* with its emphasis on the counterpoint of sound and image, came directly from Eisenstein's excitement in the discovery of *Ulysses.* Joyce's use (if not invention) of the "interior monologue" dominated all of Eisenstein's first sound-film projects. On December 14, 1928, unable to try out interior monologue on film, Eisenstein experimented on himself, hastily writing (mostly in English) a "stream of consciousness à la Joyce (somehow set off by V[aleska] Gert)," who was in Moscow at this time, working for Tairov.

> Blode ! ! (Blodsinn) [Stupid!!(Nonsense)]
> If I'll be quite disappointed in my art potence—I'll write my very scrupulous autobiography in that super-exact manner of Joyce's descriptions of Bloom. Putting all the associations that [cluster?] around the sentence or idea I am writing. . . .

In May 1928, for the first time since his theater classes at Proletcult, Eisenstein resumed formal teaching at GTK (State Cinema Technicum, later GIK and VGIK). He hoped to arrange his ideas and methods into a book, *Direction.* The remainder of the year was filled with "corrections" and the montage of *The General Line.* (Andrei Burov, architect of the model farm in the new film, discussed with Eisenstein a film *about* architecture.) In August, Tokyo's leading Kabuki theater visited Moscow, giving Eisenstein his first, exciting experience of Japanese theater and enhancing his theoretical and experimental progress. He invited actor Ichikawa Sadanji to his GTK classes to demonstrate Kabuki's relevance to film.†

---

*Originally published the summer of 1928.

†The essays that show the immediate stimulation of his experience of Japanese art are "The Unexpected" (1928) and "The Cinematographic Principle and the Ideogram" (1929); both are translated in *Film Form.*

EISENSTEIN READING JOYCE's <u>ULYSSES</u>. GAGRI, 1928.

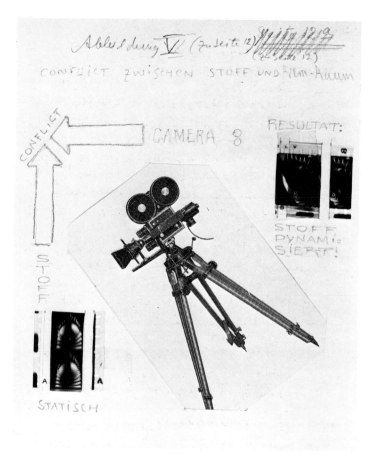

EISENSTEIN'S COLLAGE FOR HIS ESSAY.

CONFLICT BETWEEN MATERIAL AND FILM SPACE
[Clockwise from left] STATIC MATERIAL, CONFLICT,
CAMERA = RESULT: MATERIAL MADE DYNAMIC!

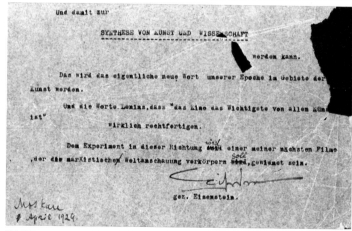

ABOVE: THE CONCLUSION TO THE GERMAN TEXT.

And we may yet have a
SYNTHESIS OF ART AND SCIENCE
This would be the proper name for our new epoch in the field of art.
And the words of Lenin, "The cinema is the most important of all the arts,"
would be fully justified
I shall devote one of my next films, which is to embody Marxist studies, to an experiment in this direction.
Moscow, April 1929

THE GENERAL LINE BECOMES OLD AND NEW

Eisenstein wrote his essay, "A Dialectic Approach to Film Form," in German, selected illustrations for it,* and prepared this photo-montage (left).

1929 Autumn *I am sent by Soyuzkino to America to study American cinema in response to the invitation of, first, United Artists, and then Paramount.*

1929 was a crowded year for Eisenstein. *The General Line* had to be completed (with changes and, pressed by Stalin, a new title, *Old and New*), and preparations had to be made for the group's trip abroad (August) and the taking of the newly cut *Old and New* with them prior to its public release in Russia. In April Eisenstein prepared texts of essays he planned to offer foreign journals. One of the *Old and New* scenarios was to be published in Germany. Perhaps the most important plan carried from Moscow was for a sound version of *Old and New* (dated August 17, 1929), the financial and technical arrangements having been assured for a London production.† On June 4, 1929, Eisenstein wrote to Moussinac: "It is my obsession to add sound to *Old and New*. Have to do that abroad. I'm still not sure if everything will go as I like it. That's why this must stay *entre nous*." Meisel was to compose the score—his third for Eisenstein—and Eisenstein outlined his ideas very precisely:

Kinds of sound:

1. Musical
2. Natural surroundings
3. Animated cartoon [rhythmically synchronized—the term "mickey-mousing" is still in use in American recording studios (1982)]

Degrees of sound:

1. Rapid [slow motion]
2. Animated cartoon [an exaggeration of No. 3 sound, above]
3. Special types of distortion of a purely acoustic sort (to be found)
   (*Volume* of sound and related volumes of sound to run counter to the norm.)

Use:

1. "Choppy" montage in relating sounds of *one* category
2. Different categories "Bull in the sky"
3. Through distortion, move glissando from sound to sound and from category to category
   Leitmotivs through *all* types (timbres) of sound
   Recording distortion of leitmotivs

---

*Reproduced in *Film Form*, between pp. 52 and 53.
†The promised financing for the London recording of *Old and New* was withdrawn.

Complex counterpoints—"That's no way to live!":
Sound, frame, and musical elements treated alike

Conflicting resolution "accompaniments":
1. In opposition to the frame
2. In words opposition to the inter-titles
3. Words or sounds unrelated to the content of the frame, but related to the perception of it (meadows and "Ach")

Multiple exposures of sound, i.e., orchestral resolutions using tones, noises and, perhaps, words during the recording
Disproportion of sounds in such resolutions
All leitmotivs are vivid and light. Simple in rhythm (easily remembered) and refined in timbres (in music, noise, artifice, etc.)

PART I

1. [Credits and first] inter-titles. Direct crescendo to explosion on "the old way"
2. Landscapes—from explosion directly into lyricism (an abrupt leap)
   —Slavonic leitmotiv
3. Peasant hut—Asian and Scythian leitmotiv
4. Sawing the hut in half—a crosscut saw
5. Dividing the fields—transition to a circular saw
6. Transition to poor peasants—deformation of the saw sound (Zeitlup) into sobbing
7. Marfa—music—Marfa's leitmotiv
8. "That's no way to live!"

Marfa throws down the plow	Boom
"That's no way . . ."	Pause
Marfa and plow	"That's no way . . ."
Marfa	Thunder
"That's no way	"That's no way . . . . ."
	(climax)

   There is a distinction between the thunder's "heavy tread" and the cutting rhythm
   "That's no way to live!"—a muffled drum beats out the rhythm of the phrase
   As meeting is introduced—a sharp fanfare might begin (cornet-a-piston)
   The fanfare becomes shrill laughter
   Distortion of the saw sound into laughter
   Animal laughter
   (The whole treatment of "That's no way to live!" is a breaking up of the explosion.)
9. Meeting—the rhythmic base is the sound (rumbling) of the explosion, dominated by a fanfare, becoming shrill and turning into laughter. Cascade of laughs
10. Agronomist—introduction of a leitmotiv—the industrial theme
11. Group—perhaps under [the music of] *Rusalka* (the wedding scene), but only a hint

PART II

1. Drought and panorama—bells
2. Procession—increasing sound of bells. Over close-ups of singers comes the music of "Lord save us" (later a chorus, but perhaps chorus is not necessary; i.e., singing might be done with closed mouths—that's better). Bowing increases in power. There is such an intensification of bells and drums that they are no longer perceived as identifiable sound. Prolonged moans over last shots of bowing supplicants. As the procession approaches the place of prayer—transition to sound of distant silvery bells
3. Prayer in the field—the complexity of the procession is increased by the introduction of a condensed rhythmic accompaniment. The accompaniment is stimulating (somewhat like the accompaniment of "Valencia"). Rapid breathing (naturalistic breathing of a dog but in the rhythm of a sheep). Then the sheep are shown
4. "A hoax?"—pause (and also in separator). Snatches [of sound]. Pause. Snatches [of sound], etc. Naturalistic sound of sniffling. And only after the shot of a cloud there is a single bleating of a sheep
5. Separator—industrial motif. Must find ecstatic gradations of timbres, corresponding to the ecstatic gradations of the shots (fountains, printed letters of the alphabet, etc.)
   Consider a line of "kind (happy) laughter" ("Path of October" collective farm, wedding, separator, skirts, finale)

PART III

1. Dream—distortion of the mooing sound (leitmotiv of bull?)
2. Clouds—distortion of mooing
3. Marfa sleeps—music resembles grandma's music-box
   Use unchoppy cutting and double exposure of sound in order to bring the corresponding mooing into foreground (alternate Marfa's music and mooing)
4. Music-box—timbre. Music is Marfa's leitmotiv.
   Then transition of the same type of construction into staccato: as bull ascends the mooing reaches a climax
5. Leap
6. Rain of milk—("prasseln")
7. Leap
8. Cloud—thunderous mooing
9. Leap
10. Rain of milk, etc. (choppy montage)
11. Beating up of Marfa—continue line of animal laughter heard at meeting
12. Agronomist—enters with the industrial leitmotiv

PART IV

1. Wedding—"lyricism"—Negro chorus. Parody on Fomka's motif with Hawaiian guitar

Growth of Fomka—crescendo of Fomka's leitmotiv. Choppy. With each jump in Fomka's growth the sound gets stronger. Without transition. This same figure is repeated in Fomka's running. There they fuse

The "Attack"—terrifying increase

Cow spreads her legs—complete pause. Then sound of gunfire and an apogee of mooing. Second pause (in darkness). Shout over pause. Theme of calves. Galloping calves. (Calves in ecstasy)

Title "The Bride"—each time with a fanfare. Distortion of fanfare sound into crying of a baby. Fanfare sound into the mewing of a cat

2. "Happy laughter"—field appears. "Ach"

Harvest—the whole *gamma* of sound effects, from galloping horses to motorcycles and ending with the rockets of the Oppel automobile. Perhaps in combination with brass instruments

Race—race gong. Stop. Catches up. Decide about unusual pauses. Then pauses will merge into chirping and into

3. Grasshopper—distant chirping. At first muted and melodic, then over [shots of] grasshopper it becomes sharp, staccato chirping against a general background of melodic sounds of the fields

4. Machines—the industrial theme in a wild tempo

PART V

Beginning—a field of rye, like an ocean tide
Typewriter—comic distortion of the industrial theme (though beginning seriously). A "Slavonic flavor" comes into the industrial theme. (Here we must find a special distortion, not of content but in the nature of the optical distortion that is achieved with 28 lens.)
Composition made from waltz and typewriter keys
Harvest—naturalistic wind and rain. Return to wind.
Title -waltz
Medals [and prizes]—superpresto. Title-waltz, extremely slow
Death [of bull]—"pure" music. Musical treatment of leitmotivs

PART VI

"Scandalous episode with tractor"—treat industrial theme in "Slavonic flavor"
"The Chase"—"Americanized" Slavonic music
Tractor parade—merging of Slavonic and industrial lines into a line of pathos
Lyrical finale—merging of both lines on a lyrical plane

General Comments

Conflict in the argicultural theme (negative) is located in the sentimental Slavonic melody and the industrial theme (positive) is treated in terms of modern Western music.

Precision in the development of leitmotivs: for example, the development of the bull theme is attached to the industrial theme. Slavonic mode is tragic (the peasant hut), tragic-lyric (the bull's death), utterly repulsive in the laughter and division of money. Industrial [theme] is "comic" with typewriter, tractor, etc. This is the key to all decisions. Follow it forcefully—and consistently.

EUROPE

"I WON'T REALLY BE SURE I'M GOING UNTIL I'M ON MY WAY BACK FROM THERE!"

1929-1930 Spring *Visited Berlin, France, England, Switzerland, Netherlands, Belgium.*

Presented lectures, notably at the Sorbonne, Paris, at Cambridge University, etc.

The first stop on the way to Hollywood was Berlin. Eisenstein, Alexandrov, and Tisse arrived there with the twenty-five dollars apiece that Soyuzkino had given them for expenses. Living arrangements had been made for them in Berlin, but from then on until they boarded ship for America they had to earn their way, chiefly through Eisenstein's name and reputation. He had brought writings to sell (the scenario of *Old and New* was published) and a friend and student, Obolensky, helped find film jobs for all of them, while Eisenstein met people and visited places that he wanted to see in Berlin (including his father's grave in Charlottenburg).

Their first jobs included work on an advertising film for beer, with Emil Jannings and George Bancroft (then in Berlin); "friendly consultation" on Mikhail Dubson's film *Giftgas*; work with Tisse on *Frauennot-Frauenglück,* a film about abortion for the Swiss producer, Lazar Wechsler; and work on a comically allegorical film on the "independent cinema" made at the Congress in La Sarraz (negative lost by Hans Richter on the train). Alexandrov and Tisse made *Romance Sentimentale* for Leonard Rosenthal (the "pearl king" of Paris) whose Russian mistress, Mara Gry, wished to sing in a film. Between November 10, 1929, and January 1930, Eisenstein shuttled between England and France. His datebook for 1930 begins with the conversations that resulted in Alexandrov's *Romance Sentimentale.*

EISENSTEIN IN SWITZERLAND HELPING TISSE WITH HIS FILM.

Jan 6		Maison de Perles de M. Rosenthal
		8 chez M. Rosenthal Parc Monceau
Jan 7		Phone Nuller[?] Tual pour Lisieux
Jan 8		[Jacques] Rivière [at] Trocadero
		[Jean] Painlevé's Musée Zoolog.
	1 heure	Darius Milhaud
	4 heures	Zervos Cahier d'Arts
	5 heures	Jean Cocteau
	9 heures	Marinetti
Jan 16	11	Samlung Van Gogh von Kröller-Müeller
[*Netherlands*]		
Jan 22	10:30	Prometheus [Films]
[*Berlin*]	11	Lenin Tag
[*Eisenstein's*	2 Uhr.	Prof. Levin & Köhler
32nd birthday]	5 Uhr.	Annie bei mir
	7 Uhr.	Schatzow
	9½	Hans Sachs
Jan 23	9	tel Sternberg
	11	H. Feld, F[ilm] Kurier
	12	Torgpredstvo [the Soviet trade office]
	12½	Michelsohn
	2½	Balazs
	3½	Alf[red] Kerr/E. Toller Montagu
	6½	Richter
	8½	Asta Nielsen
Jan 26	5	Einstein W. R. Kaiser
Jan 28	9	Départ pour Bruxelles
Feb 5	7:45	Ches les Cadix les Cadix Sadoul,
[*Paris*]		Jourdain, Vaillant
Feb 6	6	A Tobis. les Essais de montage de Sons
Feb 7	12	Chez M. Siccard [?]
		Déjeuner avec De Layr.
	4:30	chez Bella Hein
	5	Ière rencontre avec Max Ernst aux
		2 Magots
	6	Film d'Edward
	7	Tobis
	8	Sicard will phone
		Balazs will phone
	12½	[Eli] Lotar
	11	at Dick's [Blumenthal?]
	2	at Hein's
		Derain (?)
	4-5	Préfecture
	9	Fashions [?]
Feb 13		Soirée chez Gunter
		Faire la connaissance de la Veuve de John Reed
Feb 14		Telephoner á Brosse
	4½	Comédie Fr-se. Répétition Cocteau
	5½	Dôme [?]
	7½	Diner chez Mme Hein
		Aragon, Eluard,
Feb 15	2¼	Comédie Française
		Répétition de Cocteau [La Voix
		Humaine]
		Scandal Eluard*
	9	Entretien avec Frenkel
Feb 16	4½	Salle Pleyel (gr)
		[Nicholas] Nabokoff
Feb 17		Lecture at Sorbonne with screening of "Gen. Line"
		[screening cancelled by police]
Feb 18		Dej. avec Max Ernst

19	4	Chez Keim. [rue] St. Peres pour Derain
24	8	Dinner at Tzara's [who introduced him
		to Gertrude Stein's circle]
25	6	Visite a Gance aux Studio de Joinville.
		Bobino. 2 × 2 + 6 (Pieds)
		"Papa" (Marseillaise)
26	2-7:30	Versailles. Palais Parc. Trianon × 2
		(Herzen's grandson) Legendre childhood
		friend
		John Reed's girl
		Evening with Allendy
27	3	Exposition d'Art nègre
		(Afrique Oceanie) Vernissage
	5-6	Ministère de Justice
	7:30	chez Léonard (Architect)
		Théâtre Palace
		"Good News" [by De Sylva, Brown, and
		Henderson]
28	2¾	Conférence Corbusier (Louvre)
	4:30	Chez Derain
		Galeries Lafayette
	9 h	avec Moussinac & Lévy
		Paris-Soissons
		Termin für Berlin
Apr. 21		Arrivée Paris 12
	1 h	Iᵉʳᵉ entrevue avec Jesse Lasky
		Hotel George V
22		Montagu telephones from Los Angeles
23	10	Rendezvous avec Mr. Kaufmann
		(Paramount) at Hotel George V
25	1	Déjeuner chez Mara Gry
		pour Mrs. Lasky & Junior
26	11:45	Interview with Jesse Lasky
		Contract with Kaufman
		photo [by Man Ray? André Kertész?]
		I recognize L[asky] son! [in the wrong
		club]
27	1½-7½	last interview with M. G. [Mara Gry]
28		Cable: Sidney [Bernstein] Pearl [Attasheva]
		Mother
	4	Campbell (contract)
	5½	chez Yvette Guilbert
29	1	Cafe de Paris. Iᵉʳᵉ séance au sujet des
		sujets.
30	5	Contract
May 1		telephoner á 11 heures
	1 h	Café de Paris
2	10:45	Consulate U.S.A.
	11:30	Tager au Paramount
3		Je signe le contract avec Dick Blumenthal

*According to Robert Phelps (ed., *Professional Secrets: The Autobiography of Jean Cocteau*, New York, Farrar, Straus & Giroux, 1970), the performance was broken up by the Surrealists, in the person of young Paul Eluard, who had managed to get in by coming with Cocteau's guest, Sergei Eisenstein. "From the balcony, Eluard started to shout that the play was obscene, that it was actually about Cocteau and his current boyfriend. The lights came up and Eluard was spotted. Hustled out into the hall, he was surrounded by a hostile crowd, and even burned with someone's cigarette, until rescued by Cocteau himself. Then the play was resumed. . . ."

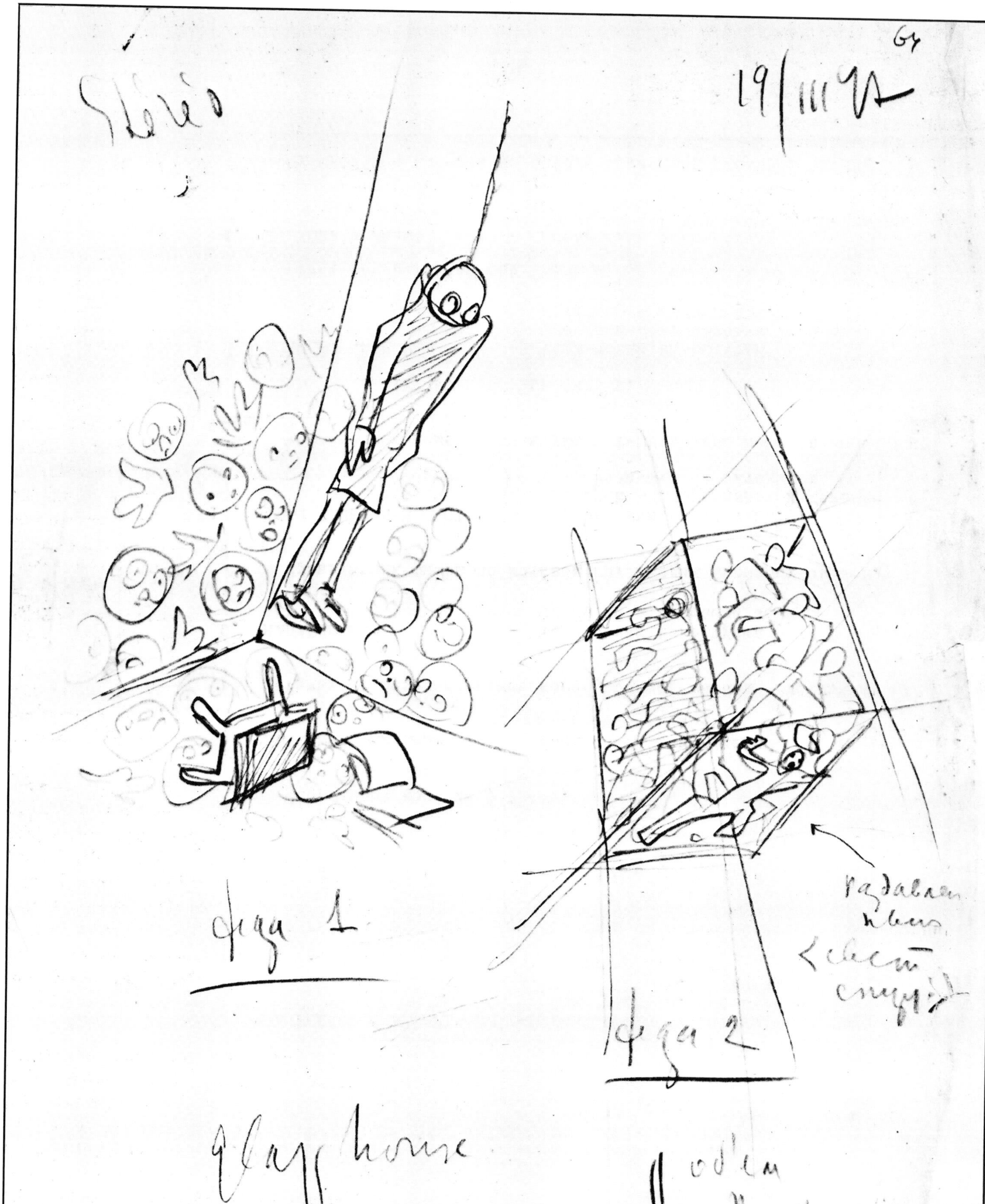
фиг 1
фиг 2
Glass house

HOLLYWOOD & PARAMOUNT

KNOWLEDGE IS COMPARING.
ON THE "TWENTIETH CENTURY," OCTOBER 13, 1930

1930 *In accordance with decision of Soyuzkino I proceed to Hollywood, to Paramount (together with cameraman E. Tisse and G. Alexandrov). Develop scenario based on T. Dreiser's novel "American Tragedy," and we part because our sociological approach to the theme does not correspond to their demands. We depart (in December) from Paramount.*

During this time I lecture on Soviet cinema in a number of American universities, Columbia (New York), Yale, Harvard, Chicago, California, and the Negro Straight College (in New Orleans.).

Once settled in a pleasant house in Coldwater Canyon, the three Russians and Ivor Montagu faced their first problem: agreeing with Paramount on a film subject. Though Eisenstein had wisely considered an American experience necessary for *Capital*, this was obviously not the subject for the American studio. Nor were they enthusiastic about *Ulysses*, *The Devil's Disciple*, or *The War of the Worlds*, all proposed to Eisenstein by their respective authors. In Paris he had discussed a film about Sir Basil Zaharoff, *Man from Darkness*, and had acquired Cendrars's agreement to film his novel about Sutter, *L'Or*. Also in Paris Lasky had proposed (and dismissed) a film about Dreyfus and Zola. Eisenstein was not tempted to film Vicki Baum's *Menschen in Hotel* (later to be filmed as *Grand Hotel*). From the *Europa* Eisenstein had telegraphed Shaw to add *Arms and the Man* to his gifts. In New York the Amkino head, Monosson, pressed *The Iron Flood* on Eisenstein. In California Lasky proposed *Die Verbrecher* by Bruckner; Bachman, appointed liaison to the Russian group, suggested *A Criminal Profession*, by Londres, and Kipling's *Kim*. Plenty of suggestions, but the first subject proposed by Eisenstein to Paramount in Hollywood was an old favorite, *The Glass House.*

As with his ideas for a film of *Capital*, Eisenstein's ideas for *The Glass House*, while never realized, are threaded through his remaining years of work and planning. The earliest project to appear among his notes and drawings is *The Glass House*. His first notes are recorded soon after his 1926 trip to Berlin, when he and Tisse stayed at the Hotel Hessler. Either this or another example of new Berlin architecture, employing a quantity of glass, started him thinking about the contradictions of a society that was able to see through all walls but maintained a code of morals that prevented it from wanting to do so.

Eisenstein was also spurred by the prospect of co-production with some Western country's film industry. German film people, who met him in Berlin, and Douglas Fairbanks, who visited him in Moscow at the height of *Potemkin*'s Berlin success, made variously serious offers of collaboration, but Eisenstein was aware that neither of his films then in production, one about the October revolution, the other about agricultural reform, would interest UFA or United Artists. One undated scrap of paper is scribbled with ideas for *The Glass House* and the name "Douglas Fairbanks Productions."

OPPOSITE PAGE: SKETCH FOR THE GLASS HOUSE, 1947.

THE GLASS HOUSE

In his search for an idea acceptable to his Paramount employers, Eisenstein's attention was caught by an article on Frank Lloyd Wright's project for a glass tower. The result was a synopsis in Eisenstein's English (shown at right) and some practical drawings that did not convince the Paramount people. Ivor Montagu gives this summary of *The Glass House* at its Hollywood stage:

The idea was this, as Sergei Mikhailovich explained it. People live, work, and have their being in a glass house. In this great building it is possible to see all around you: above, below, sideways, slanting, in any direction unless, of course, a carpet, a desk, a picture, or something like that should interrupt your line of sight.

Possible, I have said—but in fact people do not so see, because it never occurs to them to look. The camera can show them to us, at any angle, and the richness and multiplicity of possible angles in such a setting can instantly be imagined. Then, suddenly, something occurs to make them look, to make them conscious of their exposure. They become furtive, suspicious, inquisitive, terrified.[*]

Reporting on the search and decision for his first subject at Paramount, Eisenstein to Pera, July 7, 1930:

Altogether I'm not greatly troubled about "Story." Whether to make "Glass House" or something else keeps me busy. Chaplin considers the idea wonderful and demands that we make only this! (And yet the authorities say that he is envious because he isn't doing it! We've enjoyed talking a lot about it.) But it's very tough with "Story," so that it and my intentions would suit—Mr. Schulberg—he's the production manager.

By July 17 Eisenstein wrote Pera that *The Glass House* was put aside for "later." Unfortunately, no one at Paramount or Coldwater Canyon could find a satisfactory solution for the project's story problem, and Eisenstein put away his synopsis and drawings (and Wright's unrealized glass tower) for the next time he would meditate on this tempting idea.

The year before Eisenstein's death (the drawings are dated March 19, 1947) he did consider *The Glass House* again, this time in connection with the possibilities for stereoscopic film. The "suicide scene" mentioned in his Moscow and New York notes is an example of stereoscopy used for shock effect.

[*]Ivor Montagu, *With Eisenstein in Hollywood*, New York, International Publishers, 1969, p. 102.

TOP: FROM EISENSTEIN'S SCRAPBOOK. FRANK LLOYD WRIGHT'S DRAWING FOR A "GLASS TOWER," THE NEW YORK TIMES MAGAZINE, JUNE 29, 1930.

RIGHT COLUMN: EISENSTEIN'S HOLLYWOOD SYNOPSIS FOR THE GLASS HOUSE.
BELOW: TRANSLATION OF GERMAN NOTE FROM THE SYNOPSIS.

> It is very right for transparency to be <u>at once</u> perceived as logical since it is connected with the <u>turning away</u> of the head; <u>besides</u> in a very commonplace scene

---

Synopsis 1.

Prologue – Symphony of years.
The idea of the years house
explanation of the existence of such houses.

Part 1. „We do not see each other"
Beginning with showing the house and noticing afterwards that the people do not see each other — they do not want to see each other.

Scene as the man who beats his wife and 4 rooms around. seeing out not noticing it. Policeman on the corner.
(2 or 3 scenes of the same type)
N.B. All this people come afterwards into action.

2 Young lovers
1 woman who washes
1 clerk in shoe store
1 laundress (woman) (or japanese)
wife + husband, who beates her
1 Policeman

This Scene logically and associatively rounded can lead to some glimpses of other usual unseeing ness thus shown (speak-easy etc.) Beginning of something important

Part 2 „Somebody comes and opens our eyes."
The poet, Christ, a technician. arrives. He knocks his head at the glass walls and tries to explain to everybody.
Part 3 They begin to notice each other but the effect is opposite — they put walls between each other.
He makes a humanitarian speech. the result: „Aimée" proclaims the nudiste - association.
[„graduation in nudity"] — the society of hypocrisy.
Begins the competition between nudiste and tailor organization

Part 4 They begin to use that they can see each other. competition becomes battle.
The poet mixed in central love affair. The mechanical men sent to rape the nudiste girl.

The nudiste chief succombes with the tailors daughter.
Suicide of the poet.
Flats, flats, flats,
Part 5 Impossibility to continue and the smashing of the house.

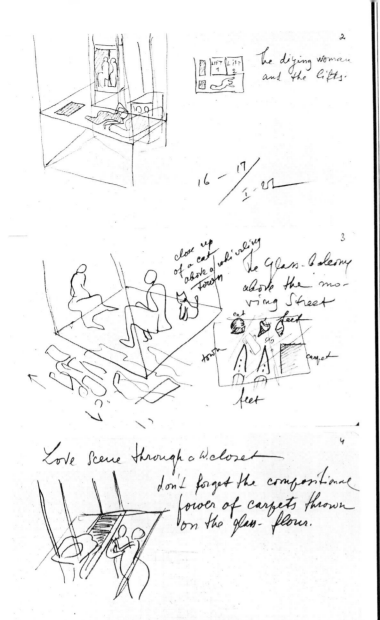

the dying woman and the lifts.

16 – 17 / I · 22

close up of a cat above of whirling forms

the Glass-balcony above the mo-ving street

cat feet town carpet feet

Love Scene through a W. closet

don't forget the compositional power of carpets thrown on the glass-floor.

ABOVE AND RIGHT: SKETCHES FOR <u>THE GLASS HOUSE</u>.

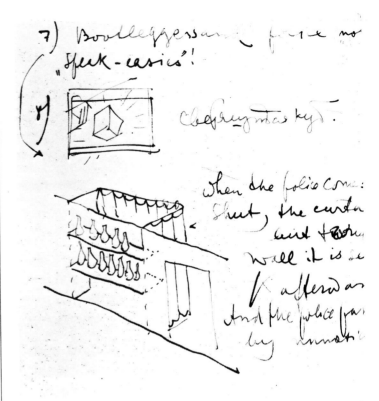

7) Bootleggers ... "Speak-easies"!

Cf [drawing the glittering cube]

When the police come: shut, the curtain but through wall it is se afterwar And the police pas by unnotic

7) Bootleggers and police / "Speakeasies"! / of [drawing] the glittering cube / When the police come, shut the curtain but through wall it is seen afterward. And the police pass by unnoticed.

BELOW: FURTHER NOTES FOR <u>THE GLASS HOUSE</u>. IN THE LAST LINES, EISENSTEIN DESCRIBES HIS ROBOT PARADE AS "LIKE THE LEGS IN MUSICAL FILMS."

48-5

·THE SAVOY-PLAZA·
FIFTH AVENUE 58TH and 59TH STREETS
NEW YORK

Robot – the mechanic man as the only "human" being. He (Robot) cannot stand the atmosphere of the Glass House and he gives the first strike to the house, and he alone persists after the crash — as the introducer of the new spirit of new humanity.

The poor girl crying at his breast.

Robot Parade (comme les legs dans des cinémas).

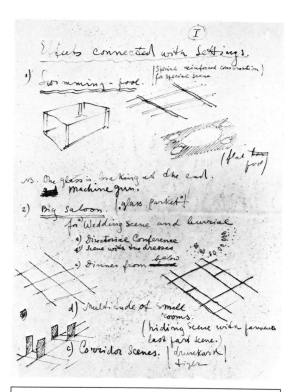

Effects connected with settings. / Special reinforced
construction for special scene. / Swimming pool. /
[flat pool] / NB. One glass is to break at the end. /
Machine gun. / ("glass parket") / 2) Big Saloon / for
a) Wedding scene and burial / b)Directorial
conference / b¹) Scene with the dresses / c) Dinner
from below / d) Multitude of small rooms. / (hiding
scene with paravents last part scene.) / e) Corridor
scenes. / drunkard / tiger

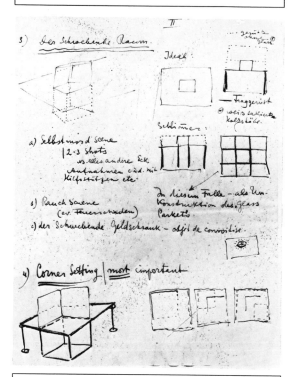

[Left side] 3)The Hovering Space
/ —Supports / white shellacked wooden lathes /
a) Suicide scene / 2-3 shots / NB. All other angle
shots, that is to say, with helping supports etc. /
Smarter / In such a case—as a rebuilding of the
"glass parkets" / b) smoking scene (fireshadows) c)
the hovering safe—the desired object / 4) Corner
setting / most important / [Right side]
Ideal:——scaffolding without glass /

SUTTER'S GOLD

The next project submitted to Paramount came closer to realization before it, too, met with unarguable obstacles. With
Blaise Cendrars's *L'Or* as the thematic base, the team explored the extensive literature on Sutter and the California
Gold Rush, then toured the original locations of the events in
northern California. The first writing step was a rough arrangement of the materials for each reel. Eisenstein's hand-
written notes for reel 3* are shown opposite, reproduced in
facsimile with a translation. The facsimile is partial, the translation complete.

At this point, Paramount's
objection was that "it would
cost too much." Eisenstein's
next move was to break
down each page of the script
to sets, people, and anything
else needed to prove that it
could be done in 57 1/2 days.

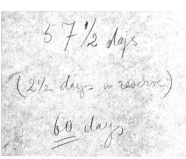

*Compare with finished script. See Montagu, *With Eisenstein in Hollywood*, pp. 170-
77.

**ABOVE: RECONSTRUCTION OF THE SAN FRANCISCO DOCKS.
EISENSTEIN MADE THESE NOTES, AND THOSE ON THE PAGES THAT FOLLOW,
FOR THE PRODUCTION OFFICE AT PARAMOUNT TO SHOW THEM HOW INEX-
PENSIVE THE SETS AND THE CASTING FOR <u>SUTTER'S GOLD</u> COULD BE.**

**LEFT: THESE CONSTRUCTION DETAILS FOR <u>THE GLASS HOUSE</u> MAY HAVE
BEEN WORKED OUT IN GERMANY.**

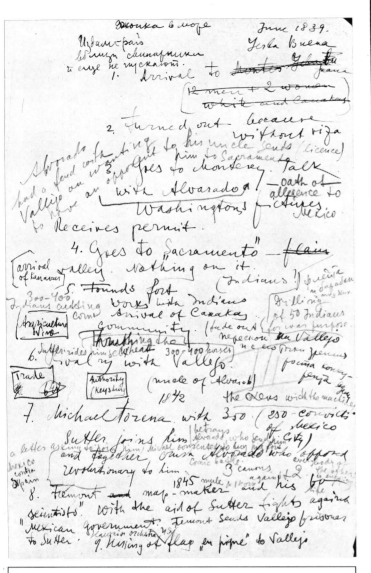

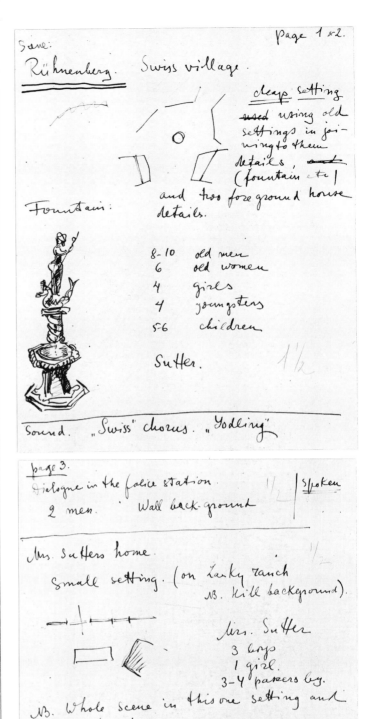

Schooner at sea
and again won't let him ashore.   June 1839
1. Arrival at Yerba Buena (12 men and 2 women / white and Kanakas)
2. Turned away because without visa (license)
3. Goes to Monterey. Talk with Alvarado. [insert] Alvarado had a feud with Vallejo about wanting to have an opponent of his uncle send him to Sacramento—oath of allegiance to Mexico. / Washington's picture / Receives permit.
4. Goes to "Sacramento" (arrival of Kanakas) valley. Nothing on it. / (Indians!)
5. Founds fort / works with Indians / arrival of Kanakas community / 300-400 Indians cutting corn / Agriculture vine / Drilling of 50 Indians for war purposes / fade out periscope [telescope?] on Vallejo and from his viewpoint / Threshing the wheat / Sutter rides himself 300-400 horses / growth of rivalry
6. Rivalry with Vallejo (uncle of Alvarado) (Trade) (Authority Keysburg [possibly intended for Samuel Kyburg or Kyburz]) 1842 the oxen with the machines
7. Micheltorena with 350 (250 convicts from Mexico City) Sutter joins him / betrays Alvarado, who sent him a letter asking him to join him. Michel consents to buy his fort and together crush Alvarado, who opposed revolutionaries to him. Comic battle. 3 cannons against 2 mules and 1 horse. Everybody of the others is enjoying life. / Mexico contra Spain / 1845
8. Fremont map-maker and his 60 "scientists." With the aid of Sutter fights against Mexican government. Fremont sends Vallejo prisoner to Sutter. Hawaiian orchestra.
9. Kissing of U.S. flag "en pique" to Vallejo.

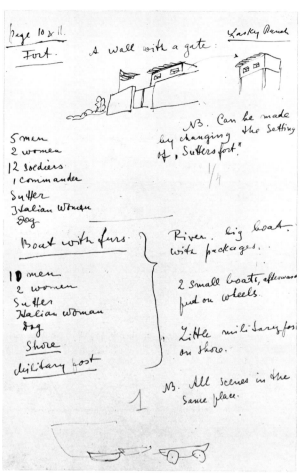

page 10 & 11.

Fort.

A wall with a gate: ___ Lasky Ranch

NB. Can be made by changing the setting of "Sutters fort."

1/4

5 men
2 women
12 soldiers
1 commander
Sutter
Italian Woman
Dog

Boat with furs.

10 men
2 women
Sutter
Italian woman
Dog

Shore.
Military post

} River. big boat. with packages.

2 small boats, afterward put on wheels.

Little military post on shore.

NB. All scenes in the same place.

1

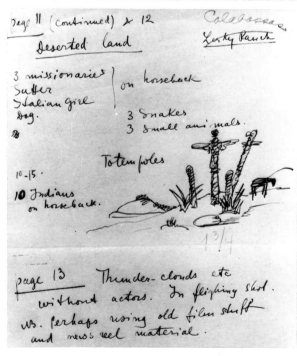

page 11 (continued) & 12

Deserted land   Calabasas
                  Lasky Ranch

3 missionaries
Sutter
Italian girl
Dog.

} on horseback

3 snakes
3 small animals.

Totem poles

10-15

10 Indians on horseback.

1 3/4

page 13   Thunder-clouds etc without actors. In flighting shot.
NB. Perhaps using old film stuff and newsreel material.

page 13 (continued) & 14,15.

Forest

Sutter
Dog
Italian Woman
4 trappers.
3 mastiffs (dogs)
1. horse

Lasky Ranch

NB. If enough water. If not : 3 shots (swimming together with scene on page 11 (Boat), but "shore" and following on Ranch.

2

(Transparency).

Setting. 10-15 "big trees" (about 15-20 feet high)

For double exposure. some shots (without actors) in Yosemite [can be done during week end, or during cutting period.]

page 16-18   Desert   2 1/2

Several shots with
Sutter
Italian woman
Horse
Dog   in desert

3-4 "gigantic" artificial cactuses.
3 artificial bushes.

all the evening material in ranch.
6-7 small dogs ("acting" Koyotes)
8 modells of Koyotes with glittering eyes [in the dark]

page 21 (continued) - 24.

Sutter fort ("New Helvetia)

Lasky Ranch

7 1/2 days

This setting is used for all connected with the fort. :

the construction of the fort. (first act) and all the scenes in this act.

The destruction of the fort (next act).

The same setting by slight changes is converted in the "Hermitage" (act "six") - by night time.

military exercise

Fremont's terrace for festival   page 23

drink store

enclosure for threshing the wheat

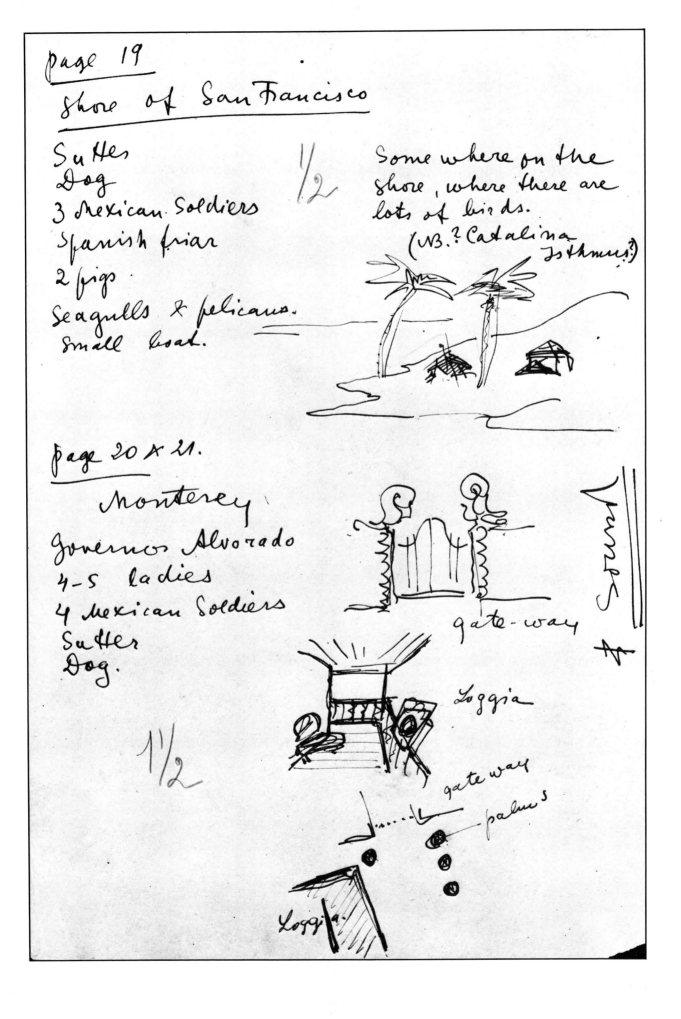

page 19

Shore of San Francisco

Sutter
Dog
3 Mexican Soldiers
Spanish friar
2 pigs
Seagulls & pelicans.
Small boat.

½

Some where on the shore, where there are lots of birds.
(NB.? Catalina Isthmus?)

page 20 & 21.

Monterey

Governor Alvorado
4-5 ladies
4 Mexican Soldiers
Sutter
Dog.

1½

gate-way

Loggia

gate way

palms

Loggia

f Sound

page 21-24 (continued)

All the indian scenes on Lasky Ranch around the setting of the fort.

35 Indians [used for all agricultural and other scenes]
Herd of horses } shot where ever You like.
Herd of cattle }

25 horses for threshing the wheat (wild with 4-5 riding indians)

10 mexican (indian) girls.

General Fremont
Sutter
Dog
8 men with Fremont.

6-8 wagons upper parts of which covered with wheat.

"120 oxen". — 12 white oxen dragging machine through differently arranged landscapes on Lasky ranch. [especially "swamp" and "hill"]
Pigeons
Lots of fruit
"wheat for treshing" - real wheat for close ups
hay etc to fill the enclosure.

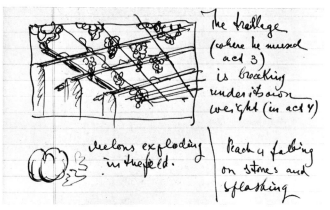

The trillage (where he mused act 3) is breaking under its own weight (in act 4)

Melons exploding in the field.   Peach falling on stones and splashing

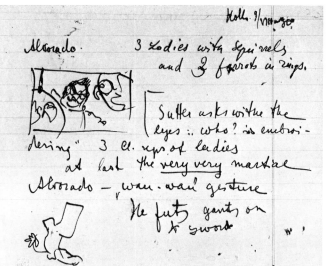

Holl. 9/VII 30

Alvorado   3 Ladies with Squirrels and 3 parrots in rings.

[Sutter asks with the eyes :. who? is embroidering" 3 cl. ups of ladies at last the very very martial Alvorado — wan-wan gesture
He puts gants on to sword

page 24-30 (continued).   1

"The advance of stone hills on fertile countries" taken in Sacramento (without actor and sound equipment) in using small elevator [there are a lot of them near the actual gold digging spots].

NB. The main part of the act — sound effects with landscapes without actors.

page 31.   page 31-36 whole travel of Mrs Sutter 5 days

Mrs. Sutter room. the same as on page 3

Miss Sutter
3 Sons [20-23 years old]
1 Young woman
Pastor
School master

Corner of Street   the same as on page 4 & 5

Mrs Sutter
3 Sons
1 Young woman
Pastor
School master
10 passers by.   Possibly a phaeton or coach (# out of the park is Lasky Ranch).

page 31 (continued).

Deck of a Ship. (corner)

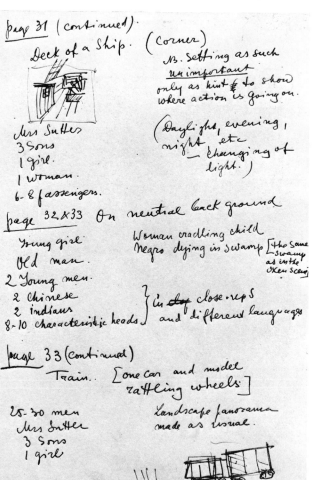

NB. Setting as such unimportant only as hint # to show where action is going on.

Mrs Sutter
3 Sons
1 girl.
1 woman.
6-8 passengers.   (Daylight, evening, night etc — changing of light.)

page 32 & 33 On neutral back ground

Young girl
Old man.
2 Young men.
2 Chinese
2 indians
8-10 characteristic heads   Woman cradling child Negro dying in swamp [the same swamp as in the oxen scene]

} in close-ups and different languages

page 33 (continued)
Train. [one car and model rattling wheels]

25-30 men
Mrs Sutter
3 Sons
1 girl   Landscape panorama made as usual.

page 34

2nd deck of a ship

Also corner but needs the crashing
of waves. Made as usual in tempest
night scenes. On a bascule.

Small setting of hold with rolling barrels
                    also on bascule.
Mrs. Sutter
Children
5-6 sailors.

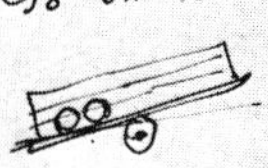

Vision

Sutter and glass painting. Horse
Trick photography

Death of Anna.   page 35 x 36

Mrs. Sutter   All in different corner
3 sons   of Lasky ranch
1 girl   and in the ruins
Sutter   of "Sutters fort"
2 indians
Dog
2 mules
1 horse

page 39 (continued) & 40, 41

Lawyers for "street scenes"
8-10
Lawyers for crowd before court of justice "and
50   the scene of the Suit [taken on
                                   same day]
Crowd
100 people.
President   3-4 windows with
Sutter   small parts of walls
3 Sons.   for interior scenes with
          1   lawyers - projected on
                   same back ground of
                   the "town of San Francisco"]

page 42 & 43

The burning house   indicated on general map.

Fire & trial 3 days

page 46 (continued) 47, 48.

Morning after festival.   [Main S. Francisco
Sutter   setting]
horse   1
1 man
60 persons for mob scenes [in different parts
                          of main setting]
All scenes outside
    (in front of saloon etc)

Sutters ride I   1/2
Sutter & horse [probably Lasky ranch]

Spanish mission
                     [somewhere in the
Sutter   hills
horse   1/2
1 friar
4 Indians.   Celebration

                  N.B. No mission.
                   Possibli one cross.
The reflection
of fire (in one or two shots of the scene)
by trick photography & double exposure.
* [4-5 close ups with words (talk) taken
   in Studio].

page 49
Sutters ride II.   Lasky ranch.
Sutter   (with artificial light
horse   1/2   - illuminating his ride).

page 50
The ruins.   Lasky ranch.
Sutter   earth blackened by fire

   1/2

                     hanging man
                     2-3 dead cows or horses
                     ravens.

Streets
Sutter   1   Among the streets of
20 passers by.   main setting of S-F.
                     with changed posters
                     & and details.

page 50 & 51 palace of justice 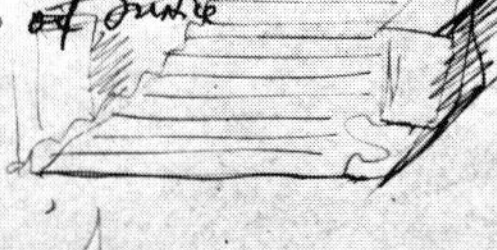
Sutter
1 small boy
2 other small boys.

          Big white staircase and upper
          part on glass (sketch of setting
                           see on a $50
                           bank note!)

Model of a big empty room.

MURDER.

Inner monologue —...I'll never have the courage to kill her... Never... No. (moaning)

Clyde is seen sitting with ~~clo~~ eyes closed. Han ~~ds~~ at forehead —

Roberta approaches him from other end of boat.

Her hand touches his "what is it clyde?" Cl. up: Hand on hand
He suddenly opens eyes. Sees her. (~~withdraws hand~~) jumps to
his feet. Camera hunts her face.
She shrieks and falls on other end of boat.
He: "o ~~pardon~~ I didn't mind to..." Steps forward.
She ~~shrieking~~ in horror jumps up.
Boat turns over ~~=~~ as result of his movem
and loss of balance
The bird's voice.
   She appears on surface
He
both are seen. He makes movement toward her.
She frightendely moves away and goes dow
He stops in his movement
Hat swims to ~~—~~ side

AN AMERICAN TRAGEDY

Eisenstein's copy of *An American Tragedy* graphically shows his growing interest in and visualization of the literary source. First, thumbnail marks in the margins, then pencil and colored pencils, and finally whole scenes growing from the text as he jots notes in both Russian and English.

We can watch the team's progress on *An American Tragedy*'s script in the surviving records of each stage of the work, from the collection in the Museum of Modern Art, beginning with Eisenstein's marked and annotated copy of Dreiser's novel (a facsimile page shown below), followed by his rough notes, his "Map of the Action," to the final collaboration of the three authors of the script.* (The surviving rough notes by Eisenstein for *An American Tragedy* are chiefly for its last two reels (13 and 14), through the trial to the film's end.)

Ivor Montagu described the process of collaboration on the two scenarios submitted to Paramount:

The team was ready . . . to work at pressure. The three were accustomed to this, indeed preferred it. Finishing *October* . . . in 1927 the pressure had been so great they had had to receive injections to keep awake.

*Published in Montagu, *With Eisenstein in Hollywood*.

AN AMERICAN TRAGEDY   325

the room beginning to whisper: "Trapped! Trapped!" And Justice Oberwaltzer at once announcing that because of the lateness of the hour, and in the face of a number of additional witnesses for the defense, as well as a few in rebuttal for the prosecution, he would prefer it if the work for the day ended here. And both Belknap and Mason gladly agreeing. And Clyde—the doors of the courtroom being stoutly locked until he should be in his cell across the way—being descended upon by Kraut and Sissell and by them led through and down the very door and stairs which for days he had been looking at and pondering about. And once he was gone, Belknap and Jephson looking at each other but not saying anything until once more safely locked in their own office, when Belknap began with: ". . . not carried off with enough of an air. The best possible defense but not enough courage. It just isn't in him, that's all." And Jephson, flinging himself heavily into a chair, his overcoat and hat still on, and saying: "No, that's the real trouble, no doubt. It musta been that he really did kill her. But I suppose we can't give up the ship now. He did almost better than I expected, at that." And Belknap adding: "Well, I'll do my final best and damnedest in my summing up, and that's all I can do." And Jephson replying, a little wearily: "That's right, Alvin, it's mostly up to you now, I'm sorry. But in the meantime, I think I'll go around to the jail and try and hearten 'im up a bit. It won't do to let him look too winged or lame tomorrow. He has to sit up and make the jury feel that he, himself, feels that he isn't guilty whatever they think." And rising he shoved his hands in the side pockets of his long coat and proceeded through the winter's dark and cold of the dreary town to see Clyde.

FACSIMILE PAGE OF EISENSTEIN'S COPY OF AN AMERICAN TRAGEDY.

good rhythm—rhythm of the wheels! / (then a burst—hang the bastard!) / briefly about money (already in whispers) / from whom (repeat trapped, trapped / silence, flashlight: Sondra) /Crumbling/ trapped, trapped / M[ason] starts up as though to launch a new attack / [illegible] . . . "That's all!"

ABOVE: THE AUTHORS. FROM LEFT, ALEXANDROV, MONTAGU, EISENSTEIN.

OPPOSITE PAGE: NOTES FOR AN AMERICAN TRAGEDY

We worked like a conveyor belt, round the clock. Paramount provided typists in relays, translators, reams of paper. Coldwater Canyon became a factory. The pattern of work was so:

Eisenstein would be closeted with Grisha [Alexandrov], narrating verbally the treatment he had planned. Grisha would go off and write it. As soon as it was written it would be typed and translated. I would take an English text, read it, and go to Eisenstein. Now he and I would go through it, discussing and making emendations. Then I would go off and rewrite it. Hell [Montagu] would receive my manuscript . . . to type fair copies. The Paramount staff would then make more copies of this final state.

This process meant, of course, that Grisha would always be two or three reels ahead of me. While he was on, say, the draft of reel four, I would still be discussing with Eisenstein the revision of reel two. Eisenstein would have to keep the whole thing in his head and switch from one to the other, like a chessmaster giving a simultaneous display.*

---

*Montagu, *With Eisenstein in Hollywood,* pp. 106-7.

26 Sept 1930
Clyde visited by:
1) Revivalist
2) 3 peasant girls
3) Psychiatrist and clerk taking notes for him (Magnus [Hirschfeld] and young man)
4) Preacher (?) (terrifying coming out of darkness only the face of a skeleton)
Necessary: that Clyde's cell be flooded with light, like a stage but the corridor, from where the visitors come—must be in semidarkness.

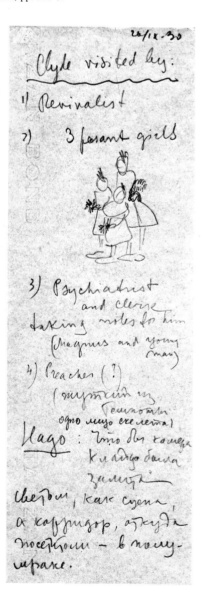

Here, the script approaches its final form. There are two drafts of Roberta's murder, leading to the final version (pp. 293–96 of Montagu's *With Eisenstein in Hollywood,* and pp. 237–41 in an Appendix to *The Film Sense*).

This draft, dated September 26, 1930, concentrates on sketching the use of the inner monologue. The second draft, reproduced on the opposite page in facsimile form in Eisenstein's English, is undated and appears to place less emphasis on the inner monologue.

Murder   26 Sep 30

Inner monologue.
Why not ??!
Joyce in literature,
O'Neill in drama,
we in cinema!
In literature - *good,*
in drama - bad,
in cinema - *best.*

Boringly they row a long time.
Each piece is *identical.*
The boat turns (like the train at the end of *Bed and Sofa*).
Drifting. Dialogue.
Fade-out.
Inner monologue (with images?)
Fade-in.
Drifting. Dialogue.
Fade-out.
Inner monologue.
Fade-in.
Drifting. Dialogue.
Fade-out.
Inner monologue.
Fade-in.
Drifting. Dialogue.
Fade-out.
Inner monologue.
Fade-in.
Drifting.

Change of intention.
(Starting point - inactivity of nature and fear. Again - "warm.")
While eating, Roberta is fully agreeable.
A hint of tenderness.
Farewell, Sondra. (Various views of Sondra fade out successively.)

He photographs her [Roberta].

Could we marry . . .?

She is clumsily tender.

He recoils from her contact.
(the decision of a moment, that has not yet reached a physical sensation for decision). Nothing more than something sharp in his movement.

A flash: Sondra?

She: Clyde! I'm afraid of you.
Sondra fades out. Roberta's image returns.
He rushes to her with tenderness.
She does not comprehend.
One. Two.
Three.

The boat overturns under a piercing shriek.
The shriek of a bird.
He throws himself toward her in the water.
She is frightened and gestures him away.
She is drowning.
He emerges.
The shriek of a bird.
He dives.
His hat floats away.
Exhausted, he throws himself on the shore.
The shore. We hear the splashing of a tired
swimmer - it is *he* who is swimming.
He sits with one foot in the water.
He begins to shiver.
Cold sweat.
He pulls his foot out of the water.
His trembling reaches its climax.
and . . . stop (including the apparatus of thought).
No more Roberta . . . All as I wished it . . . I didn't kill . . .
I agreed to marriage . . . Providence . . . helped . . .
Sondra . . . Sondra . . . Sondra!
Life! . . . Hurry. Conceal evidence . . .
Is Roberta really drowned? . . .
In a fever of activity
Changes his clothes.
Wrings out the wet ones.
Effect of a naked man in cold black water. Shirt.
A slight trembling. White cold legs.

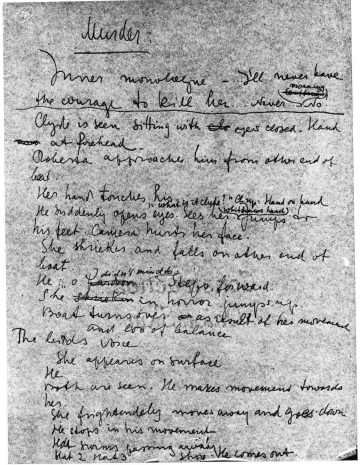

THE SECOND DRAFT OF THE PLAN FOR THE MURDER SEQUENCE.

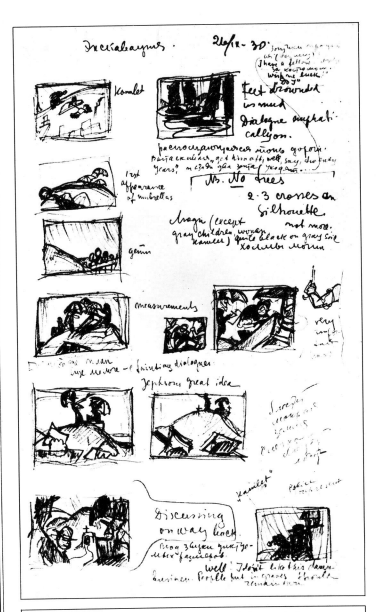

EXHUMATION 26 Sept 1930 [Reading left to right]
Hamlet / Feet drowned in mud. Dialogue emphatically on. The
spreading slush on road. Drawling "get him off, well, say twenty
years," and behind two umbrellas leave [insert from above]
Looking down on umbrellas (without faces): dredge / I have a
fellow . . . behind the clothes. "Wish me luck!" "Do I." 1st
appearance of umbrellas / NB. No trees / 2-3 crosses in
silhouette / not more. People (except gray children, women,
Hamlet) quite black on gray soil / mound graves / children
/ measurements / very important hand / same shot—more detailed
with fainting dialogues / Jephson's great idea / wet earth shines
/ shovels slightly shine / "Hamlet" / Police representatives
/ Discussing on way back / Under sound of dictated measurements.
Well! I don't like this damn business. People put in graves
should remain there.

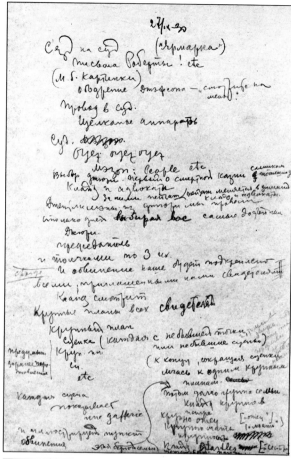

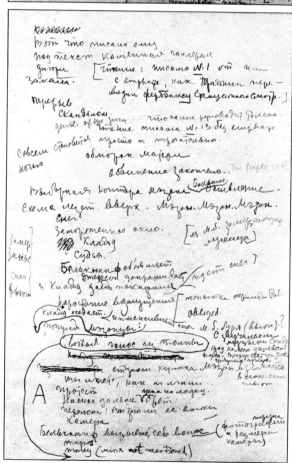

THE FIRST ROUGH NOTES FOR <u>AN AMERICAN TRAGEDY</u>.

27 Sept 1930 ("Fair")
Arrival at the courtroom
    Roberta's letters! etc
    (perhaps snapshots)
        Approval of Jephson—"look at me"
    Walk through the courtroom
        Clicking of cameras
Courtroom. Oyez, Oyez, Oyez
    Mason: People etc.
Selection of jury. First is asked about capital punishment
        his Yes is too hasty
Clyde and lawyers
    Behind them a landscape, the landscape turns wintry
        Clyde and lawyers.
Gentlemen of the jury, we have spent so many days in
    selecting you, the most trustworthy
        Jury
        Foreman
        in stages of 3
    [charge] And our charge will be supported by
        all the witnesses we have summoned.
        Clyde watches.
    Close-ups of all witnesses.

[worked out and arranged in advance]	Close-up short scene (each from a new angle or a new scene)
	Close-up scene (scenes get shorter and shorter rushing etc. to a single close-up.)
Each scene shows une gafferie and illustrates a point in the indictment	This poor family (the Aldens) Then a long hold on the family group

        close-up of Clyde in fear
        close-up of father ["father"]
        close-up of mother ["mother"]
        close-up of sister ["sister"]
    Clyde is startled whispers "God"   Pause.

Here is what she wrote to him	
Jury	(Reading: Letter N. 1 with the same
Sunset.	emphasis as Trainin used in translating "The Station Master" for Fairbanks.)

Eruption of a disturbance
    Gentlemen of the jury . . . we are guided only
    Reading of letter N. 13 without emphasis
    Simple and touching
[Night falls] Mother faints
        The indictment is concluded—"The people rest."
Mason's election headquarters. Big excitement. Graph on
charts climbing up. Mason. Mason. Mason.

Snow	
Frost	Frosted window (NB. Maybe a puddle freezes over.)
Cold	Clyde
Snow	Judge Belknap makes an announcement
Storms	Jephson questions and Clyde testifies
snow is falling	Attempt to blacken Roberta's
Indignation mounts	name. Obliged.
Mason's followers parrot him???	With the sound of music
Clyde slumps	Sondra at the wheel of a cheap Ford.
Snow grows heavier— maybe a blizzard?	All around statues of Justice. Dirtied.

Mason bangs his fist and thrusts himself into the
cross-examination.
Perhaps you were lying . . . Protest
A further thrust. Price of boat. Shouts.
Change of mood: You tore her hair. Belknap tears out one
of his hairs
    (type of photograph and size of camera) The camera
maps
money (Miss X not mentioned)
"Bastard" voice from the crowd

(maybe?) Sondra's note
mother's arrival. Fully hopeful. (money and the
governor will receive her today)
Mother caresses him, cradling him in her arms "baby boy"
—"You did not . . . in the depths of your heart . . .
You did not intend . . . to . . . kill?"
—". . . Yes, mother . . . I   gazes radiantly (hope
did . . ."   Mother turns   for salvation and reconciliation)
to stone.   Calmed, like a child he snuggles
Hand stops caressing.   and whispers innermost thoughts
He pats her hand. /
. . . in your heart . . .
(he doesn't hear) / He doesn't see her,
nestles at her knees . . . but I never <u>did do</u> it . . .
Mother incredulous and stony
Jephson runs in and hurries out
Clyde: "Good luck!"
Snatches Sondra's note
The Governor. Start with details of Governor's mansion,
very opulent, then to the governor, who is quite plain.
". . . See in me but the father . . . I have too . . . children . . .
mother . . . As Mother . . . do you really believe him pure and
innocent like before God? Could he have done it?"
Mother starts to say "My son . . ." With her mouth partly open
she stops herself—"like before God"—her eyes open wide.
Clyde's voice. Yes, mother . . . I did . . .
She shuts her eyes. Her head is bowed.
Long pause. Gray can be seen in the part of her hair.
Loud ring. She opens her frightened eyes.
The governor slowly removes his finger from the bell. He is
solidly built and is full of importance. Distant. And without
tricks (tableau).
Sorry. There are no arguments to review the case. God help you.
(maybe it should be a clerk who says that, while the governor
walks out, closing the door.)
She makes a move as though to say something.
She turns like an automaton. The clerk shows her out.
The closed door. She comes to her senses.
But he's innocent. Innocent!! . . . <u>Is</u> he?
Transom [of cell] opens with a crash. Close-up—spittoon.
A broom sweeping around the spittoon. And around the room
In semi-darkness one can distinguish the shape of an armchair.

Mother and son are praying (singing a psalm)   [Clyde wears
. . . ."But I want <u>to live</u>!" (thrashes about)   electrocution
Mother goes on singing.   dress]
He is at her feet sobbing.
She sings.
"to <u>live</u>!"
In the garden the singing can be heard.
Piercingly: "to live"   [and the mother in black is <u>alone</u>
The garden in full bloom.   in the same spot.]
The door is closed with a screech. (faintly—to live . . .)
The landscape blazes with color.
The transom closes. (Perhaps upper shutter is lowered cutting off
the landscape. At first slats (scraping sound) then solid wall
(muted.)
to live . . .
Again the landscape.
The lowered transom we saw open now is shut [with drawing].
A long pause.
The dying echo of the transom.
A sputter as switch is thrown (an instant's flash of light).
A hymn is heard from the darkness.
Yellow smoke.
Houses.
San Francisco.

                                            Street preachers
for B.P.S. [Schulberg?]   I don't think this is the best way
"Mary, let's better marry"   to bring up children . . .
or she says it and he   They seem to be kinder than
agrees.   usual . . . today

A "Map of Action" was prepared of the whole novel, to make sure no important juxtapositions by Dreiser had been omitted. These are the last chapters of Book 2:

Chapter 45. pp. 48-56

Arguments for and against murder interrupted by letter from Roberta announcing threat and return, and telephone reply arranging to meet her at Fonda for little trip.

Chapter 46. pp. 57-64

Meeting at Fonda. Separate railway carriages, with their separate thoughts, to Utica.

Chapter 47. pp. 65-79

Grass Lake. Big Bittern, promising her marriage. The boat, its overset and the murder.

Eisenstein and his collaborators enclosed this note with the completed script, submitted to Paramount October 5, 1930:

Gentlemen:

So here we see the miracle accomplished—*An American Tragedy* presented in only 14 reels. Still, we think the final treatment must not be over 12. But we withdraw from the final "shrinking," leaving it for the present "in extenso," so as to have the possibility of making this unpleasant operation after receiving the benefit of notes and advice from:

1. The West Coast Magnates.
2. The East Coast Magnates.
3. Theodore Dreiser.
4. The Hays Organization.

Accordingly, gentlemen, we have the honor to submit to your "discriminating kindness" The Enclosed Manuscript and—*Honi soit qui mal y pense.*

The Authors

FROM THE SCENE SHOWING THE EXHUMATION OF ROBERTA'S BODY.

Unknown to the Eisenstein group, the scenario had powerful enemies. Here is a memo from David Selznick to B.P. Schulberg, October 8, 1930:

I have just finished reading the Eisenstein adaptation of *An American Tragedy.* It was for me a memorable experience; the most moving script I have ever read. It was so effective, that it was positively torturing. When I had finished it, I was so depressed that I wanted to reach for the bourbon bottle. As entertainment, I don't think it has one chance in a hundred.

. . . Is it too late to try to persuade the enthusiasts of the picture from making it? Even if the dialogue rights have been purchased, even if Dreiser's services have been arranged for, I think it an inexcusable gamble on the part of this department to put into a subject as depressing as is this one, anything like the cost that an Eisenstein production must necessarily entail.

If we want to make *An American Tragedy* as a glorious experiment, and purely for the advancement of the art (which I certainly do not think is the business of this organization) then let's do it with a [John] Cromwell directing, and chop three or four hundred thousand dollars off the loss. If the cry of "Courage!" be raised against this protest, I should like to suggest that we have the courage not to make the picture, but to take whatever rap is coming to us for not supporting Eisenstein the artist (as he proves himself to be with this script) with a million or more of the stockholders' cash.

Let's try new things, by all means. But let's keep these gambles within the bounds of those that would be indulged in by rational businessmen; and let's not put more money than we have into any one picture for years into a subject that will appeal to our vanity through the critical acclaim that must necessarily attach to its production, but that cannot possibly offer anything but a most miserable two hours to millions of happy-minded young Americans.

David O. Selznick

Although the studio had liked the script and sent the group on a tour of New York City and upper New York State, scene of the original case which was Dreiser's source, their excursion ended unhappily. In Jesse Lasky's New York office they heard the news.

"Gentlemen, it is over," they were told. "Our agreement is at an end."

Eisenstein's last desperate suggestion, made to both M-G-M and Universal Studios, was for a film of Edgar Lee Masters' *Spoon River Anthology.* The proposal was rejected.

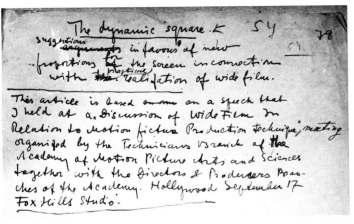

The dynamic square. 54 78

suggestions arguments in favour of new proportions for the screen in connection with the practical realisation of wide film.

This article is based an on on a speech that I held at a Discussion of Wide Film In Relation to Motion Picture Production technique, meeting organized by the Technicians Branch of the Academy of Motion Picture Arts and Sciences together with the Directors & Producers Branches of the Academy. Hollywood September 17 Fox Hills Studio.

NOTES FOR AN ARTICLE ON THE PROPORTIONS OF THE WIDE SCREEN.

One of the last of his extracurricular duties in Hollywood was to address a meeting of the Academy of Motion Picture Arts and Sciences during a symposium devoted to the problems of the wide screen.

Four years later, in July 1934, Eisenstein summed up the Paramount experience for an American friend.

> Am shown *The Virginian* as the ideal of a picture. "Our main audience is the small towner; he is the one who pays."
>
> 1) The martyrdom of the Jesuit missionaries in the United States during the civilization (probably: horrors of the red skins torturing the father Jesuit—great stuff for blood-thirsty "bolshi").
> 2) Pacifistic "Broken Lullaby"—produced later on by Lubitsch.
> 3) Above mentioned "Grand Hotel."
>
> Other proposals from us
>
> 1) Gold Rush to California—*Sutter's Gold* by Blaise Cendrars. I actually completed the scenario on this, but Paramount was afraid to produce it. Opposition from Daughters of the American Revolution and other patriotic organizations. Panic about bolshies treating the subject of gold.
> 2) Basil Zacharoff, etc. etc.
> 3) stock market crash.
>
> Finally agreed upon subject of "American Tragedy." Strict instructions: treat story as police story about "a boy and a girl." Controversy started with that. [Must be] no social background, no story of development and growth of character. My question: Why take Dreiser book? Pay him $100,000—if such a point of view—easier to take any story out of everyday newspaper. Second big controversy when asked if in my treatment Clyde Griffiths is criminal or not. Main point in my treatment—conditions of education, bringing up, work, surroundings, and social conditions *drive* characterless boy to crime. And electrocuting him afterwards. "Such a film would be a monstrous accusation against American society," says Paramount. We added nothing, just accentuated the important sociological points with Dreiser's objective method—all are in the book.

QUÉ VIVA MÉXICO!

JE NE FAIS PAS DU CINÉMA
JE FAIS DU MEXIQUE ET DU MOI.—MAY 22, 1931

1930-1931 *I film, with the concurrence of Soyuzkino and Amkino together with a group of friends of the Soviet Union (headed by Upton Sinclair), a film "Thunder Over Mexico" through the whole territory of Mexico (along with cameraman Tisse and G. Alexandrov).*

The effort to bring home a film to show for their time abroad resulted in Eisenstein's greatest film plan and his greatest personal tragedy. Details will be found in the Eisenstein-Sinclair correspondence.* (Finding Sinclair's proposed contract too loose, and sensing trouble ahead, Montagu did not accompany the group and returned to England from California.)

As Eisenstein's group traveled through Mexico, the shape of the film grew clearer—four novellas with prologue and epilogue. The structure of Anita Brenner's *Idols Behind Altars* suggested to Eisenstein this solution of the problem. But the arrangement of these parts changed with time, circumstances and money. Eisenstein prepared the earliest of the "scenarios" in April 1931, and sent them to Sinclair to show to the backers of the project. The finished version of this "sales script," carefully tailored for financial and religious inspection, was first published in *Experimental Cinema.*†

*Most of this correspondence has been published. *See:* Harry M. Geduld and Ronald Gottesman, eds., *The Making and Unmaking of Qué Viva México!*; Marie Seton, *Sergei M. Eisenstein*; and Montagu, *With Eisenstein in Hollywood.*
†No. 4, 1934; reprinted by Ernest Lindgren, London, 1951.

ABOVE: FILMING A WOMAN'S PROFILE AGAINST THE PYRAMID AT CHICHÉN ITZÁ FOR THE PROLOGUE. OVERLEAF: THE COMPOSITION AS IT APPEARED IN THE FILM.

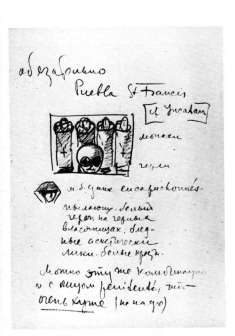

Absolutely
Puebla St. Francis (of Yucatan)
monks / skull
perhaps even
encapuchonnés
Searingly white
skull
against black robes,
pale, ascetic faces,
white crosses.
May use same
combination with
the face of a
penitente, which is
much worse (better
not).

OPPOSITE PAGE: FILMING A COMPOSITION FOR "CONQUEST."

Prologue

Each of the planned six parts of *Qué Viva México!* was to be dedicated to an artist: the Prologue, dedicated to Siqueiros, embodied the composition of his fresco "The Worker's Burial" (see below). The fresco itself was so mutilated that it was eventually destroyed altogether.

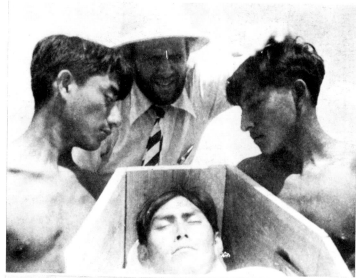

"THE WORKER'S BURIAL." DAVID ALFARO SIQUEIROS. UNFINISHED FRESCO, 1924–1925. NATIONAL PREPARATORY SCHOOL, MEXICO, D.F.

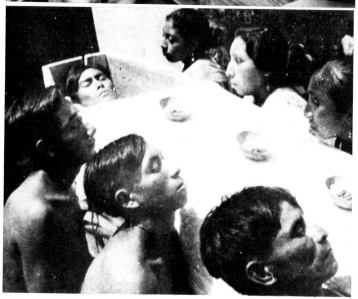

ABOVE AND OPPOSITE PAGE, NEAR COLUMN: FILMING THE PROLOGUE, INCORPORATING THE COMPOSITION OF SIQUEIROS'S FRESCO.

Conquest

Synthesizing two actual rituals, Eisenstein filmed the Stations of the Cross (with three Christ-*penitentes*), a possible transition between the Spanish tone of "Fiesta" and one of the later novellas. When Tisse saw this footage later he said, "We weren't sure where it was to be used."

STATIONS OF THE CROSS.
65 · <u>QUÉ VIVA MÉXICO!</u>

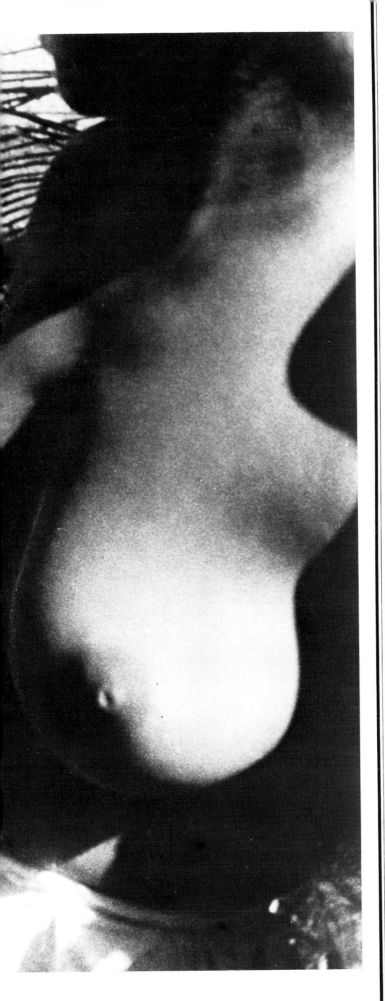

Sandunga
DEDICATED TO JEAN CHARLOT

The matriarchal society in Tehauntepec required a change from all the styles in use for the other novellas: the "story" almost disappeared in the event shown (preparations for a wedding and the wedding), the compositions became horizontal and passive, and Tisse's photography turned away from his well-known sharpness to a softening of all images.

Fiesta
DEDICATED TO THE MEMORY OF FRANCISCO DE GOYA

This novella was planned to be composed of all of the most Spanish elements in Mexican life, its content to be built around one afternoon's bullfight program. The story was a triangular drama, husband, wife, and mounted picador, ending in a miracle—to be filmed in Moscow. The picador (Baranito) was selected so that his role could be filled later in Moscow, and his scenes were shot (see photo below) so that they could be completed later.

ABOVE: EISENSTEIN REHEARSES THE EPISODE OF THE THROWN PICADOR.

OPPOSITE PAGE: THE CONCLUSION OF "SANDUNGA," WITH NATURE AND THE WEDDED PAIR IN TOTAL HARMONY.

ABOVE: THE DAWN HYMN, IN THE HACIENDA COURTYARD.
BELOW: THIS MOMENT OF ECSTASY WAS INTENDED FOR THE DANCERS' SCENE. THE SKETCH AT BOTTOM SHOWS AN EPISODE LEFT UNDESCRIBED IN THE VARIOUS PUBLISHED SCRIPTS. LUCIANO, THE MASKED LEADER OF THE DANCERS, MAY BE GIVING INSTRUCTIONS FOR THE REBELLION.

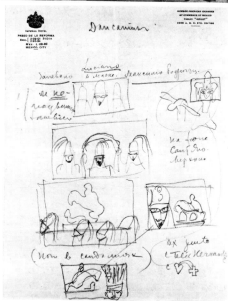

Dancers
[Top] The chorus leader and also <u>not</u> moving. / Luciano in mask / Máximo Rodríguez. [Center] In background, Santiago on horseback [Bottom] (feet in sandals) / their joining with Felix Hernández

FILMING THE PUNISHMENT OF THE HOOVES.

Maguey

This novella was eventually separated from the rest of *Qué Viva México!*, cut by other hands, and released as *Thunder Over Mexico.* These are Eisenstein's rough cutting notes for the beginning of "Maguey," interlacing the dawn hymn of the peons, the formal meeting of Sebastián and María, and the pulque industry of the hacienda (see facing page).

> *Quelle finesse en tout cela* and how amusing, when you recall that since eight o'clock until the setting sun, filming the cruelty to the peons in the days of the tyranny of Porfirio Díaz. In the pounding of horses' hooves, between the passions of the Indio and the cold malice of the Spanish. Pull these together in the loop of the lasso. It is with such a lasso that we pull together the crumbling pieces of the conception. And for the day something monistic is accomplished.
>
> *Et je crois que c'est le seul, et le vraiment parfait bonheur.*
>
> *Et un bonheur impossible à communiquez à autres . . .* Grisha pushes balloons [?] with the little Venuses at the "Distillo Federal." Tisse knocks billiards over a green cloth . . . *Communiquez!*

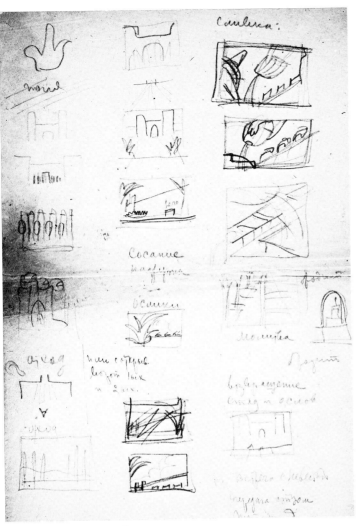

SKETCHES FOR "MAGUEY."

[First column]	[Second column]	[Third column]
maguey	sucking juice	Pouring: prayer
the way out	burros	pressing returning
and continue	with opening second	of herd and burros
	half in 2 parts	meeting with bride
		giving over by father
		the way back

EISENSTEIN DIRECTS MARÍA IN THE SCENE WHERE SHE FINDS THE BODY OF SEBASTIÁN.

"LAS SOLDADERAS." JOSÉ CLEMENTE OROZCO. FRESCO, 1926. NATIONAL PREPARATORY SCHOOL, MEXICO, D.F.

Soldadera

This fresco was one of many works by Orozco on which the scenario and the plan for the film were based—and this segment of *Qué Viva México!* was to have been dedicated to him. Another source used was a large collection of historical photographs of the Mexican Revolution.

In *The Kindness of Strangers* Salka Viertel gives the history of the last months of *Qué Viva México!* and explains why "Soldadera" was not filmed and the entire project was brought to a halt.

Berthold [Viertel]'s prediction that twenty-five thousand would not be enough for a film had come true. The year had passed quickly and the money was about gone. First the rainy season, which lasted three months, had detained Eisenstein's shooting; then the search for locations and his becoming ill caused further delays. Eisenstein asked me to persuade his Pasadena sponsors to invest more money in the film. Through Upton I succeeded in the difficult task and the millionairesses agreed to increase the financing. But Mrs. Sinclair insisted that the "irrational artist" be put under the strict control of her brother, Mr. Kimbrough. There were telephone calls and letters, and finally Eisenstein agreed, appointing me to be his representative when the rushes were shown in Los Angeles. As he had no facilities in Mexico for developing the film the negative was sent to the Eastman Laboratory in Los Angeles. The Mexican Consul had to see the rushes to be sure that nothing detrimental to Mexico had been filmed. My job was to explain to the Pasadena ladies why Eisenstein had photographed this or that from different angles (for example, the bare breasts of a dark Mexican girl, or two parrots sitting on twin coconuts).

It was useless to explain that, even unedited, the film revealed Eisenstein's intentions and also the passion and concentration with which he worked. Then suddenly I was no longer told when the rushes were to be shown, and a letter from Eisenstein [in German] informed me of what had happened.

Mexico, January 27, 1932

Dear Zalka! (He always wrote my name with a Z).

It seems to be your fate that I should be heaping my despair upon you! In my Paramount days and after—but this time is the most desperate of all! I don't know how much Sinclair keeps you *au courant* about our activities and difficulties. If he does I may be as doomed in your eyes as I am in his. However, this is the situation:

You know that instead of the four months schedule and $25,000, which would have merely resulted in a pitiful travelogue, we have worked thirteen months and spent $53,000, but we have a great film and have expanded the original idea. This expansion was achieved under incredible difficulties inflicted upon us by the behavior and bad management of Upton Sinclair's brother-in-law, Hunter Kimbrough. I am blamed for all sins committed and I accept it, under the condition that from now on I myself should be responsible but not Mr. Kimbrough. Or we three, I, Alexandrov, and Tisse, should manage the whole thing until its completion. But I am facing a situation which, so far, had been completely unknown to me: blood relationship and family ties. Mr. Kimbrough was recalled, but then sent back with "increased powers" *as my supervisor*, which means that now he has the right to interfere in everything I do and make all the cuts! He presented me to Sinclair as a liar, blackmailer, and God-knows-what-else. My direct correspondence with Sinclair stopped, our only contact was through Kimbrough who, an ambitious man, poisons our existence and creates an atmosphere in which it is impossible to work. I wrote this to Sinclair, whereupon he abruptly halted our work of thirteen months. The last part of my film, containing all the elements of a fifth act, is ruthlessly ripped out, and *you* know what this means. It's as if Ophelia were ripped out from *Hamlet*, or King Philip from *Don Carlos*.

We saved this episode, the best material, story and effects, which have not been exploited before, as a climax and the last to be filmed. It tells the story of the *Soldadera*, the women who, in hundreds, followed the Revolutionary army, taking care of their men, bearing them children, fighting at their side, burying them, and taking care of the survivors. The incomparable drama and pathos of this sequence shows the birth of the new country. Exploited and suppressed by the Spaniards, it emerges as a free Mexico. Without this sequence the film loses its meaning, unity, and its final dramatic impact: it becomes a display of unintegrated episodes. Each of these episodes now points toward this end and this revolution.

Now to our practical achievements: We have 500 soldiers, which the Mexican Army has given us for 30 days, 10,000 guns and 50 cannons, *all for nothing*. We have discovered an incredible location and have brilliantly solved the whole event in our scenario. We need only $7,000 or $8,000 to finish it, which we could do in a month, and then we would have a truly marvelous film—and when I say it I *mean* it!—a film with such mass scenes as no studio could attempt to produce now! Imagine! 500 women in an endless cactus desert, dragging through clouds of dust, household goods, beds, their children, their wounded, their dead, and the white-clad peasant soldiers in straw hats following them. We show their march into Mexico City—the Spanish Cathedral—the palaces! For the meeting of Villa and

Zapata we will have thousands of sports organizations—again without pay—with the cathedral bells ringing the victory of the first revolution. And all that has to be sacrificed because of $8,000 and quarrels—by the way, I am absolutely right and have documents to prove it—Sinclair stopped the production and intends to throw before the people a truncated stump with the heart ripped out!

I have exhausted my powers of persuasion. I shall do everything he wants . . . I accept Kimbrough, everything, anything . . . if only they let me finish this film. I have worked under most incredible harassment, no, not worked—fought. When I see you in Hollywood I will tell you what we had to go through and what probably is still ahead of us.

I myself am incapable of persuading these people. Zalka, you have already helped in this cause. We, all three of us, are convinced that this is our best film and that it must not be destroyed. I beg you, Zalka, go to Sinclair. As you were authorized to see all the rushes, he will certainly use the occasion to pour out to you everything which caused the present situation; or better, you could ask him and I am sure influence him . . . A film is not a sausage which tastes the same if you eat three-quarters of it or the whole *Wurst*. You will hear horrible things about me (first, they are not true, and second, I know you don't care and I beg you to think only about the film). The situation is different now. I have an ironclad plan. I know the locations precisely; General Calles has promised us all the facilities: Those are concrete things! And we are now familiar with conditions here and know exactly how to handle the production. Use your Medea flame and convince him (but especially *her*) to let us finish our film.

We were due to leave but Kimbrough postponed our departure for ten days, to clean up odds and ends of what we have shot. Our only hope is that meanwhile a miracle will happen and that the *Soldadera* episode will be filmed. Help us, Zalka! No, not us, help our work, save it from mutilation! If they have no money, ask for their consent to let us get it elsewhere. It seems incredible that this amount could not be raised as business. Even here the money could be found, not from philanthropists, but from businessmen, but the Sinclairs are so frightened of businessmen that they prefer to destroy all that they now have.

Wire immediately that you have received this letter and that you take our cause to your heart, regardless of what they tell you about me. One does not write such letters often.

Your,
Sergei

I phoned Upton Sinclair and asked if I could come to Pasadena and talk with him. After a brief consultation with his wife, he said that he and Mrs. Sinclair had a luncheon date in Hollywood and they would come to my house afterward. When they arrived Upton was, as usual, warm and friendly, but, I could feel, uneasy. Mrs. Sinclair, at first gay and charming, launched soon into a ferocious attack on Eisenstein. I was prepared for it and did not interrupt her, until she said that in Hollywood the Russians had been squandering money like mad, giving "wild parties" for Paramount executives. She knew for sure that the cost of one of them was four thousand dollars. (I was curious how she had arrived at that sum.) She said further that Eisenstein was immoral and a megalomaniac. I asked if she seriously believed these fantastic stories. Berthold and I had been at the party Eisenstein and his "collective" had given for the Schulbergs, at which Mrs. Montagu had been the hostess. It had been a simple, utterly "uncapitalistic" dinner, and like Upton, Eisenstein was a teetotaler. Mrs. Sinclair smiled at my guilelessness. But my greatest mistake was in saying that I could not understand what Eisenstein's private life, and the way he entertained, had to do with his art and talent.

"Of course not!" said Mrs. Sinclair. "But why should fine, trusting people spend their good money to support irresponsibility?"

I suggested that perhaps it would be advisable that less "fine and trusting people" should take over the financing of the film. I added that I knew a producer who would buy the existing film material and pay off the Pasadena group. Upton seemed inclined to give in; I sensed that he did not quite approve of his wife's severity toward Eisenstein.

David O. Selznick was then the production head at RKO. He was young, and it was said in Hollywood that he was brilliant and heading for a great career. Oliver [Garrett], who did not like producers, told me that Selznick was the only man in the industry he did not mind working for. The telephone conversation was quite long; then Oliver returned saying that Selznick wanted to see me at his office.

My interview was brief but promising. Selznick authorized me to tell Upton Sinclair that he would like to see all the film Eisenstein had shot, as he intended to buy out the Pasadena group and finance the picture himself. Of course, he did not believe that eight thousand would be enough to finish it.

That evening Eisenstein telephoned from Mexico and I told him of Selznick's offer. Afterward I called Upton, repeated what Selznick had said, and added that I had talked to Sergei. But Mrs. Sinclair was adamant. She was determined to call an end to the Mexican venture, and that was that. "Mr. Eisenstein was notified days ago that the production would be stopped. The film belongs to the Pasadena group and can neither be sold nor financed by anybody." That was final.

He and his companions waited a whole month in Laredo, Texas, for visas to the U.S. . . . We talked often over the telephone. Sometimes I could do him a small favor. Before he left America, he wrote:

> I am very sad because I am not going to see you anymore and I have the feeling that all I have to ask you this time is to send me a family photo of all of you. You and Berthold have been our best friends in the stormy and hard times. I hope the great distance will not interrupt our friendship . . . (Then, recovering his boyish, unsophisticated humor:) Thanks to our guardian angel, Mr. Kimbrough, we are sitting now a month in this lousy hole . . . I remember that when they are shooting the *Faust* film in Berlin the publicity chief of UFA said to me: "Goethe intended Mephisto to be a mixture of filth and fire." Three years later I saw the film and the same publicity man (now with another firm) added: "Unfortunately, we forgot the fire." Mr. Kimbrough is also a mixture, but it is difficult for me to say of what.

> (And later:) We are heading now for New York. We hope to cut the film in Moscow. I am really homesick and very glad about it. I have decided to change the plan of the whole film and to use everything I have shot, but in a different continuity. I hope it can be saved.

His last letter was from Moscow, in 1936.

> I have just returned from the Caucasus where—strange as it may sound—I have been shooting a new film [*Bezhin Meadow*] . . . I am slowly recovering from the blow of my Mexican experience. I have never worked on anything with such enthusiasm and what has happened to it is the greatest crime, even if I have to share the guilt. But there are things which have to be above all personal feelings. Let's not talk about it anymore.

TOP: FILMING A SCENE FOR THE EPILOGUE.
ABOVE: "WOMEN (INDIAN) IN WHITE AND BLACK . . . DIEGO [RIVERA] STYLIZED."

Epilogue

Dated December 17, 1930, dedicated to Posada, Eisenstein drafted a rough but complete shooting script for the Epilogue. It shows how the Epilogue would have accomplished its main purpose—to draw together the several threads of the preceding novellas and the Prologue. It opens with a bit of theater.

To obtain General Calles's promises of army and supplies for "Soldadera," Eisenstein was asked to make a short film of the general's soldiers and other uniformed

outfits on parade. In the intervals of filming the display for Calles, while the various parade sections were organized on the street, the roof of the hotel was used to film the costumed skeletons in the Posada manner (*calaveras*) for the Epilogue.

Skeleton introduces 2 November, in Mexico—the Day of the Dead. Skeletons (all) to be whitened with <u>priming</u> paint—eyes to be blackened (perhaps with varnish).

Choose skulls of <u>primitives</u>—more character and disproportion in the faces.

The spoken text is rhythmically broken by a clacking of the teeth. (movement of the jaws should <u>not</u> correspond with the text.) . . . the curtain falls . . . a bell . . . three candles . . . skull . . . belfry . . . funeral arches . . . women in black—on their knees, etc.

[child's costume sequence was originally begun here, and then held for later]

setting up arches / women (Indian) in white and black (peon?) Diego [Rivera] <u>stylized</u> / candles / ritual food / food in the form of coffins, skulls, crosses / table set with food / child's costume placed on chair / parents on right and left of costume / long shot of whole family at long table / conversation with the dead from the same angle /

solemn litany for the dead by the groups at cemetery in black (daybreak)

food on tombs . . . candles . . . praying . . . many people and many candles . . . people more <u>genre</u>.

skulls and masks of skulls, alternating . . . more maskers . . . masker singing.

portrait of Díaz (man beneath Díaz) [scene on tomb]

maskers and in front of them . . . a corridor . . . Díaz calavera . . . maskers run by, laughing

Bishop [skeleton] . . . gentleman [skeleton] in top-hat group laughs and sings . . . children dance in skull masks . . . faces on tombs [these last two shots originally in reverse order] . . . children chewing sugar skulls . . . paper streamers over saloon . . . playing with bones.

saloon, in front of it: calavera—general, bishop, top hat [skeletons] kiss one another . . . quarrel with bones . . . calavera—Zapatista [skeleton] . . . Lady [skeleton] . . . toreador [skeleton] . . . embrace

calavera—groom and bride [from "Maguey" novella]

fight . . . lying on the tomb . . . Aztec skull (stone one, in museum)

kiss . . . and [?]

skull (clay) . . . removal and murder of masks . . . after removal . . . stone . . . clay . . . masks

mask on naked infant . . . naked infant gurgles when mask is removed . . . feet trample masks

infant shouts . . . life.*

THE SHOOTING SCRIPT FOR THE EPILOGUE.

---

*A facsimile of the first page of this script is reproduced in *Sight and Sound*, Autumn 1958, p. 306.

A CALAVERA. ENGRAVINGS BY JOSÉ GUADALUPE POSADA.

EISENSTEIN FILMING GENERAL CALLES'S SOLDIERS ON PARADE IN EXCHANGE FOR HIS USE OF THE ARMY IN THE LAST NOVELLA, "SOLDADERA."

<u>BELOW:</u> **A LAST MEMO FOR THE EPILOGUE.**

<u>LEFT, THIS PAGE AND OPPOSITE PAGE:</u>
THE COSTUMED SKELETONS FROM THE EPILOGUE.

THE LAST PARADE
(L'AGONIE)

"BLACK MAJESTY"

L'AGONIE

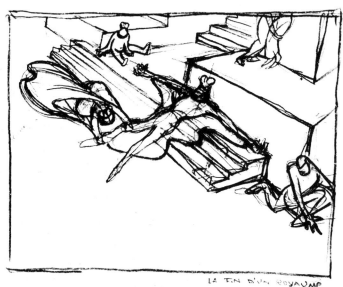

LA FIN D'UN ROYAUME

ABOVE: SKETCHES FOR SCENES FROM <u>BLACK MAJESTY</u>.

OPPOSITE PAGE: THE DESIGN OF A WHOLE SEQUENCE FOR <u>BLACK MAJESTY</u>, SHOWING FROM ABOVE THE MOVEMENTS OF THE HERO HOLDING A CANDELABRUM.

[PARENTHESIS: HAITI]

On March 21, 1931, while waiting for bright sunlight in Mérida, Eisenstein began to sketch key scenes for a film of the Haitian Revolution, an idea inspired by John Vandercook's dramatic *Black Majesty*.

This was another subject that he clung to stubbornly. An early record he left of his interest is dated in Paris, before the signing of the Paramount contract. On his return to Moscow in 1932, with the hope of Paul Robeson's participation. Eisenstein was delighted to hear that Anatoli Vinogradov, learning of Eisenstein's interest in the subject, had written a novel about Haiti, *The Black Consul;* this would give more weight to Eisenstein's proposal to the Film Committee. Robeson accepted the leading role (either of Christophe or Dessalines) and Solomon Michoels was to play Toussaint l'Ouverture. The project was cancelled even though Robeson had come to Moscow to discuss the production, which had been officially announced. Still, Eisenstein could not let go the story's great potentialities, as we see in this sketch for the candelabrum scene ("scene with the lustre"), which he transformed into a lesson for his students at GIK in 1933.*

Eisenstein's morale was at its lowest in January 1932. He had realized that he might not be allowed to complete his great Mexican plan. However, he received news of appreciation of his work in several quarters which revived his faith in himself as an artist.

This, by Jean Cocteau, was from the English edition of *Opium,* sent by a friend to Eisenstein in Mexico. Although Eisenstein had little respect for Cocteau as an artist, after meetings with him in Paris (his parodies of Cocteau's drawings are extraordinarily acute), he was keenly aware of the prestige of Cocteau's praise.

I have seen funny and splendid films; I have only seen three great films: *Sherlock, Jr.,* with Buster Keaton, *The Gold Rush* with Chaplin, Eisenstein's *Potemkin.* . . . On re-reading these notes (October 1929), I add: Bunuel's *Un Chien Andalou* . . . it must be admitted that one of the numerous successes of *Potemkin* is that it does not seem to have been filmed or played by anyone.

(1930) I knew Eisenstein. My view was correct. At the last minute he invented the steps where the massacre took place. This stairway takes its place in Russian history. Alexandre Dumas, Michelet, Eisenstein, the only true historians.

More encouragement came by way of William Hunter's *Scrutiny of Cinema,* published in London in 1932. Though Hunter's comments on Eisenstein's films were not *all* praise, more importantly they showed understanding, which was highly valued by Eisenstein.

*Vladimir Nizhny, *Lessons with Eisenstein*, New York, Hill & Wang, 1962.

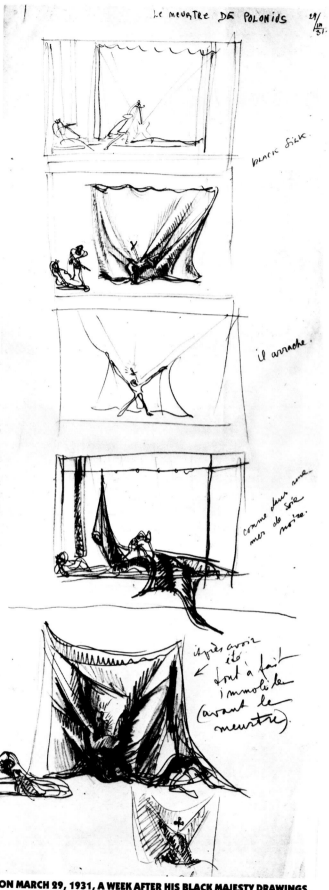

BLACK SILK

il arrache.

comme dans une mer de soie noire.

après avoir été ← tout à fait immobile (avant le meurtre).

ON MARCH 29, 1931, A WEEK AFTER HIS <u>BLACK MAJESTY</u> DRAWINGS, EISENSTEIN SKETCHED A SCENE THAT WAS CLEARLY INTENDED FOR THE THEATER: HAMLET'S MURDER OF POLONIUS.

The Murder of Polonius / Black Silk / He pulls [the curtain] / As in a sea of black silk / After having done this everything is immobile (as before the murder)

An essay published in *Virginia Quarterly Review*, October 1931, by Prince Mirsky, contained the most serious discussion of his work yet to appear.

It was only with the rise of the Soviet school of film directors that the inherent kinship of the art of cinematography with science was brought out, and the new art entered on a path that had only occasionally and desultorily been trodden by its elder relatives. This happened with the release in [1926] of Eisenstein's famous film, *The Battleship Potemkin.* . . .

Eisenstein's revolution . . . is only a recognition of the inherent but undeveloped possibilities contained in the scientific technique of the new art. It is a step forward in the understanding of scientific laws rather than in the accumulation of scientific data, a philosophical rather than a technological advance. Eisenstein may be compared to Galileo, whose importance in the history of science does not reside so much in the new observations (however important) made by him as in the realization of the fundamental importance of exact measurement for the construction of physical science. What makes the new Soviet school important not only for the art of the cinema but for modern culture and philosophy in general is that it introduces a new attitude towards the creative process itself, a new way of producing imaginative values. To a certain extent Eisenstein's revolution reproduces the revolution undergone by painting in the Quattrocento when mathematical calculation was introduced into the creative process of the painter, but the much more complex technical basis of cinematography as compared with painting, and the infinitely larger scientific background of modern civilization, promise to make the new transformation more solid and stable than could be the case in the Quattrocento.

This understanding on his own intellectual level gave Eisenstein so much pleasure that he transcribed large portions of the essay before leaving Mexico.

Réaliser !"

"

Cézanne.

ON THE EUROPA

1932 Spring *Returned to the USSR. In autumn I accepted the Faculty of Direction at the State Institute of Cinematography. Working on pedagogic and scientific research. Also work on script ideas and on developing projects.*

Also sailing on the *Europa* were Noel Coward, Alexander Woollcott, and Dorothy Thompson. Eisenstein was invited to share a table with this "gathering of wits." Just before sailing, he had received a cable from Sinclair, which must have put him in a good humor:

BON VOYAGE. ALL FILM WILL FOLLOW ON NEXT SHIP.
For the rest of his life Eisenstein kept this broken promise on display above his desk, along with a more positive reminder, written on a card of the *Europa* (above).

BELOW: SOME OF THE BOOKS BROUGHT HOME BY EISENSTEIN FROM AMERICA.

MAXIM MAXIMOVICH MAXIMOV
I AM PERFECTLY SURE THAT MM NEVER
— NOVEMBER 16, 1932

On October 13, 1932, Eisenstein wrote to Kenneth Mac-Pherson, editor of *Close Up*:

> At the present time I am finishing the licking of my Mexican wounds—it looks as if the picture is lost for ever. . .as soon as the thing is definite you will get an article about this "chef d'oeuvre inconnu"—the film that nobody will see. . . .
>
> . . .for the comedy on which I am working at present is the next theoretical step after things which were worked out and discovered upon the *American Tragedy*. . . .
>
> Between the work I am doing, I am rejoicing myself by some amusing little research work; and this is for the moment *D. H. Lawrence.*

The year after his return to Moscow was one of Eisenstein's most painful years. Negotiations with Sinclair through friends continued until Eisenstein learned that his film had been turned over to other hands and that the "Maguey" novella had been stretched into a commercial feature film *Thunder Over Mexico*. This led to a nervous breakdown and an extended stay at Kislovodsk. The scene at home was scarcely more encouraging: soon after Eisenstein's return, Boris Shumyatsky, who had agreed to Sinclair's treatment of Eisenstein and to the destruction of the Mexican film, proposed a musical comedy to Eisenstein; Eisenstein declined, but Alexandrov—without consulting Eisenstein—accepted the idea. Eisenstein's two counterproposals both were rejected: *The Black Consul*, in which Paul Robeson had agreed to play Chris-

SKETCH FOR THE SATIRE MMM.

tophe, and *MMM* (a satirical idea planned as early as 1928), a fantastic comedy with Maxim Strauch to play the newly appointed head of Intourist in an unnamed Russian city. *MMM* was completely planned before it was halted.

The action of *MMM* ranges (in the hero's nightmare) through Russia's history. Here is the last scene of the prologue, with a deliberate echo of *Don Giovanni*:

[Max] heard a giggle
Was turned round
Stumbled. . .
Over a threshold
Of what seemed a door.
But, perhaps not. . .
No, it's a door.
Someone let him in
And closed it
With a hollow boom
And with a rumbling
Echo. . .
Over the threshold,
he found himself. . .
In the town cathedral.
Boom. Gloom.
All around dimly glimmered faces
In the reflections
Of icon-lamps
Images
Of ancient
Russia
"Lord, help us!"
Saints on the frescoes
Patriarchs
Pious
Boyars
And princes
And heavenly birds
Sirins
And Alkonosts
Around galleries.
Forgetting tact,
And shame,
And respect
For the past,
With the whirl
Of a dazed head,
In a drunken ecstasy
And a fevered frenzy
Of self-love
As conceited
As some Don Juan,
Challenging the Commander,
Max
Cast a challenge
To Holy Russia:
"I summon you all!
Come!
I will convert you
In three days
All of you
At the very least
Into union members!
I belong to Rabis [Workers of Art]
I am Boyarsky [president of Rabis]
himself
I will fashion you
In the image of Boyarsky
Of the trade union!
I'll sign you up as shock-workers!

b.

c.

JUDITH GLIZER (STRAUCH'S WIFE) BEING REHEARSED AS THE VAUDEVILLE ACTRESS MARRIED TO MAXIM MAXIMOVICH.

I'll make you members
Of the Komsomol [Young Communists]!. . ."
And Maxim's shadow races
Across the severe faces
Of the frescoes
Across patriarchs
And saints
Suddenly. . .
A frescoed patriarch nodded to him.
"I'll come"
Came rushing
Through the silent vaults.
Sobered up at once,
Maxim
Flew
Like a cannon-ball,
Leaving behind him
Cathedral,
Crosses,
Bells
And "the unsleeping eye."
An invisible choir
Joined in
"I'll surely come."

d.

TRANSLATIONS OF NOTES WRITTEN ON CHARACTER SKETCHES ABOVE AND AT LEFT.

a. V. Khenkin in the role of the tram conductor

b. The whiskers play on the lyre! 29 Jan 1933

c. A deliberate anachronism—ribbons, stars, medals. [The Patriarch of All Russia to be played by Naum Rogozhin.]

d. [The legendary Bird of Alkonost (with overtones of alcoholism), to be played by Novikova.]

TRANSLATIONS OF NOTES WRITTEN ON SKETCHES ON OPPOSITE PAGE.

[Clockwise from bottom left]

Changes in the shape of whiskers

Novikova and Strauch

Executioner / Sings without words / Ida declaims to his singing. [At bottom] Duet on executioner's block

Silk shirt below knees / "My white hands are aching from hard work" / The Executioner

CLASSROOM: GTK, GIK, VGIK

. . . MUST BE IN FULL CONTROL OF METHOD —TO MAKE IT SERVE PRACTICE.—MAY 1931

1933-1934 *Work in State Institute of Cinema: headed Department of Direction and supervised the Direction faculty. Worked on large theoretical work on Direction (to be published this current year [1937?]). Work as consultant on various scripts.* (N. B.: *My pedagogical work started in 1922, Directors' Workshop in Proletcult; in 1928 in State Technicum of Cinema.)* [*For a record of Eisenstein's lectures of 1933-1934, see* Lessons With Eisenstein.]

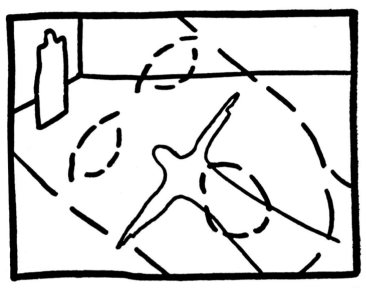

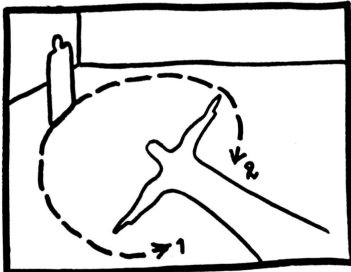

ABOVE: FROM EISENSTEIN'S BLACKBOARD SKETCHES ILLUSTRATING HIS LECTURES ON MISE-EN-SHOT. DRAWN FROM THE LESSONS ON THE MURDER OF THE MONEYLENDER IN <u>CRIME AND PUNISHMENT</u>.

OPPOSITE PAGE: EISENSTEIN TEACHING HIS CLASS AT THE FILM INSTITUTE.

MOSCOW

In England the Montagus received word of the fall of MMM, the rise of *Moscow*, and Eisenstein's continuing work on "the book."

Eduard Tisse to Ivor Montagu, June 6, 1933

> We are hard at work. The comedy that we were planning with Sergei Mikhailovich has been postponed, and we are now preparing a grandiose production, a big historical film, *Moscow*. The work is big. Shooting is to start in February 1934.
>
> Grisha has gone on independently and is working on a comedy called *Jazz*. This film is being made by our two disciples, Grisha—Sergei Mikhailovich's disciple, and cameraman Nilsen, who was mine. As for Sergei Mikhailovich and me, we are now in the category of "elders." Therefore we have resolved to turn away from light comedies and to make huge screen canvasses as befits our age.

Eisenstein to Ivor Montagu, undated

> I am working very hard on my book. Please do not laugh. It is the only important work I am doing at the present. Although at the same time I am supervising the writing of a play by Zarkhi, which I want to produce on the legitimate stage in autumn, when I have finished my book etc. I hope to start film production early in spring.

Pera Attasheva to Ivor Montagu, December 21, 1933

> About S. M.'s book—it's in progress, but of a very slow kind indeed. Nevertheless—it will be finished before 15th of February. He will begin the production of *Moscow* film at the end of March (that's in the case of failure of Mexican affairs).

"Your unhappy old S. M. E." writes to Ivor Montagu, April 27, 1934

> The whole Mexican affair has raised a certain disgust for everything connected with films. And I am not quite sure if I can exist without film interests. . .Besides that I'm terribly tired after the very hard work during this season at GIK and the still harder work on the book. I have now to correct the manuscript and then it will be finished, but I nearly have no force to do it. Head empty and no capacity to work . . . . My plans for the future include even . . . staging a show in the . . . theater!

Moscow was the first of several unrealized projects to follow the structure of *Qué Viva México!*: different, contrasting epochs within a historical unity. The surviving sketches for it indicate a boyar period before Peter, the heavy industry of Peter I—both Piranesi's prisons and the Moscow Metro stations, then in construction, were used for its design—and Moscow in 1812 (all on following page).

ONE OF TWO PIRANESI ENGRAVINGS OWNED BY EISENSTEIN.

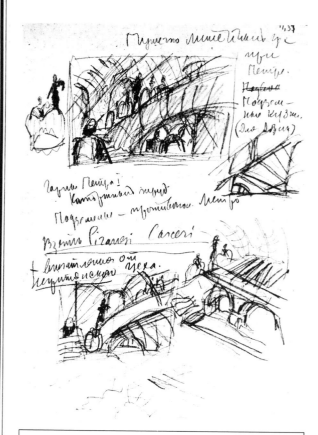

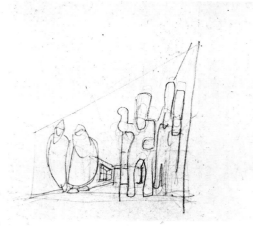

THE BOYARS IN CONTROL, WITH THEIR ASIAN HAREM.

Cannon foundry during Peter's reign, underground smithy. / Peter's furnaces. Underground passages. Metro. / Borrow from Piranesi Carceri / impression of Negro workshop.

In "burning Moscow / fragmented speech is itself / transformed into slogans / —16 Jan 1934 Around campfires at night, / an accumulation of remarks, / The words of campfires. / Whispers. Calls. Become speeches. Shots of Alexander and 1812 and "1905" / (but not in the style of Chervyakov's exercises) Crowded shots during Peter's reign: / one feels the urge to break through / and into the 19th century

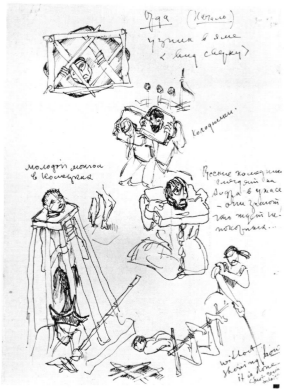

THIS DRAWING OF THE TATAR VICTORY MAY BE RELATED EITHER TO MMM OR MOSCOW.

[Tatar] <u>Hordes</u> (beginning) / prisoner in hole (seen from above) / stocks / young Mongol in stocks / Russian prisoners with a look of horror—they know what awaits rebels . . . / [whipping feet] without showing <u>how</u> it is done—(just ready to do it).

FROM LEFT, MEI LAN-FANG, TRETYAKOV, EISENSTEIN.

The *Moscow* project ended tragically. Nathan Zarkhi, known best for his scenarios for Pudovkin, was working on the *Moscow* script simultaneously with his play, *Moscow the Second*, that Eisenstein also was to direct. Zarkhi was killed in an automobile accident, ending both projects. Other projects took their place this year, only to vanish unrealized.

When André Malraux came to the Soviet Union for the Writers' Congress in 1934, there were discussions about the filming of *La Condition Humaine*; he and Eisenstein developed a treatment during their stay in the Crimea. The last document on this project is dated August 8, 1934, a contract with Mezhrabpom-Film for Eisenstein to work as "consultant" on the film. It is possible that Eisenstein's essay on Chaplin (*Film Essays*, pp. 123-24) contains the only published fragment of this treatment.

The Haitian project, *Black Majesty*, was revived for a short while. Paul and Eslanda Robeson arrived in Moscow at Eisenstein's invitation. Robeson still wanted to play Christophe, and Solomon Mikhoels was to play Toussaint l'Ouverture. The Robesons remained in Moscow for discussions with the film authorities (Boris Shumyatsky then headed the film industry) without coming to any decision about *Black Majesty*.

On October 27, 1934, Eisenstein married Pera Attasheva without publicity.

1935 *By decree of Central Committee of USSR I am awarded the title of Honored Art Worker.*

MEI LAN-FANG

By January 1935 Eisenstein's interest had shifted from Japanese to Chinese culture. Later that year, Eisenstein attempted at the Newsreel Studio to record a scene, "Duel at Rainbow Pass," from the Moscow performances of Mei Lan-fang and his troupe.

MOMENTS FROM "DUEL AT RAINBOW PASS."

BEZHIN MEADOW

FROM THE STOREHOUSE OF CREATION NOTHING IS COMPLETELY LOST.

"Bezhin Meadow," one of the short genre stories by Turgenev in the collection *A Sportsman's Notebook*, tells how Turgenev, losing his way while returning from one of his hunting hikes, stayed the night at a bonfire kept by the boy horseherders. The ghost stories they told each other to keep awake, revealing so much about the Russian peasant child of 1850, were recalled by Alexander Rzheshevsky when he was commissioned by the Komsomol organization (the Communist Youth League) to write a scenario on the theme of the farm work of the Young Pioneers. He went to live for two years in the village of Bezhin Meadow, to observe and record the contrast between the Russian peasant child as Turgenev knew him and as he is today.

He brought back a scenario vivid with new Soviet village life and the heroism of Young Pioneers on a collective farm. The central figure of Stepok was modeled on Pavlik Morozov, a boy whose work of guarding the harvest threatened the sabotage activities of his family; they murdered him. Early in 1935, when Eisenstein chose Rzheshevsky's script for production, the original plan was to make two versions of the film, one for general release and the other for children's cinema audiences. Among the many alterations in this ill-fated film, that plan was abandoned.

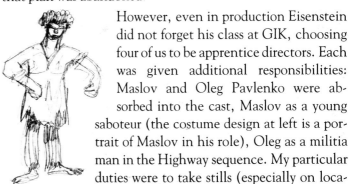

However, even in production Eisenstein did not forget his class at GIK, choosing four of us to be apprentice directors. Each was given additional responsibilities: Maslov and Oleg Pavlenko were absorbed into the cast, Maslov as a young saboteur (the costume design at left is a portrait of Maslov in his role), Oleg as a militia man in the Highway sequence. My particular duties were to take stills (especially on location hunting), help with actor selection, and to keep a production diary (from which the following italicized excerpts are quoted).

> Costumes. Boy Komsomols: white shirts; girls: white blouses; old men and women: black shawls, skirts, jackets, coats, shirts; others: dominant tone—gray (dun color); Maslov: coarse shirt; Zaitzev: (bearded) in black; Protopov: in short coat, peasant style; props: rifle fire with smoke; badges of Voroshilov marksmen.

ABOVE: ONE OF THE FIRST SCENES IN THE FILM: STEPOK AT THE BURIAL OF HIS MOTHER.

OPPOSITE PAGE: TISSE AND EISENSTEIN FILMING THE ROAD SEQUENCE IN <u>BEZHIN MEADOW</u>.

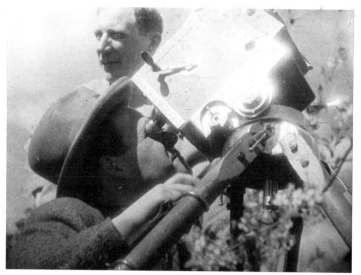

**ABOVE: FILMING THE PROLOGUE IN THE APPLE ORCHARD.
BELOW: FROM LEFT, TISSE, EISENSTEIN, A STUDENT.**

While the crew and cast were chosen, Eisenstein continued his usual unceasing stream of drawings.* There were sketches for all phases of the film, both large concepts and minute details.

> . . . for movements of separate bodies and massed bodies, for ideas that are drawn before they go into the scenario, for series of compositions to maintain a part of the narrative in one key, for series that are building a climax, for faces that he is looking for and faces that he has found and is fitting into the scheme, for backgrounds to be sought, settings to be built, costumes, objects, details, everything. As practical as these drawings are, as exercise or as plan, Eisenstein's reliance on them is not a hampering thing. [Later I saw production designs being used as blueprints, both in Moscow and Hollywood.] The drawings are as loose and elastic as the scenario will remain to the last shot. I have seen more than one filming day pass without Eisenstein referring once to the script—so reliant is he upon the firm mental images he keeps with him. He says that all plans are to prepare you for the new ideas that the day's work brings.

While we waited for the location scouts (assistant Gomorov and administrator Gutin) to return from the south, we took advantage of the season to film the short poetic prologue, an evocation of Turgenev, in the old apple orchards of Kolomenskoye.

> These first shots were taken with an understanding of Turgenev's place in and contribution to the history of literature and art. In the wake of romanticism, Turgenev was attracted by the impressionists, who were in turn attracted by the Japanese printmakers; Turgenev's introduction of impressionism into literature was the key the episode needed. As Turgenev extracted the essence of an already extracted Japanese accent on detail, on isolation, on the perfected ensemble of seemingly chance selection, so out of Turgenev's style and background a cinema approach was extracted. The problem for these first few compositions became one of showing the audience <u>how</u> Turgenev saw the things around him. The impression of this brief prologue must not be that of turning over a collection of Japanese prints and Chinese drawings, but of examining, lovingly, the corners and details of a landscape lit by the soft last light of romanticism, selected by an artist fascinated by the eyes of the Orient.

Most of the actor selection for mass scenes would be done on location, but the central character of the boy, Stepok, who was needed in all scenes, had not been found as the schedule for the expedition came closer.

> Two days a week, for four steady hours, those chosen during the week by the assistants and agencies are shot into his view, five at a time; the second (his first) selection is indicated, these are photographed and registered. Those for mass scenes are chosen with almost as much care as for the speaking roles. Out of more

---

*In the later general destruction of all materials connected with this banned film, Eisenstein himself, who was archive conscious and normally saved all significant documents, kept none of the hundreds (probably thousands!) of work drawings that I had seen and had watched him work on through the first version of the film. Among the few survivals are marginal sketches in the preserved copy of his shooting script—and one costume sketch that I begged for as he was cleaning off his desk in Kharkov. Eisenstein said, "Oh, don't bother with that—I'll give you a good one when we get back to Moscow." But I took it.

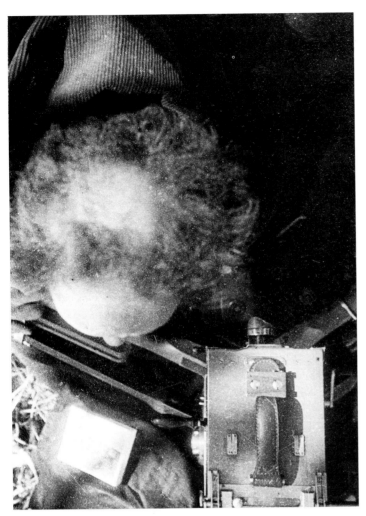

EISENSTEIN AT THE CAMERA.

VITKA KARTASHOV'S SCREEN TESTS FOR THE ROLE OF STEPOK.

than 2,000 children, the assistants chose 600, which Eisenstein narrows down to 200, and still the boy to play the hero hasn't been found. No one made a deep enough impression on Eisenstein to be given a screen test. Attasheva, working as an assistant, was sent to Leningrad to look for possibles, but Stepok wasn't there, either. Crisis. The expedition was to start any day, and Stepok was a vital part of the episode to be filmed on the first location. Of the four leading characters, only one had been decided upon—the boy's father. At the first reading of the scenario, Boris Zakhava, director of the Vakhtangov Theater and without previous cinema experience, was given this role.

And then, in the next to last prepared viewing of children, Eisenstein saw Vitka—"He IS Stepok." He is a quiet eleven-year-old, interested in mathematics, but not movies—the son of an army chauffeur, Kartashov. He seemed to have everything (and everyone, including Rzheshevsky) against him: his hair grew in the wrong way, insufficient pigmentation of the skin gave him great white blotches on his face and neck, and at the test his face grew stiff and dull—until he was told to ask us riddles, when he produced a clear, fine, almost compelling voice. Only Eisenstein was able at once to see the positives, later clear to all. A make-up man was some help; more importantly, Vitka expressed the role as Eisenstein imagined it, not as an actor, but as a child, as a Young Pioneer, with a quick and broad intelligence, an expressive face, and a surprising emotional range.

Armavir

Scouts had meanwhile been looking for locations. It had been decided before they left that the real Bezhin Meadow could not be used, that a "synthetic" village would be composed, employing backgrounds from various places in the Soviet Union. To avoid confusion among his assistants, Eisenstein made a map of this synthetic Bezhin Meadow.

With the return of the scouts, a plan was agreed: Armavir for two weeks, to film mass scenes for the film's Highway episode, then Kharkov for about a month, to film all the acted scenes for this episode, with the help of the Kharkov tractor plant.

So, at six o'clock on the morning of June 15, a chartered plane carrying a group of seven and all of our cameras and apparatus took off from Moscow airport and flew almost directly south. By four o'clock we found ourselves 1,500 kilometers from Moscow, in the Azov-Black Sea district, on the Stalin State Farm, the second largest _sovkhoz_ in the USSR and so far uncontaminated by a kino expedition.

Kharkov

Because this Highway episode represented the most difficult part of the film, Eisenstein chose it for the first to be filmed, so that the rest could be built around this accomplished climax. It occurred midway through the film, which covered a twenty-four-hour action, from the morning of one day to the next, harvest day. (The highway itself was one of the repeated uses of a road symbol.) In this episode, four fugitive incendiaries, who have been forced out of their refuge in the village church, are being taken away under guard by two militiamen. They try to cut across the highway, along which peasants are moving to the harvesting camp. When the harvesters learn who these men are, they threaten violence; but the boy Stepok, stepping between the two groups, relaxes tension with a joke. The militiamen are able to proceed with their prisoners.

THE SABOTEURS ARE HALTED BESIDE THE HIGHWAY.

THE HARVESTERS WANT TO LYNCH THE SABOTEURS.

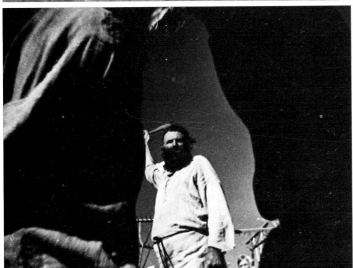

TOP: FILMING THE HARVESTERS' TRACTORS ON THE HIGHWAY. EISENSTEIN AND HIS ASSISTANT GOMOROV ARE TO THE LEFT OF THE CAMERA CREW.

ABOVE: BLACKBEARD THREATENS THE SABOTEURS WITH AN AX.

STEPOK STOPS THE ANGRY PEASANTS WITH A JOKE.

A YOUNG PIONEER GUARDING THE HARVEST ON A WATCHTOWER.

Taking advantage of the generosity of the State Farm and the fine weather, and because we were way ahead of schedule, we used the marvelously filmic acres of ripe grain to film some shots for the finale of the film, when the body of murdered Stepok is brought back to the village: Young Pioneers salute from their watchtowers as the body is carried past, in a series of unusually beautiful and bare compositions, a pair of guards high in their towers and another pair, in close-up, below. Almost invariably these shots were taken with the 28. lens. When I asked Eisenstein to explain the choice of the 28. lens for these compositions, he said that lenses can be used as instruments are used in orchestration. Different lenses produce different tensions. There are flat lenses, such as the 150., which produce little depth, little tension, and little emotion. Then there are the less-corrected lenses, such as the 28. and the 25., which give a wide and sharply rounded image, producing a positive sense of strain in the spectator. These shots, coming near the end of the film, should bring a calculated, gradual expansion of the heart, and here the greatest tension of both lens and of composition (far and near) may be advisable. This exquisite precision in the choice of lenses is one of Tisse's contributions to the Eisenstein-Tisse partnership.

EISENSTEIN AND TISSE FILMING STEPOK ON A WATCHTOWER.

Although three and sometimes four cameras filmed constantly, very few of the shots would appear on the screen just as they were taken. Although we had no sound equipment until we got to Kharkov, the finished sound was considered with each day's work. Eisenstein explained the mystery: "On the editing table this episode will be handled in the same way as a composer works on a fugue in four voices. The material we're filming here is only one of those voices. Most of it will be used for rear projection and transparencies when the second voice will be worked out, with figures and close-ups in the foreground. . . . The third and fourth voices (or theses, or motifs) are in sound—sound and speech." **

No possibilities of this first voice were neglected, even though Tisse (looking like the White Rabbit) had to climb every morning into his hole dug under the road to film machinery passing over him in different combinations arranged the night before. We worked from six in the morning until seven at night, then washed hilariously before dinner at the little hotel, had a conference on the day's achievements and the morrow's plans. "Well, have we come up to the record set during Potemkin, *when 75 different shots were made in one day's filming on the steps?" "No, but 45 on three cameras and a hand camera is still pretty good." "Not good enough! Don't let the old battleship shame us."*

Pera Attasheva wrote to Ivor Montagu from Moscow, July 14, 1935:

> We started the filming of the new film called "Bezhin Lug" (Bezhin Meadow?). S. M., Eduard and rest of them all are in Charkhov on the location. I am the only one staying here—looking for actors. And looking for other location near to Moscow. . . 70 percent of the film must be taken on the location—and the summer is not perfect at all.

Attasheva's efforts to find the necessary locations nearer Moscow were successful. By the time we left Kharkov and the elaborately prepared Highway, we were able to film an early sequence—Stepok with his dead mother—outside the same village where the apple blossoms had been filmed for the brief prologue.

January 15th 1936
Experience in Sound
Audiovisual polyphony:

For the scene in which Stepok sobs and buries his face in his mother's shoulder, Zaitsev suggests that music should be used to convey his crying. Vulgarity as a method!

To challenge his point of view I worked out a concrete solution—and out of that came some basic deductions. (N.B.: It's always this way, not something thought up from thin air or something outside concrete emotional and visual impact.)

In the scene "Stepok and his mother's corpse" distinctly:

I { The boy's crying—by acting in shot
"The indifference of nature"—by the composition of the shot
The mother's death—music in the shot

This is the correct polyphonic schema.
It would be vulgar to do it this way:

**Vladimir Nilsen was to be in charge of the film's multiple and process shots.

II { Crying with acting
Crying with the composition of the shot
Crying with the music

This would be a case of "creeping" synchronization, while the former example shows a correct solution— *expressive* synchronization.

Synchronization must *not* be *descriptive* but in *imagery*. (N.B.: Example II might be used in moments of 101 percent intensity, as a unison of the ancient Gregorian plain chant that Huysmans so enjoyed. This would comprise the "face" of a composition. In a word, "real time.") To be more precise:

Music—the mother's corpse. In a certain composition in this scene the dead woman is filmed as "the dead Peasant Mother," not as "the corpse of a certain peasant woman, who lived at a certain place and was of a certain age." (N.B.: I always remember in *The Youth of Maxim*: "The song bursts out." "Nothing can gag the mouth of revolutionary song." "The whole prison sang." That is what *should* have been, but this is what was filmed: the technique of inserting the not very clean fingers of the prison guards into the prisoners' mouths to prevent the escape of any kind of sound from those mouths.)

Generalizations—"the *image* of death" through music is expressive. The depiction of "the image of death" as a corpse is not expressive. The "anecdote" of the boy's crying—if shown in proportioned composition within the frame—can create a monumental-lyrical image that conveys the monumental-lyric, severe, cosmic quiet of nature ("how quiet it is").

Another example: a composition like Auswuchs [outgrowth] visually perceived (images) of landscape, in an *identical* setting. Here we also have a disjunction (quite impossible in painting!); image-imaged, expressed as "this sort of nature" in a single *montage* piece (with an appropriate structure of composition), but in another montage piece of a *different image*, not of nature, but of a landscape, a tall old man and a crying boy, but placed in a composition of the same structure as in representing nature, i.e., where *both* depiction *and* the composed image are integrally attached to the subject's anecdote.

Examples: the skiffs in *Potemkin* illustrated the "graphic" continuity of compositional movement from shot to shot.

From the same source we find examples of unity in imagery structure, moving through a row of montage pieces.

This imagery has an overtonal-complex order (graphic, light, angle, color, etc. in a totality, during possible conditions of non-concurrence and correspondence with each separate element).

This does not disturb the ranks of indications and spontaneously separated correspondences (for example, through the sustained tonalities and textures of the pieces). We can unify through a detail—such as a branch against the sky. But, for example, graphically—however, and it works! But not as graphic-calligraphically, as in the analyzed example in *Potemkin*.

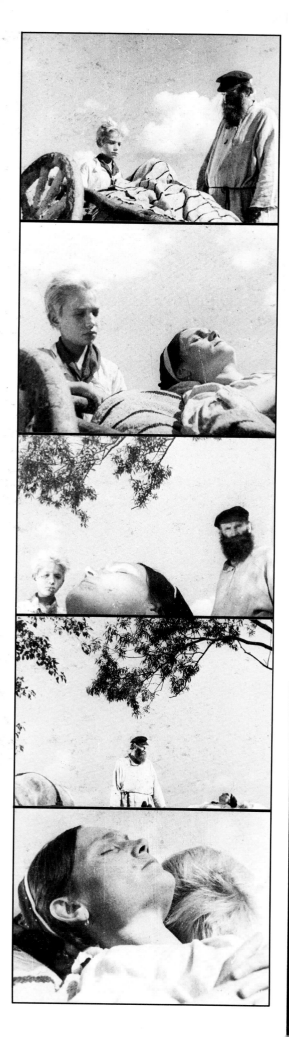

(Kolomenskoye Village 5-6 Aug 1935) fac. Planirovka

1. Savitsky from B → B, into B₁: "Why did your father beat her up like that?" (make this a close-up)
2. Stepok in A makes a turn "Because of me." Sees the feet of the dead woman. Runs to cover them (into A₁)
3. Savitsky from B₁ → B₂: "But why?"
4. Stepok from A₁ → A₂ (turns, leans on wagon. Pause): "Because she had given birth to a son like me" (reaches over to touch the head of the dead woman from A₂ → A₃—cut)

5. Here use (additional shooting) close-up of dead woman's head, covered by burlap [drawing] added shot Stepok's voice over her shot: "Because she understood me . . ."
6. Stepok in A₃, throws off the burlap. Stepok and Savitsky pull it away.
7. Stepok (in A₃): " . . . and she won't talk any more?" (general and close)
8. Savitsky (close): "Not a murmur . . .
9. Shot of dead woman (chiaroscuro) . . . never . . ." (Savitsky's voice over)
10. Stepok (in A₃) throws himself at his mother. Looks into distance, Then: "Mama, let's go away. Mama, get up." Straightens up, begins to hurry Savitsky. Runs up to him in B₃ (A₄)
    Pulls at Savitsky: "Let's hurry etc."
11. Savitsky: "She won't go any faster now, see him sucking" (turns his head to point to the colt)
12. The sucking colt.
13. Stepok looks there, then at his mother, sobs and pushes his head in her shoulder.
14. Savitsky: ". . . it's so quiet" (2 variants).

Post-synchronization and added shots for synch scenes.

Pick up shots:
1) for "It's so quiet":   Can be shot anywhere
2) Face of dead woman: She, Stepok, Savitsky
3) Ride along "Linkin" 29 km.   and add variant
along Kashirskoye Chaussée.

ABOVE: COMPOSITION FOR THE FRAMES AT LEFT.
LEFT: STEPOK'S DEAD MOTHER.

The Hut

An Eisenstein sound film will be visual-sound counterpoint, in his own words—the highest plan for the realization of conflict between optical and acoustical impulses. He has also said that the ideal form for the sound film is the monologue. In the Family sequence, filmed in the studio, both of these ideals find expression. The father is taunted by the presence of the boy who has "betrayed" him. Being weak, and not quite drunk enough to beat the boy, his only outlet is to goad him with scorn and anathema into making some move that can be answered with a blow. The dialogue for the scene is literally a monologue by the father, and the sequence will be edited as a conflict between the rising hysteria of the father and the increasing calm of Stepok, culminating in shrieking drunken fury and Stepok's decision to leave home forever. In an interior set, built in exaggerated perspective, you sometimes <u>see</u> the back of Stepok's upright head and <u>hear</u> the new pitch of anger it provokes in the father. Sometimes the conflict appears in the same shot: Stepok's face and the father's face dancing behind it in frustrated brutality. Sometimes two visuals convey the same side of the conflict, but expressed in opposites—as in the shot where the father's hysteria is shown alongside the silent, still, and concentrated hate held by the grandmother for the boy.

Eisenstein's directions are the most sensible I have seen in practice. With both skilled and unskilled actors, he first solves their physical problems: What are my torso and limbs and head doing at this point? How will my movement over to there be managed? Does this movement convey the desired meaning? With skilled actors, and this now includes Vitka, he talks over the scene, uncovers the scene's emotions (but never once showing how a face must act), and goes through it once or twice without the camera, enlarging on details and making changes, seldom drastic ones. Then the camera is brought into action, the shot set up, and while Tisse arranges the lights and Bogdankevich the microphone, the scene is played through several times. When it is taken, if Eisenstein or Tisse or the actor is not satisfied, it is retaken. In customary manner, a long dialogue sequence is filmed first straight through for sound-strip and mise en scène, before being broken into the more telling middle and close shots.

Filming came to an abrupt halt when Eisenstein came down with smallpox. In his personal selection of every object that was to decorate the next interior set, the church, some germ, waiting on an icon or holy banner, chose the atheist Eisenstein for the only case of smallpox known in Moscow for about two years. The last entry in my production diary* is dated October 20, 1935:

---

*The last scene I worked on was the Church Porch, though my last job on *Bezhin Meadow* was as courier between Eisenstein and Isaac Babel, who had agreed to collaborate on a drastically altered script. I have since read a lurid anecdote of this collaboration, resembling nothing that I witnessed. Months were to pass before production could be resumed. I was offered a job in New York and Eisenstein advised me to accept it, loading me with scripts and documents (chiefly relating to his Hollywood projects) that became the present Eisenstein Collection at the Museum of Modern Art.

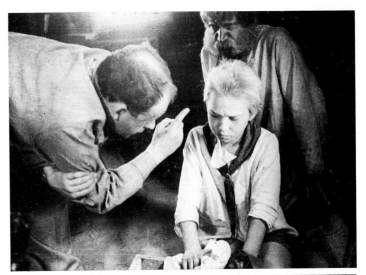

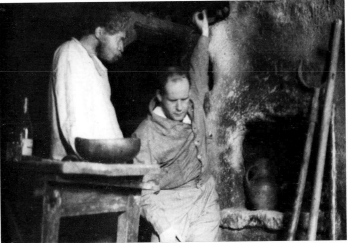

ABOVE: EISENSTEIN REHEARSING THE BOY AND HIS FATHER IN THE HUT SCENE.

BELOW: ON THE CHURCH PORCH: A CAPTURED SABOTEUR (MASLOV) BLESSED BY STEPOK'S GRANDMOTHER.

Moscow. Potilikha
1/II 1937.

My dear Jay!

I was very very happy to get news from You and all the lovely things You've sent me. It was a pleasure and a sorrow. For strange as it may seem — I'm missing You here! You know I was never too sentimental — I'd say on the contrary — but You formed a certain link with things I even have no opportunity to talk to anybody now! I mean by that my theoretical ideas and the trend of thoughts surpassing the purely professional side of art producing! Most of the time with You I was pretty biting and disagreable — but that was a sort of self protection against ... oneself: against things that drive me mad — things I cannot but drown in book form being chained to producing other things! You were allways provoking and touching my most secret "wounds" — the side of my work which is so

Now both these things can fit marvellously together — taking the race and national problem within the poem about revolutionary Spain, but all that means ... two more years of nothing doing about the book !!! Well it is not quite sure about the next film — and if not this film, then I hope to rob a couple of months out of my director's biography — and still accomplish what I ought to.

Another feeling of sorrow overcame me in another direction: Your letter made me feel out of touch with the outer world: I felt myself in no connection with what is going along on the other side of the ocean — what people on the other side of the ocean — what people think about, what they write about, what is going along in the arts and Sciences. Well I can imagine that not much, if anything, is in progress there in the modern way. But discoveries, research etc must be going ahead. Could n't You hold me a little bit ... au courant "of what is happening in the fields I am interested in. May be it would n't be too difficult to send me from

my opinion the really most important of what I have to do — and which I am not doing. So that's why our intercourse had a certain mixture of pain and pleasure —well as any masochistic pasttime! Now nobody and nothing is tickling me in this way: and when I by accident jumps out of production for an hour or so, I feel like Peer Gynt in the scene where he watches the rush of leaves on the earth which happen to be his ideas that never got form ... I hope that in three-four weeks I'll be through with the shooting. Quite a few people have seen the rushes and are very highly impressed — all of them feel in it a "return and revival" b reborn "renaissance" of film poetry (that was the first thing Feuchtwanger said when he saw them). As soon as I'm through with the picture I must put myself at work on the book. But there will start again a new tragedy: primo: there are plans for Spain. secundo: Paul Robeson who was with a concert tour here has put himself at my entire disposition for the time from July to October!

time to time even the ... "Times" book review, so as to know what is published and printed over there. Also some about what is going on in arts and art science — You're in the center of all that there. Thanks for the books You made note of for me (the one promised to be sent never arrived). And write me more often — not waiting for immediate answers!

My best regards to all the nice people of the museum and all my excuses to them for not writing: I had to become grippe so as to have an opportunity of writing to You! And no views of re-becoming small pox again and having a month and a haft of Kislovodsk !!!

Well! Thank very very much again and hope to hear news from You as soon as possible.

Allways heartily Yours

P.S. Do You (or the museum) need anything from here? Just write about it.

LETTER WRITTEN JUST BEFORE THE COMPLETION AND SUBSEQUENT BANNING OF BEZHIN MEADOW.

REHEARSAL WITH THE DYING STEPOK.

> *After a quarantine of three weeks (with daily radio bulletins), he'll convalesce for a month. . . . Mid-December will see work resumed on <u>Bezhin Meadow</u>, with scheduled completion in May 1936. In hospital he celebrated his thirty-eighth saint's day.*

But on May 12, 1936, when convalescence permitted, he wrote to Ivor Montagu: "As to 'Bezhin Lug'—I expect to be through with it in autumn if everything continues to be all right."

1937 Jan. *The High Commission of the All-Union Committee on Affairs of Higher Education in the Commissariat of People's Education verified and bestowed upon me the title of Professor of Film Direction at the Higher State Institute of Cinema Science (for Academy).*

The first letter I received from Eisenstein—in February 1937—does not mention this high honor, but it does announce a film about the war in Spain. As for *Bezhin Meadow*, its shooting is to be completed in three or four weeks. But by March 17 the shooting had been completed, edited, screened (both versions) for the film unions, bitterly criticized, and banned and shelved.

> . . .two catastrophes: the ruin of "Mexico" and the tragedy of "Bezhin Meadow."

VISHNEVSKY: <u>WE, THE RUSSIAN PEOPLE</u> AND [UNTITLED: SPAIN]

Vsevolod Vishnevsky, one of the few at the *Bezhin Meadow* execution to defend Eisenstein, now used his political and artistic authority to right the series of wrongs. He published a pamphlet accusing the film authorities of conspiring to destroy a great Soviet artist. He sketched two scenarios for Eisenstein to make: *We, the Russian People* and an untitled film about the war in Spain.* For the latter, Eisenstein devised a single set for the entire action, incorporating some details ("Souvenirs de Taxco") of a Mexican town in his synthetic Spanish set.

Pera Attasheva to Ivor Montagu, July? 1937

> What do you think about Robeson playing the part of a Morocco soldier in Spain—that is the new idea, instead of "Black Majesty" (sweet dreams! while Shumyatsky sleeps!)

---

*There are notes for its production dated, Kislovodsk, June 1937. Roles were indicated for Paul Robeson, Waylund Rudd, Hans Klering, Maxim Strauch, Judith Glizer, Pera Attasheva, and Mikhail Rosenfeld.

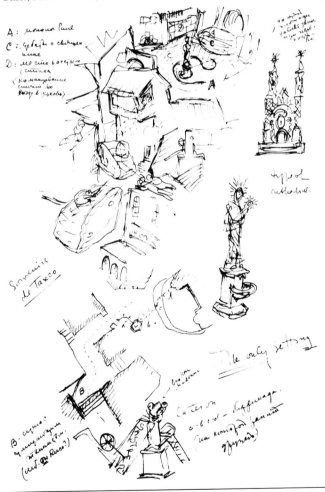

[Reading from left to right] A: Paul's monologue / C: debates with the priest / D: place of execution / (walls / the commanders stand in the church door / On this square the tanks press on (around church and fountain?) / type of cathedral / Souvenirs de Taxco / <u>The only setting</u> / B—scene with the dying tankist (perhaps <u>he</u> is Ruso?) / broken Madonna [arrow] / later on a-b-c-d—barricades (on which the friends are wounded)

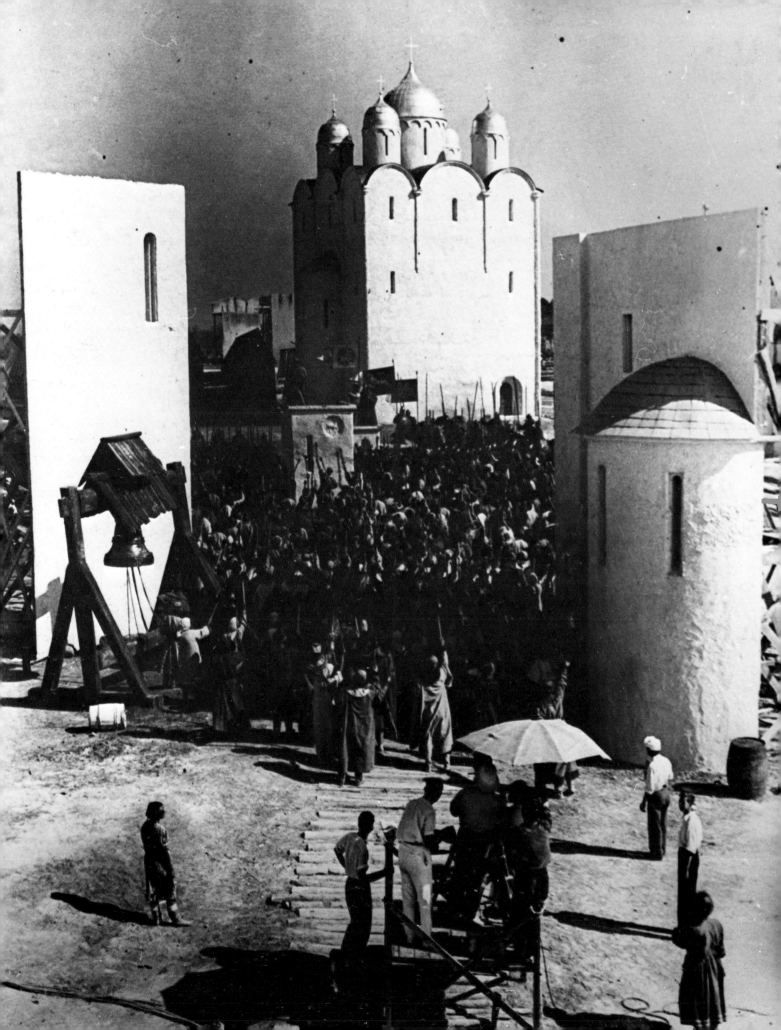

ALEXANDER NEVSKY

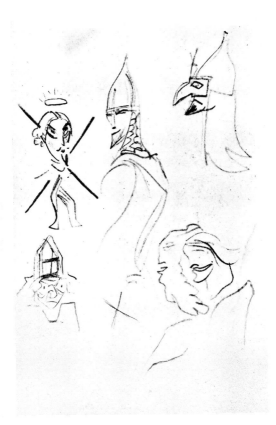

ABOVE: AN EARLY PROBLEM: WHAT WAS TO BE EMPHASIZED IN ALEXANDER'S CHARACTER? COULD A SAINT OF THE ORTHODOX CHURCH BE TRANSFORMED INTO AN ACCEPTABLE HERO FOR SOVIET AUDIENCES OF 1938? THE SCENARISTS FOUND THE SOLUTION IN NEVSKY'S PATRIOTISM. BY THE TIME THE FILM WAS FINISHED, EISENSTEIN WAS ABLE TO DESCRIBE IT TO THE MONTAGUS AS "AN ANTIFASCIST ENGINE."

OPPOSITE PAGE: FILMING THE PEOPLE OF NOVGOROD AS THEY DECIDE TO RESIST THE GERMANS.

In January 1938 the all-powerful head of the Film Committee, Boris Shumyatsky, was replaced by Semyon Dukelsky. This change affected all who worked in Soviet films—especially Eisenstein. Shumyatsky had led the campaign (with the emotional cooperation of the Sinclairs) against *Que Viva Mexico!*; he took pride in the abortion of MMM, of *Moscow*, of *The Black Consul*; and the new humiliation of Eisenstein through the banning of *Bezhin Meadow* was so satisfying as to make Shumyatsky positively gleeful. His removal now renewed Eisenstein's hopes that he might make films again.

At this time Eisenstein was working with Pyotr Pavlenko on a scenario of twelfth-century Russia, and its hero, Saint Alexander Nevsky.[*]

Despite Shumyatsky's departure, however, their published script was attacked (probably through force of habit), but the temporary defeat of the anti-Eisenstein group did clear the way for a production, proof of Eisenstein's planning methods and efficiency, and an indication of his eventual rehabilitation.

Ever since his victory in finishing *Potemkin* for its scheduled gala premiere, Eisenstein had tried to demonstrate with each succeeding film that length of production is not a way to guarantee quality of result. As films and shooting schedules grew longer at Mosfilm, he propagandized for longer and more careful *preparations*. The interruption of two films (*The General Line* and *Bezhin Meadow*) had broken carefully swift schedules, but the *shooting* time of *October*, regardless of the months of unavoidable discussion in the cutting room, still was considered a remarkable achievement. Its shooting script (almost unrelated to the published "literary script") was so devised that Eisenstein was able to hand over certain sequences for Alexandrov to film while he shot or prepared other sequences. Tisse sometimes worked with one, sometimes with the other. By 1937-1938, when *Nevsky* was being prepared, the useful Alexandrov was occupied with his own career. Dmitri Vasiliyev (unrelated to either of "the Vasiliyev brothers" famous for *Chapayev*, 1934) had shown himself to be a dependable assistant director on two difficult films, Romm's *Lenin in October* and Raizman's *Last Night* (both in 1937) and Eisenstein chose him to take charge of several scenes in which the principal actors did not appear, scenes that Eisenstein had fully worked out on paper, beginning with several pieces of the Battle on the Ice. With careful planning, *Alexander Nevsky* was completed and given to the studio five months before it was due.

The scene of the Battle on the Ice, because it was the most difficult one in *Alexander Nevsky*, was filmed first, in a summer heatwave. This was done at the suggestion of Dmitri Vasiliyev. A leveled field near the Mosfilm Studio (see p. 98) was covered with sodium silicate to give the color and texture of a frozen lake. Tisse converted the summer sky into a wintry one by means of filters.

---

[*]The Film Committee gave Eisenstein the choice of Nevsky or Sussanin (hero of Glinka's opera *A Life for the Tsar*). Eisenstein chose Nevsky, "because nothing is known about him."

TOP: THE LEVELED FIELD NEAR MOSFILM TURNED INTO A FROZEN LAKE.
ABOVE: FILMING THE TEUTONIC KNIGHTS' ATTACK.

THE RUSSIAN FOOT-SOLDIERS ARE SEEN GETTING INTO POSITION FOR ANOTHER TAKE OF THEIR ATTACK. EISENSTEIN IS IN THE FOREGROUND.

[Top] The proportions of the group of knights are wrong. They should be farther away and smaller
[Center] Of course the crack should be across but it should also follow a direction from Alexander to the knights.
[Bottom] Part A moves away from B—the crack widens and then the whole [of the] ice breaks away.

CAVALRYMEN REHEARSE THE FINAL DUEL. APRIL 10, 1938. THE HORSEMAN PORTRAYING NEVSKY BECAME A HERO OF WORLD WAR II, GENERAL TROKHACHOV; THE OTHER, LEV DOVATOR, WAS A DISTINGUISHED CAVALRYMAN.

EISENSTEIN SHOWS THE ACTOR PLAYING THE GERMAN KNIGHT HOW TO BATTLE-AXE GAVRILO, PLAYED BY ALEXANDER ABRIKOSOV.

12 Apr 1938 / von Balk (mounted) / Gavrilo / Savka / Knecht

ABOVE: EISENSTEIN AND TISSE WITH THE CAMERA CLOSE TO THE SURFACE OF THE WATER FOR THE OPENING FISHING SCENE.

BELOW: EISENSTEIN SHOWS SERGEI BLINNIKOV, PLAYING TVERDILO, HOW A TRAITOR BOASTS.

BOTTOM: EISENSTEIN DEMONSTRATING THE DEATH SCENE OF THE ARMORER IGNAT, PLAYED BY DMITRI ORLOV.

Perhaps because so many unrealized projects preceded *Alexander Nevsky*, it echoes more of Eisenstein's earlier ideas than did any other film completed by him: compositions and sequences from *Qué Viva México!* and *Bezhin Meadow* especially are to be noted.

It may be merely coincidence, but Prokofiev's score also has a variety of familiar echoes—Berlioz's *Corsaire* overture, Nedda's minuet aria in *I Pagliacci*, and a Handelian organ piece for the *Black Monk* are a few that have been recognized.

An early idea for the finale was discarded in production. In it Nevsky goes to the camp of the Golden (Tatar) Horde, and is poisoned. A century later his place is taken by Dmitri Donskoy, who defeats the Tatars at Kolikovo Polye. (This unused conclusion is translated in *Three Films*.)

The Missing Reel

Although parts of Shklovsky's essay on Eisenstein's career derive from the posthumously published memoirs, there is a surprise in his description of the completion of *Alexander Nevsky*.

When the filming was finished, Sergei Mikhailovich lived and slept in the cutting room. In cinema there's never enough time. The sun sets too soon, snow falls too early, then the sun melts it too fast; film people always work under pressure, and they can't even find enough time to splice their shots together. In those last weeks on *Nevsky* the people began to work day and night, quite confident that their working day contained twenty-five hours, and they turned out to be right, after all, for they succeeded. With no thought of time Eisenstein would edit, fall soundly asleep, then wake up and go on editing. . . .

One night the Kremlin telephoned—Stalin wanted to see the film. Without waking the director, the crew gathered up the reels and hurried them off to the command screening. Though the film was much liked, Stalin did not see the entire film. One scene, of a brawl on the bridge at Novgorod, was being given its final cutting by Eisenstein; the reel containing the fight was on his table and the messengers had overlooked it. This reel was never screened and the gap was not noticed. Afterward, when the forgotten reel was brought to the attention of the official in charge of the Kremlin screening (Dukelsky?), it was decided the film would be released as it had been approved. That is how it went out to the public—and not a single critic noticed anything wrong. *

---

* The reel is *still* missing.

SOME SURVIVING FRAMES FROM THE MISSING REEL. TOP LEFT: THE MERCHANTS OF NOVGOROD DECIDE NOT TO RESIST THE GERMANS. TOP RIGHT: NEVSKY'S ARRIVAL SUPPORTS THE WORKMEN, WHO WANT TO RESIST. BOTTOM: THE DIVIDED PEOPLE OF NOVGOROD AS NEVSKY ARRIVES.

ABOVE: A PAINTED BACKDROP OF TREES IS RIGGED UP TO BE FILMED BY A WIDE-ANGLE LENS, LATER TO BE COMBINED WITH A SHOT OF THE CATHEDRAL AND BRIDGES.

[Upper right] Zvenigor, bridge / 10 Apr. 38
[Left] Stand of trees creates the horizon, all hopes rest on 28″ lens.

1st Zvenigorodsk Version.

Effective shot of Alexander and his troops filmed against the sun as they arrive in Novgorod for the People's Assembly.

The bridge is in segments. Cathedral.

Dear Jay!

It was a real pleasure to get Your letter! I hope that from now on we will have a continuous and regular correspondance. The idea of Your magazine is fine. I will let You know quite soon if I'll be able to contribute to it an article which I hope to finish soon: — an article quite amusing in its idea: "El Greco y El Cinema"! Can You imagine a machine of some 26.000 words (!) solely occupied with the problem, how cinematic in all directions that old Spaniard behaves! C'est piquant! The thing will need quite a lot of Greco pictures and details as well as other illustrations. It is the result of a certain "elephantiasis" undergone by one of the chapters of one of the books I'm constantly writing. I've started to work on "Vol I" of "Peyцucesza" but strange as it may seem, I'm "still so tired after "Nevsky" — who was a hell of a job to be made on so short a schedule —

that I cannot concentrate on the work, as concentrated I should be! Will see how everything will turns out. Also with the Greco article. Please write me as much as You can and about everything of importance and interest in books, in the arts and so on. Thanks for the hint about Mrs. Rosen: have written to her and if we start our book exchange ("raquet"!) a new — everything will be all right with part of the books. What about the Film Library? And sure I will be glad to have a glimpse of what You're doing about our movie history.

What about the "snobbishness" around Nevsky: I'd like to know as much as possible about everything — unfavorable even more than favorable (what is written in "Nation" and.. "New Republic", what in magazines? What do people say about him)

The next film will be not so very soon: it will probably take the whole of next summer. I'll try like hell to manage something with the book during the time the script and preparations are done. Awaiting news from You as soon as possible (and all sorts of details for the book about which I'll write specially) with all my love Yours

Best regards to Sylvia and Kirstein.

A PROGRESS REPORT RECEIVED AFTER THE AMERICAN RELEASE OF <u>ALEXANDER NEVSKY</u>.

RESEARCH PHOTOS FOR <u>FERGHANA CANAL</u>.

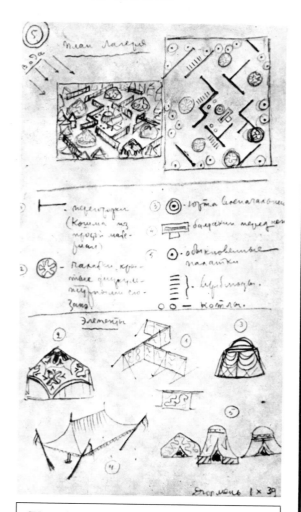

[Upper left] Plan of the camp / water [Center]
(1) Partitions (made of plain, coarse material)
(2) Tents covered in figured shapes (3) the
commander's yurta (4) canopy in front of his
yurta (5) ordinary tents, camels, cauldrons
/ Elements / Diurmen 1 Oct 1939

FERGHANA CANAL

In two early moves toward preparation of *The Great Ferghana Canal*, Eisenstein commissioned a photographer friend, Max Penson, to record a number of Uzbek scenes for the three parts of *Ferghana Canal* and sent Prokofiev this letter.

Moscow 26 July 1939

My dear Sergei Sergeyevich,

I hope that you are thoroughly contented in the Caucasus and feel wonderful. Our trip to Central Asia was crowned with success—we shall be making a long and complex film with its release for screening to be approximately in May of 1940. I cannot imagine such a film without you and therefore without delay I took the liberty of sending you an expanded libretto, which the Central Committee and the Studio have already accepted as a basis. Apparently, there are to be no particular deviations, and I made rough markings in the libretto of what I hope you will delight me with. In my opinion, the stuff is damned fascinating and might prove very substantial.

Deadlines: I think you ought to fly out here in September or October, so that you can see Samarkand and Bokhara (which are very interesting) and to absorb the *couleur locale* of Uzbekistan a little. The basic part of the work will fall in December–January, when we hope to deliver the nearly completed second and third parts and will have to prepare material for the first part (Timur, etc.). And, subsequently, in April, the final cut, completion, glosses, and last touches.

Now in essence: the marginal notes, in my opinion, are sufficient, intelligible, and knowing me "a little" you will see immediately how I myself visualize them.

The main theme is, of course, the theme of water. It distinctly emerges four times:

1) Menacing (Timur), destructive
2) Lyric (small irrigation ditch of Tokhtasyn and the daughter's dance)
3) Menacing (uprising of the poor), destructive (in a different aspect with respect to No. 1)
4) Victorious–celebrative (setting in motion of the canal. It seems to me No. 2 is broadened to the loftiest inspiration—added to it the elements of No. 1 and No. 3)

The second theme is very curious. This is the theme of the sand. Sand is a bastard when it advances in dunes across the desert, but at night it sings. A rare, ringing rustle. And a very terrifying endlessness (*perpetuum mobile*).

The duel between the water and the sand must, of course, come out very forcefully (with the victory by the sand). The sand itself labors:

1) A thirst-dying town (introducing its theme)
2) The victory of the sands (the finale of Part 1)
3) The advance of the sand (through the second part and in particular in the finale: by the death of the girl. N.B.— through her dance—through the background too.)

The third group—this is Tokhtasyn's song (ephemeral) and

SHOOTING TESTS FOR <u>FERGHANA CANAL</u>.

THE SHOOTING CREW, INCLUDING TISSE, HIS CAMERA ASSISTANT, AND EISENSTEIN (SEATED).

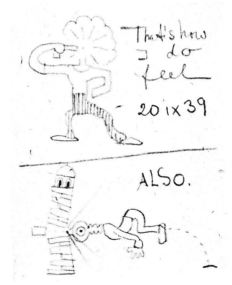

EISENSTEIN'S REACTION, DATED SEPTEMBER 20, 1939.

apparently somehow coming through her (the song) the theme of labor in Part 3.*

Tests were begun on location, but the *Ferghana* project was stopped. These tests were later incorporated into a documentary film about the building of the canal.

*Translated by Ronald Levaco.

Tower of Timur

This series of drawings illustrating the cruel Tower of Timur was sketched by Eisenstein during one very productive day in Tashkent (Diurmen?), while *Ferghana Canal* was in preparation. They were apparently not drawn in the order shown here; Eisenstein placed them in this order later on. The purpose was to detail the construction of the tower, in human layers, covered with clay.

[Upper left] Two rows and covering of clay
[Below] One arrangement for the layers

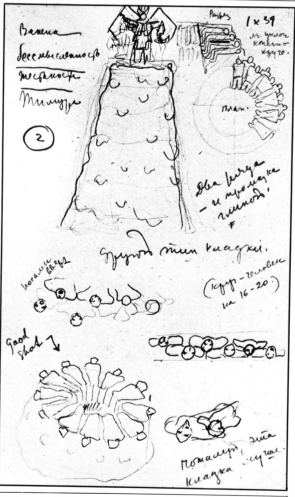

[Upper left] Important to show senseless cruelty of Timur [Right of tower] Cross-section / 1 Oct 1939 / NB. Angle of finished circle. / plan / Two rows and covering of clay / [Center] With noses up / varying types of layers / circle—of 16-20 persons / good shot [Bottom] This arrangement of layers probably better.

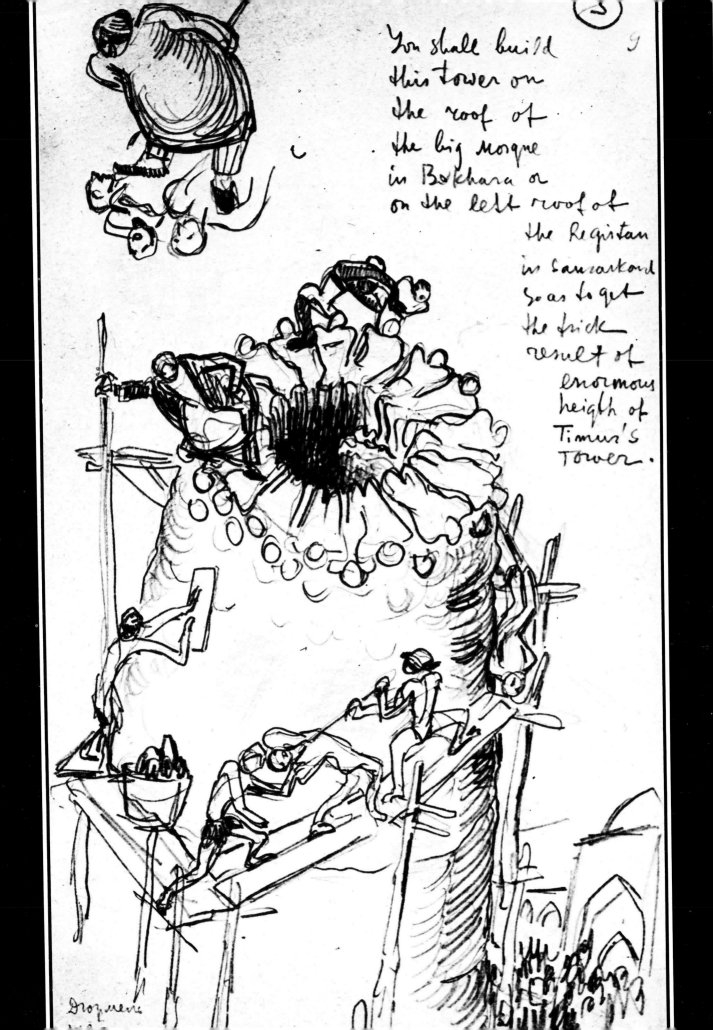

You shall build
this tower on
the roof of
the big mosque
in Bokhara or
on the left roof of
the Registan
in Samarkand
so as to get
the trick
result of
enormous
heigth of
Timur's
Tower.

(4)

Showing how
very easy
it is to get
the effect
you desire

You just put it
on the roof of the
Big Mosque in Bokhara.

Dewirmain
1 x 39

(5)

На 20 персон круг

20 persons to a circle.

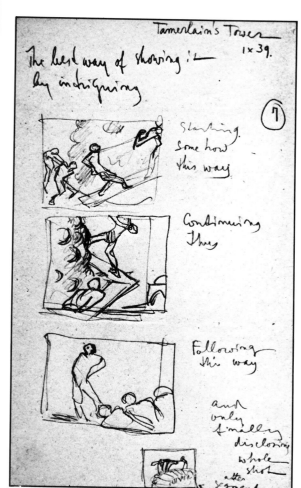

Tamerlain's Tower
1 x 39.

The best way of showing it —
by intriguing

(7)

Starting
some how
this way

Continuing
thus

Following
this way

and
only
finally
disclosing
whole
shot
after & forward

(8)

Триумф Тамерлана
на башне из живых людей
обмазанных глиной.

Четыре каждый < a w. five(?)

< перед прорывом плотины >

Ташкент
1 x 39

Triumph of Timur atop the tower made of live
bodies covered with clay. Four to each layer (or
maybe six) before the dam breaks / Tashkent 1 Oct
1939

EISENSTEIN, AS PRODUCER, ADVISING MIKHAIL ROMM ON <u>DREAM</u> (1943).

Someone in the higher echelons of government must have grown self-conscious about the best Soviet directors, including Eisenstein, being left unused in the actual production of films. In any case, these "best" were given new appointments as "artistic heads" of the leading Soviet studios: Eisenstein at Mosfilm, Dovzhenko at the Kiev Studio, Ermler at Lenfilm, Yutkevich at Soyuzdetfilm. Romm and Roshal did some of their best work at Mosfilm with the production guidance of Eisenstein.

BOOK ON DIRECTION

Possibly induced by the crisis of 1936, Eisenstein frankly stated his preference for writing and research over the making of films. His book *On Direction* grew with every lesson he gave at GIK, lessons determined by the outline of his book. Here are two triumphant gestures celebrating the book's progress.

EISENSTEIN USES A MAY DAY PARADE FLOAT TO EXPRESS THE PROGRESS ON HIS BOOK. LEFT: PATHOS ECSTASY CENTER: EXPRESSIVE MOVEMENT RIGHT: DRAMATURGY OF THE FILM FORM

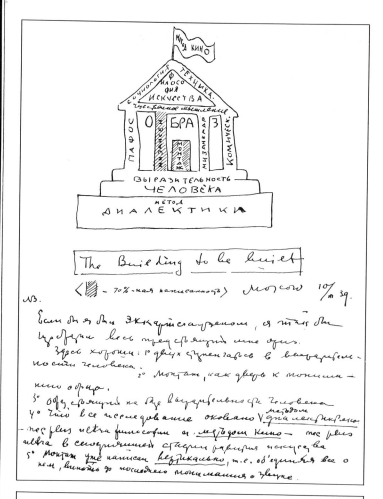

The Building to be Built.

If I were an Eckartshausen, this is how I would picture my whole future opus.

The good things here:
1. that there are two stages in the expressiveness of man.
2. that Montage appears as a door to the understanding of the image.
3. that the image rests on a basis of man's expressiveness.
4. that the whole research is held together by the <u>dialectic</u> method—the ne plus ultra of philosophy and the <u>method of film</u>—the ne plus ultra in today's stage of the development of the art.
5. that montage is <u>already</u> written *vertically*, i.e., uniting everything in itself, including the latest understanding of sound.

WAGNER: DIE WALKÜRE

YESTERDAY THEY PROPOSED THAT I STAGE WALKÜRE AT THE BOLSHOI.—DECEMBER 21-22, 1939

The German-Soviet Non-Aggression Pact, signed in August 1939, had three direct effects on Eisenstein's work. First, *Alexander Nevsky* was withdrawn quietly from distribution in the Soviet Union; second, production of *Ferghana Canal* was halted (the coincidence in timing, though unexplained, cannot be ignored); third, the Bolshoi Theater invited him to stage *Die Walküre*, "in the mutual interests of German and Russian cultures."

Eisenstein eagerly accepted the new challenge as it presented an opportunity for him to learn more through Wagner and to pay homage to that master on a stage almost entirely closed to him (the only current Wagner production was *Lohengrin*). Wagner's idea of combining theater, music, literature and myth into one medium concurred with Eisenstein's vision of film as synthesis. Determined to make each moment of the opera count in dramatic effect as well as thematically, he began at once to explore the literature on the *Nibelungen*, starting with the vocal score of *Die Walküre* (shown above). The absence of the *Ring* from the Bolshoi repertory since 1914 gave Eisenstein the tremendous advantage of a quarter century free of oppressive staging tradition.

It was an ideal situation, and within the week he began sketching ideas for unifying the production. A tree was the natural first thought, inspired by Wagner's set directions and the action of Act I—but what an evolution from first idea to the tree seen during the overture by that first-night audience of November 21, 1940!

ABOVE: ANNOTATED SCORE FOR THE SECOND SCENE OF ACT I OF DIE WALKÜRE.

THE PREMIERE OF DIE WALKÜRE.

[Upper left] If possible / swinging in three planes. [Upper right] 24 Dec 39 The tree full of / amorous murmurs. / a bit too vertical / (somewhat) pulled in height. / NB. Perhaps / branched in pieces— / more exactly / the coccyx / must stick up / toward Heaven.

What a Dantesque thing! in this tree full of characters!

NB. And this is no accident. Wagner writes to Mathilde Wesendonck, London, 30 Aug 1855: "At present I'm reading a canto of Dante every morning ere I set to work: I'm still stuck deep in Hell; its horrors accompany my realization of the second act of Walküre . . ."

If tragic in Act II—Why not sensuous in Act I?!

Хундинг
со слугой

и

Зигмунд.

16/I-40

ABOVE: REHEARSING BRUNNHILDE (MARGUERITE BUTENINA) WITH THE VALKYRIES.

ABOVE: THE INTERVENTION OF WOTAN.
OPPOSITE PAGE: HUNDING WITH HIS PACK (LEFT) AND SIEGMUND.
BELOW AND RIGHT: PLANNING THE RIDE OF THE VALKYRIES.

Clouds must move - or background and somewhere to be frozen on gaz.

The flying horses ought to be with some pieces of gaz like ... and have a human being inside to move the head, legs, tail

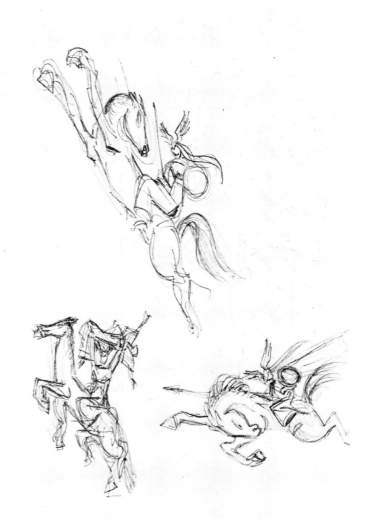

113 · WAGNER: DIE WALKÜRE

Another evolution to be observed in the drawings is the entrance of Fricka. Eisenstein's earliest idea for this least attractive and most "moral" of the gods was somewhat elaborate, but, close to final rehearsals, it was scaled down, and the original complicated vehicle was simplified though her rams are still pulling Fricka's chariot onto the stage.

Eisenstein had cherished the hope that he could follow *Die Walküre* with *Siegfried*, the next (and third) opera in the four-opera *Ring* cycle. However, reception of the November 21 opening performance was so cool*—both critically and publicly—that he abandoned the idea of proposing the whole *Ring* to the Bolshoi administration.

Instead, he returned to his work at Mosfilm and there resumed his search for film ideas to submit to the Film Committee. He was at work on two scenarios by Lev Sheinin, *The Beilis Case* and *An Empire's Prestige* (about T. E. Lawrence), which he had proposed on May 19,† but his hopes for these

ABOVE: REHEARSING THE GODDESS FRICKA BEING DRAWN BY HER RAMS. EISENSTEIN IS IN THE BACKGROUND.
BELOW: SKETCH FOR FRICKA'S RAMS.

were dashed by a telephone conversation with Andrei Zhdanov on January 11, 1941. Another project of 1940, to be made with color film, did not survive. Set in the Middle Ages, this was an attempt to link the studio's suggestion of a film about the Black Death with Eisenstein's wish to work on Giordano Bruno.

In October 1940, while waiting for the long-delayed premiere of *Die Walküre*, he drew up this credit-debit accounting of his professional career:

Successes	Failures	Unrealized
Mexican [19]21	Gas-Masks [19]24	U.S.A. [19]30
Sage [19]23	October [19]27	Mexico [19]32
Do You Hear,	Old & New [19]29	Bezhin M. [19]39
Moscow [19]23		Ferghana [19]39
Strike [19]24		Walküre [19]40
Battleship [19]25		
Al. Nevsky [19]38		
(50%)		

*The coolest were the Germans, for whom the gesture had been made. Alexander Werth left the Bolshoi premiere just behind two officers from the German embassy; their comment: "Deliberate Jewish tricks."

†Eisenstein's promised schedule:
    scen. for No. 1 – can submit 15 Oct 1940
    shooting to begin Spring 1941
    scen. for No. 2 – can submit 15 July 1940
    shooting to begin in Sept
    can complete film by 1 May 1941

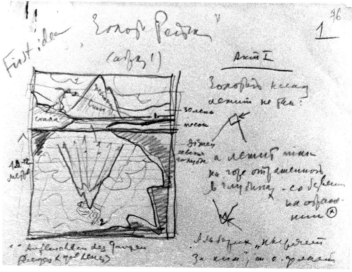

A PLAN FOR **DAS RHEINGOLD**.

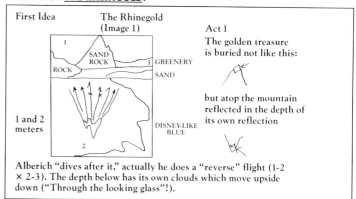

First Idea	The Rhinegold (Image 1)	Act 1

Alberich "dives after it," actually he does a "reverse" flight (1-2 × 2-3). The depth below has its own clouds which move upside down ("Through the looking glass"!).

OPPOSITE PAGE: A PLAN FOR **SIEGFRIED**.

if ever the whole "Ring"
should be produced.

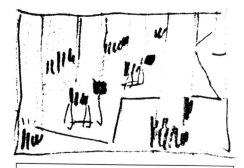

He [Boris Godunov] runs for a long time through a maze of pillars. Each pillar ringed with candles. March 1940.

Vladimir Andreyevich in the cathedral. Of course, without light! 20 March 1942.

ABOVE: OUT OF THE PLANNED SEQUENCE ABOUT BORIS GODUNOV IN THE PUSHKIN FILM (AT TOP) CAME THE IDEA FOR A STYLE THAT DETERMINED <u>IVAN GROZNY</u> (ABOVE).

CLOCKWISE FROM LOWER LEFT: NIKOLAI KARAMZIN; GEORGES CHARLES D'ANTHÈS; NIKOLAI I, TSAR; NATALIA (NÉE GONCHAROVA) PUSHKIN.

PUSHKIN: <u>THE LOVE OF A POET</u>

After the disappointment on the *Ring*, Eisenstein returned to his first sketches for a film on Pushkin for which he had made daring plans in color. While in Asia he had drafted passages for a book on *Pushkin and Cinema*. This may have led to the ambitious project, *The Love of a Poet*, for which he proposed a totally original use of color film. As research material, he collected portraits of four of the chief characters. The following pages show his drawings, amounting to a very complete mise-en-scene. This work must have been a refreshment for him. Eventually out of it, and especially out of his plan for the monologue in *Boris Godunov* (March 1940), came the idea and the style for his last film, *Ivan the Terrible*.

PUSHKIN   **6 MARCH 40**
First outline

Prologue
Hannibal. Scene: A black among whites. One against all. Like the germ of an image that develops later on (in Part III). Pushkin alone contra all of society and [Tsar] Nikolai.

I. Stage of Pushkin's life similar to Mayakovsky's "yellow blouse." Brawler. Woman-chaser. Playful with his muse. Light-hearted ("when can he find time to write down his poetry"). Gypsies. Odessa. The Vorontsovs. Departure with Rayevskys. Themes for "Gypsies."

II. Pushkin in his Mikhailovskoye exile. Great. Profound poet. Wisdom of the people–Arina Rodionovna. Social protest. Against Nikolai–"I have attained the highest power" [*Boris Godunov*]–as accusation. Pushkin's arrival [in Petersburg]. Pushkin travels through snowstorm: conceives his "demons." Through blizzard to Petersburg. Opera. "Istomina" based on *Eugene Onegin* (Ulanova). Sees Goncharova for first time. Quarrels with neighbor for not applauding enough. Rushing sleigh. Pacing. Pistols. Duel *comique* with fat man.

III. Pushkin and struggle with Nikolai. Liaison between Nikolai and Natalie should be presented as it appeared to Pushkin—he knew and he didn't know, just as we don't know: was it or wasn't it? Duel. Death. Etc. Fearful aspect of Petersburg in motifs of "Queen of Spades," gambling houses, "Bronze Horseman," etc.

Outline I

> Dawn breaks over the gypsy camp, lost in the vast steppe. Camp wakes. Old man (startled by the approach of a gypsy).

> ". . . It's getting bright. The old man
> Circles the silent tent.
> 'Wake, Zemfira, the sun is rising.
> Awake, my guest! It's time, time!
> Leave, children, your bed of pleasure!'"

Pushkin wakes in the arms of Mariula.
(Epilogue of "Gypsies":

> "And for a long, long time
> The name of lovely Mariula
> I tenderly recalled.")

[Pushkin] emerges from the tent against a background of the waking camp.

Leading a bear Mariula's husband (or established lover?) approaches. (Image of Aleko—minus the fashionable Byronism—just the face) A germ of jealousy in the scene.

Mariula:

> Old husband, angry husband, (and continues)
> Stab me, burn me
> I am strong and unafraid (wordless tune)
> Neither knife nor fire

The fury of her man breaks out.

A crowd of young women interfere.

Pushkin is shoved aside.

Gypsy leads Mariula away.

The camp begins to move.

Pushkin, beside an old grave, gazes after the moving camp (as in "Gypsies").

He whispers: "Old husband, angry husband" in different tones.

And we see rolling melons.

Ripe tomatoes–like bloodstains.

Turks. Greeks. Fish. Turbans. Feluccas. Harbor. Bazaar. Odessa.

Pushkin in the center of the bazaar (somewhat playful).

House of the Turkish woman and Bazaar constructed on the Odessa steps.

Charging horses down the steps amidst rolling watermelons.

Under circumstances of near scandal—he sees her.

On a veranda the black eyes and half-veiled face of a Greek woman.

Her servant at the gate.

Pushkin with the Greek woman.

Their tête-à-tête is disturbed. The chase after Pushkin (who is wrapped in a woman's gown or something). The servant leads him out through the terraced garden. He is chased from the house.

Greek woman in tears.

Pushkin hugs the maid and jumps over the wall.

Hesitates on another wall, charmed by the vision of a "Bryulov maiden" hanging out the wash.

Pushkin is transfixed. Stares. Murmurs: "Old husband, old husband . . ."

Pushkin and the maiden.

But cries and pursuit are all around.

She takes him to the gate. He runs away.

Vorontsov's office. Pushkin's place is vacant.

Vorontsov comes to the desk. "Where's Pushkin?" (first mention of Pushkin's name)

On the desk Pushkin's report on the locust. We can't see the text, only the heading on the cover and Vorontsov's anger.

Vorontsov on his way to his wife.

Madame Vorontsova, in a darkened room opening on a veranda, in someone's embrace.

She lifts her head, listening.

The man holding her also lifts his head.

It is Pushkin.

Both listen. Distant jingle of spurs. (Compare: Onegin's meeting with Tatiana at the end of the poem.)

Vorontsov's spurred boots.

Vorontsov's walk.

Pushkin hurries to escape.

Through the veranda—

Into a flower bed. Whistling:

"Angry husband, old husband . . ."

Vorontsova turns as the enraged Vorontsov enters.

"What a protégé you have . . ." etc.

And angrily reads aloud the report on the locust.

Vorontsova bursts out laughing, quickly hides her face in the cushions.

Her husband almost chokes with indignation. He notices a pair of men's gloves and a top hat on the chair. He grabs them.

Vorontsova is frightened.

But Vorontsov is already on his way back to the office.

Pushkin is at his desk–busy.

Writing very attentively.

All the staff stand except Pushkin, who is too busy with his work.

He writes on and whistles the melody of Mariula's song.

Over his shoulder we see: "Old husband, angry husband,
              Stab me, burn me . . ."

The furious Vorontsov sees it too.

He grabs the paper.

Throws the report at Pushkin.

Pushkin jumps to his feet.

Vorontsov hands him his hat and gloves. Pushkin is thrown into confusion: trouble coming!

On the street a carriage drives up.

It is Rayevsky and his two sons. They see Pushkin and Vorontsov through the windows.

Greetings are exchanged.

And Pushkin is already with the young Rayevskys.

Vorontsova in tears with her confidante.

Old Rayevsky tries to pacify Vorontsov.

Vorontsov shows him the order for Pushkin's exile to Odessa.

And about the reasons: how Pushkin copied Miloradovich's pamphlets by heart.

However, it's decided that Pushkin can go with Rayevsky.

And there, on the veranda, is Vorontsova, waving a tearful goodbye.

The Rayevsky family and Pushkin go off in the carriage.

Vorontsova waves.

The Greek woman waves.

The Turkish woman waves.

And many, many others.

The carriage moves on.

The "Bryulov maiden" waves.

Pushkin jumps from the carriage.

And embraces the maiden.

Runs to catch up with the carriage.

The Polish women wave.

And far into the steppe the gypsy camp is on the move—Mariula is humming: "Old husband, angry husband . . ."

Her dark gypsy watches her jealously.

"I love another . . . ." etc.

And the rest can be heard over the shot of Rayevsky's carriage disappearing in the distance.

CONTINUITY FOR THE TSAR'S PRIVATE CABINET.

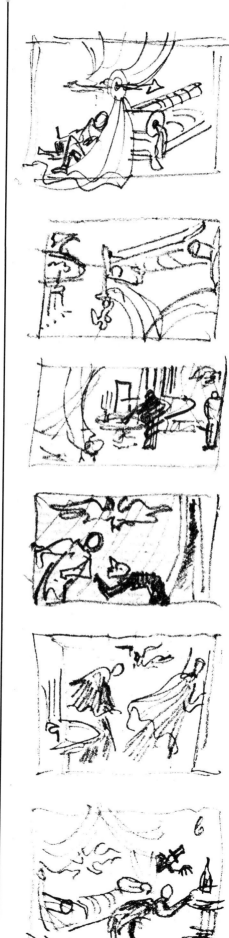

18 Dec 1940

Scenes to follow thus:

1. Bribery of the footman (outside door)
2. They come into close shot / touches the corsage puts lips on shoulder
3. Corner of fireplace and a candelabrum
4. Corner with a hidden door. Door swings open.
5. General shot. In doorway stand (Tsar) Nikolai and a young woman (pair on couch) do not hear. Nikolai steps ahead of his lady and approaches them.
6. Nikolai stands over them, hiding his lady behind him, coughs (?)
7. Panic. With lady behind him, rolls his eyes as if furious and then benevolently: "I am older than you, my dear fellow, let me have your place." Close-up 7a.
8. A grabs B and takes her quickly inside. At the same time pushes D forward. Her face is concealed by a black half-mask. She wears a short black cape. As she moves she falls onto the couch in the same position as the previous lady, Nikolai bending over her.
8. Door opens discreetly: the footman. In a panic he shuts door.
9. The arrival of Pushkin and Natalie.
10. She throws off her ermine wrap onto his arms. (As they go up the stairs she puts on her mask.)
11. They walk through the door (seen from the back). In the background, tumult. They enter.
12. Spies are dozing behind the curtains of the "tent."
13. Close-up (I).
14, 15. Then (a kind of Percier et Fontaine).
16. A table with flowers and candelabrum—a white Cupid.
17. (1) Benkendorff. (2) Nikolai arrives and starts eating gluttonously.
18. Benkendorff's spy reports: "They've arrived." Benkendorff reports to Nikolai. (2) "Costume?" (3) "Harlequin." B. throws domino cape over N., puts one on himself and both
19. Run out.
20. Spies: Spy A reaches for bottle / Spy B intercepts him and grabs his arm.
21. Struggle for bottle. Suddenly they see a second one and grab for it. They hear a noise.
22. Quickly they hide.
23. On the swinging curtain—the glitter of the golden, two-headed eagle.

Pushkin / The stairway of the masquerade ball / mirrors / Before Pushkin (if needed) / then D'Anthès already in the ballroom (other image) / arrival of D'Anthès couple *Everybody* masked except Pushkin! [7 July 1940] / (That's not as good although it gives possibility to reveal their relationship while removing coats and his lack of attention to her.)

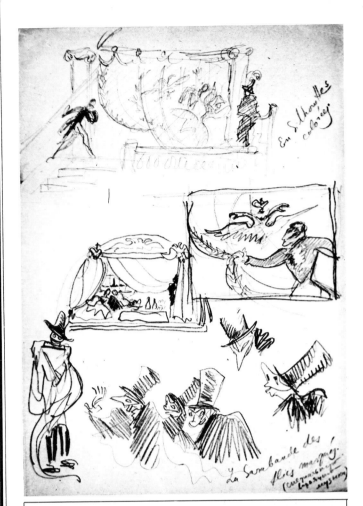

In colored silhouettes / The sarabande of masked spies (special variant in music)

8 July 1940—Later on introducing scene of Pushkin's search through dancers. Pushkin hears someone sobbing behind the column—Catherine is in tears. He talks to her, friendly, comforting. And suddenly the thought . . . if D[Anthès] is not with her, it means . . . he leaves her and rushes through the dancers. / Through the sarabandes of the cotillion / Note: Dramatize D's lack of attention to Catherine, as a springboard and not for information. [Translation of notes (to drawing) not reproduced.]

bluish pink / Profit by their love / blue-rose of these silhouettes with black [shadowed] faces and colored! / pearly gray and fog around. NB. Maybe white nights.

ARRIVALS AT THE BALL.

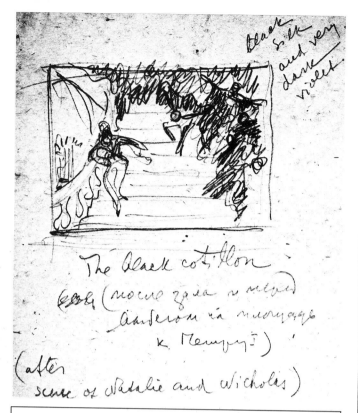

Black silk and very dark violet. / The black cotillion (after the ballroom and before he runs out into the square, towards the Peter I monument) / (after scene of Natalie and Nikolai).

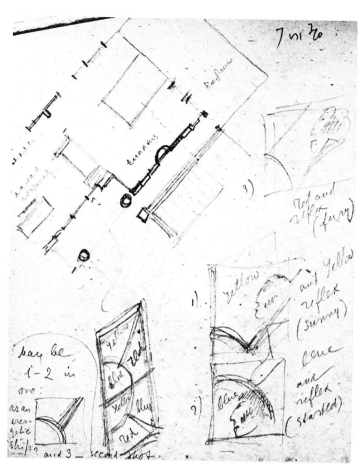

PLANS FOR THE COLOR SCHEME OF THE FILM.

[From left] Maybe 1-2 in one: as a energetic stripe? and 3— second shot / yellow/red/blue/yellow/blue/red / 1) yellow and yellow reflex (sunny) / (2) blue and reflex (startled) / (3) red and reflex (fury) [7 July 1940].

Montage plan: / a whirl of blood-red and black / Pushkin / top hats / seen through top hats—Pushkin running / Pushkin's run / down the stairs / and out, to the / Bronze Horseman. / Everything is white / The only black images / are Pushkin Darkened windows / Top hats / Footmen in black caped coats / / spotted below /

TWO IDEAS FOR PUSHKIN'S FLIGHT FROM THE BALL. THE ONE IMMEDIATELY ABOVE IS A PLAN TO SHOOT THE SCENE THROUGH THE TOP HATS OF THE GUESTS.

THE BRANCHES OF THE TREES GROW SPARSER AS PUSHKIN AND HIS SECOND APPROACH THE SITE OF THE DUEL.

A later manuscript, written during the war, concentrates on the color plans for Parts 2 and 3 of his Pushkin film. It was the plan dated March 4, 1940,[*] which follows, for "the nightmare monologue" from Pushkin's tragedy, *Boris Godunov*, that suggested a style for *Ivan Grozny*.

Boris's monologue—its cinematic solution a nightmare ("and bloody boys revolve before my eyes"). Red carpets of the cathedral. Red flames of the candles. Their light casts red streaks, and the icons look spattered with blood.
The Tsar darts through the great rooms.
Blue. Purple. Orange. Green.
The colors rush to meet him.
A color nightmare rages around the Tsar. The camera whirls through the multicolored rooms and parapets of the Kremlin Palace.
The poet saw in Boris the image of Tsar Alexander, the murderer [of the Decembrists].
The fire in the Mikhailovskoye fireplace flares up.
To the poet it seems that Tsar Nikolai stares at him through the flames (a quite legitimate transposition for film).
The poet's hand is drawing nervously on a sheet of paper
Gallows
Gallows, gallows, gallows.
"And perhaps I . . . I too . . ." Nervously he remembers the Decembrists.
He stares into the fire.
The vision of Nikolai returns his stare.
He crumples the paper in his fist.
The crumpled paper is hurled at the evil vision—as Luther's inkwell was thrown at the devil.
The vision vanishes.
The paper with the gruesome gallows drawings is consumed by the flames of the dying fire.
Along with the final burst of flames we hear the clashing of gendarmes' sabres.
The bright, blood-red flame plays across a gendarme's helmet.
Tsar Nikolai has recalled Pushkin to Moscow.
Thus begins the building of the red theme of blood. In "Requiem" it will appear on Danzas's cap-band.
A lively stream drives along the island.
"Stream" is not the right word, for it is winter and it is the movement of sleighs over the snow.
No one pities him.
Few will feel sorry for him a few hours later, when his blood will pour steaming onto the whiteness of the snow.
No one pities him.
But he—is pleased.
Politely nodding to passing sleighs he says something funny to his companion.
The companion (an officer) pays little attention.
He fidgets in his seat.
His behavior is strange, ill-mannered.
He is trying to attract the attention of the people in passing sleighs.
He wants them to notice something that he is carrying.
But he doesn't want [Pushkin] to be aware of it.
What he is holding is a flat case, the kind that carries pistols.

*Eisenstein made two versions, both in color, on this date. The first has been reproduced and translated in John Halas, *Visual Scripting*, New York, Focal Press, 1976.

People stare at the curly hair sticking out from under [Pushkin's] top hat.
Another futile attempt to attract attention to the flat case.
Another funny comment from the curly-haired companion.
No one feels sorry for him.
And he—is pleased.
He is on his way to a duel.
And he is very glad that no one interferes.
They pass a luxurious sleigh.
In it sits a fashionably dressed woman.
But the woman is near-sighted and does not recognize the curly-haired gentleman.
Although this curly-haired poet is her husband.
I always imagined that Pushkin's duel—all duels, in fact—took place in the morning. As in the staging, for example, of the Onegin-Lensky duel in the opera. The duel, however, actually took place during the day. More precisely [between four and five] in the afternoon.
Pushkin and Danzas (he was the uneasy officer who tried so desperately to attract the attention of the passers-by and prevent the approaching tragedy about which he was not entitled to speak openly) continued their ride through the glittering, fashionable crowd to the site chosen for the duel, on the Petersburg Islands.
So many familiar faces.
But not a single person whom he could stop.
Not a single one who would stop them.
[It was Danzas who] later recalled that Natalie was among those who passed Pushkin.
The music grows happier and more playful as Petersburg's society amuses itself sleigh riding.
Sergei Prokofiev's Requiem, still remote, begins to be heard as a musical subtext—grave and dark.
Through the gliding sleighs of Petersburg's highest society, Pushkin moves toward his death.
The Requiem grows stronger, its power made more palpable by the glittering dash of sleighs.
Colors grow dim and faded. (Visible motif—the blue frosty air absorbs color. The frost dims the flame-red of moustaches and sideburns. Snow sifts down from the trees—an intricate veil that extinguishes the shimmer of colors.)
A fleeting burst of cherry-red—it's the satin of Natalie's muff.
Natalie, the "cross-eyed madonna."
A dim-gray tonality dominates now.
And the contrast of black and white.
Snow.
The silhouettes of the duellists.
There is only one spot of color.
Bloody.
Red.
Not on the chest.
Not on the shirt.
Not on the vest of the poet.
—In the sky!
The blood-red circle of the sun.
Without rays.
The sun is a raspberry hue—as it is when it hangs low over the horizon on freezing days, and peers through the black silhouettes of trees, etching the outlines of Petersburg's empire fences, street lamps, and the spire [of the Admiralty].

Duel: white and black and blood-red disc of the setting winter sun. Into it, *into the sun*, ride the galloping horses carrying the body of the dying poet in final shots of the duel sequence. The branches at the end should probably be covered with frost.

Black, gray, white.

N.B. Probably artificially made.

Very typical for St. Petersburg winter evenings.

Light filters through the stained-glass door to the mezzanine and a flickering red spot falls on the white fingers of the frightened Natalie.

The poet is carried into the house.

It was not she, his wife, whom he wished to see first.

The one he asked for first was—Karamzina, wife of the historian.

The red spot from the stained glass now looks like blood.

Impossible for Natalie to wash it off, as it was not possible for Lady Macbeth.

Natalie hides her hands.

Her magnificent white dress is splattered with the different colors of the stained glass.

The pristinely white dress of Natalie (who wore it in all the pale-violet scenes—the courtship, the wedding with its evil omen of the dropped ring) is suddenly transformed into the motley of Harlequin. She jumps from her seat to allow Karamzina, all in black, to pass.

Natalie is caught in the vortex of all the rays filtering through the stained glass.

Now her white dress looks like the masquerade costume of Lady Harlequin—that appeared in all the scenes of Pushkin's most searing jealousy and in the scene when he and d'Anthès both burn with jealousy for a third rival.

The blood-red velvet of the Tsar's avant-loge, and the omnipresent black figure of its guardian angel—one of Benckendorff's spies—hold a mysterious silence over the scene, composed in the spirit of Tolstoy's comments[*] on the amorous adventures of Nikolai I.

Nuances of action in different scenes require a variety of color motifs. But the scenes have begun to weave themselves around a single theme which for me, unquestionably, was the most beautiful in the poet's biographical materials.

Tynyanov's hypothesis: Pushkin's silent love for Karamzin's wife. (N.B.: See Yuri Tynyanov's essay "Silent Love" in *Literary Critic*, 1939, 5-6; also Tynyanov's novel.) I don't know how much is fact, how much is fiction. But I am certainly convinced that there are many enchanting possibilities for plot development hidden in this hypothesis.

---

*In his notes for *The Love of a Poet*, dated December 18, 1940, "Nikolai and the Lady in Loge C," Eisenstein refers to Tolstoy's research materials for *Hadji Murad* and to chapter 15 of that novella.

КОМИТЕТ ПО ДЕЛАМ КИНЕМАТОГРАФИИ ПРИ СНК СССР

ПРЕДСЕДАТЕЛЬ

Всесоюзного Научного Инженерно-Технического Общества Кинематографии

(ВНИТОК)

Москва, Дом Кино, Васильевская, 13.   Телефон Д 1-46-59.

Dear Jay!

First of all my hearties(t) greetings and the great pleasure that finally our countries are cooperating. And here the preface to the booklet.

I plan the thing in such a form:

1) Possibly somebody's introduction concerning the problems as such, it's importance etc (may be written by You?)

2) My preface.

3) Montage 1938 (according to text published in "Life and Letters to-day" because of the examples from Milton and and other english poets.

4) Montage Vertical N. 1

5)   —   "   —   N. 2

6)   —   "   —   N. 3.

Am finishing (at last!) the Greco article! Am working on english version of very large article about Griffith and the history of montage through the arts. Will add to it probably a survey of the idea of the Close Up through art history. These three articles could make another little booklet: first because this one will need illustrations. Secondly because the completion of the articles may take some time and I'd like the first booklet to be published as soon as possible.

With all my love

P.S. Am adding a set of photographs for the Nevsky diagram.

EISENSTEIN'S PROPOSAL FOR HIS FIRST BOOK

"MY POSITION AT WORK."

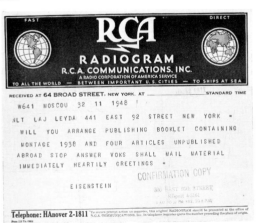

THE FIRST PUBLISHED BOOK

In August 1941 I received the above cable.

I replied with enthusiasm, spoke to Robert Giroux, then at Harcourt Brace, and in due course received more details from Eisenstein.

The booklet became his first book in any language, *The Film Sense*. Faber & Faber took the English rights, and for many years other countries translated this as the first book by Eisenstein. The first copy of *The Film Sense* reached him in Alma-Ata, on January 22, 1943, his forty-fifth birthday.

This must be the first time in my life that I am absolutely satisfied—with my first book and how it came out.

I can't imagine how it could be better.

Jayka is an absolute brick.

Even the dust-jacket [designed by McKnight Kauffer] is the one I would have chosen: absolutely boulevard in appearance—yellow with black, like the cover of a detective novel.

On it my face with an absolutely obscene glance and a Giocondo smile.

This was cut from a photo by Jiménez in Mexico in 1930. In my right hand near my shoulder I held a sugar skull from the objects associated with "death day".

With the skull removed what is left is a semi-ironic expression on my face and a lustful eye looking out from under a slightly raised left eyebrow.

Exactly like the sort of face used for "he knows your future" or a booklet on hypnosis, animal magnetism, etc. Wonderful. Splendid.

Eisenstein made this note of a future motto he would like to add to *The Film Sense*:

> **The other day even M. Daudet was to be heard—**
> **babbling of audible colours and visible sounds**
> R. L. Stevenson, "A Note on Realism"

IVAN GROZNY

PART I

Before the full script was submitted to the Film Committee, it had grown into two full-length films, and it was in this form that the literary treatment was published at the end of 1943.

However, when filming began in the small studio in Alma-Ata (the former House of Culture) to which the Mosfilm and Lenfilm Studios had been evacuated in wartime, *Ivan Grozny* had become *three* full-length films, to be filmed simultaneously, for the studio could accommodate only one large set at a time and the same set was required for Parts I, II, and III. This situation made possible such publicity photographs as the one below with Eisenstein alongside both the old Ivan and the boy Ivan, playing scenes in the same reception chamber set.

The two-part scenario was expanded to three parts, making the interior scenes the larger part of the filming task. As Tisse was reluctant to take the responsibility for these studio scenes, Andrei Moskvin, the skilled Leningrad cameraman, who had filmed the works of Kozintsev and Trauberg, was assigned to *Ivan*'s interiors.

FROM LEFT: CHERKASOV, THE BOY ERIC PYRIEV, EISENSTEIN.

ABOVE: FROM PART III, A SKETCH OF IVAN AND HIS BROKEN STAFF.
OPPOSITE PAGE: THE FINALE FOR PART I: THE TSAR IS WAITING TO BE INVITED BY THE PEOPLE OF MOSCOW BACK TO THE THRONE.

TOP: IN THE WORKSHOP WHERE EISENSTEIN'S SKETCHES WERE TURNED INTO SETS. FROM LEFT, TISSE, EISENSTEIN, AND JOSEF SPINEL, THE DESIGNER.

BOTTOM: EISENSTEIN (IN WHITE) AND CREW FILMING THE SIEGE OF KAZAN. TISSE AT FRONT CAMERA. IN THE TENT, IVAN, PLAYED BY CHERKASOV, PLACES HIS HAND ON THE SHOULDER OF KURBSKY, PLAYED BY NAZVANOV.

RIGHT: THE CLIMAX OF PART I: IVAN AT THE COFFIN OF ANASTASIA. ANDREI MOSKVIN AT CAMERA.

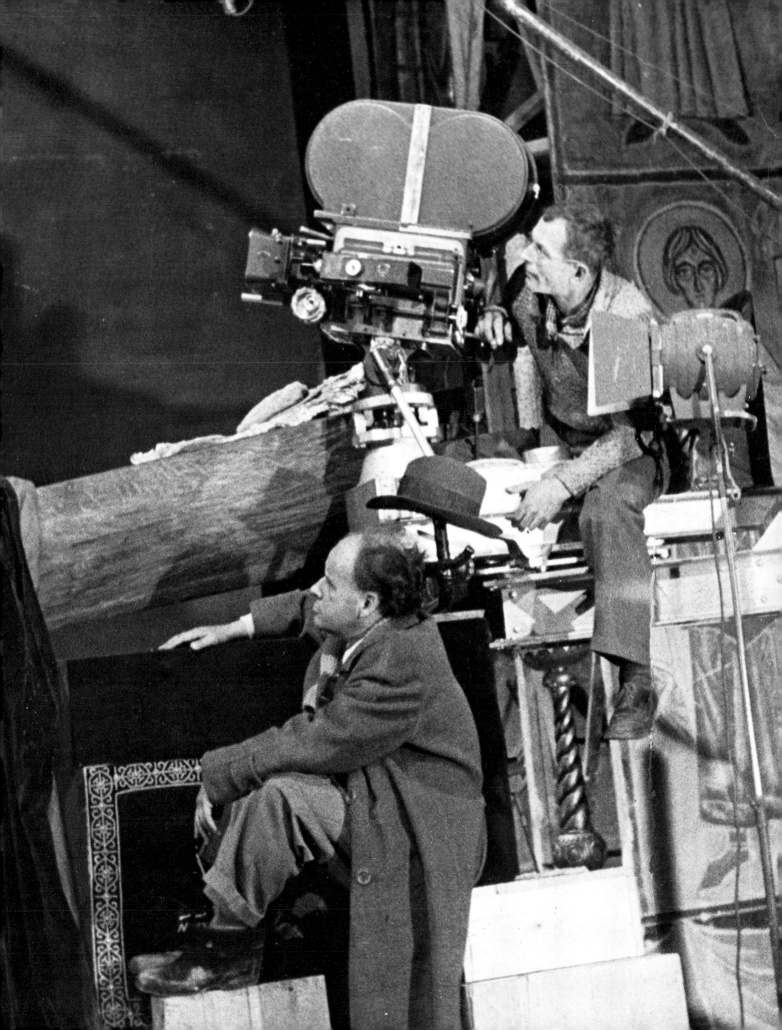

All of the drawings for the finale of Part I, the procession appealing to Ivan to return to Moscow, which appears to be one of the most intricate *mise-en-scènes* for the film, are dated November-December 1942. Several variants were planned and filmed.

BELOW: FROM EISENSTEIN'S SCRAPBOOK. WOODCUT FROM ONE HUNDRED VIEWS OF FAMOUS PLACES IN EDO. HIROSHIGE, 1857. HIROSHIGE'S HAWK MAY HAVE INSPIRED THE COMPOSITION ABOVE.

For the finale. 29 Dec 1942.

ABOVE AND BELOW: FRAMING IDEAS FOR THE PROCESSION.

High angle shot from Ivan's point of view looking down from the porch. [From left] clergy / 26 Dec 1942 / clergy boyars group [around a circle] / people run forward / boyars / people

THE TSAR WAITING FOR THE PROCESSION TO INVITE HIM BACK TO MOSCOW.

> "Save thy people, O Lord . . ." 27 Dec 1942.

TOP: FILMING IVAN AT THE MONASTERY.
JULY 24, 1942.

CENTER: MOSKVIN AT CAMERA; EISENSTEIN
AT RIGHT IN OVERCOAT.

BOTTOM: SKETCH FOR THE SHOT.

> "Saddle the horses—we gallop to Moscow."
> NB. Only Ivan is without a robe.
> 27 July 1942.

ABOVE: EISENSTEIN WITH MIKHAIL ROMM AS QUEEN ELIZABETH. THE SCENES WITH QUEEN ELIZABETH WERE LATER DELETED.

Queen Elizabeth with the boyar Osip Nepeya. 2 Apr 1942.

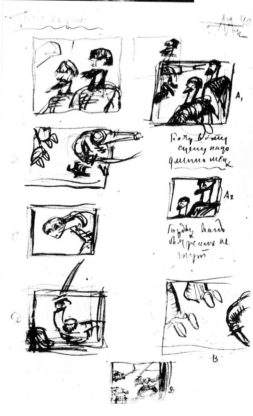

Queen Elizabeth and the young Blount. ". . . learn diplomacy, dear boy!" 18 Mar 1942.

A-1 This scene requires boyars with long necks.
A-2 The boyars do not bend their proud necks.

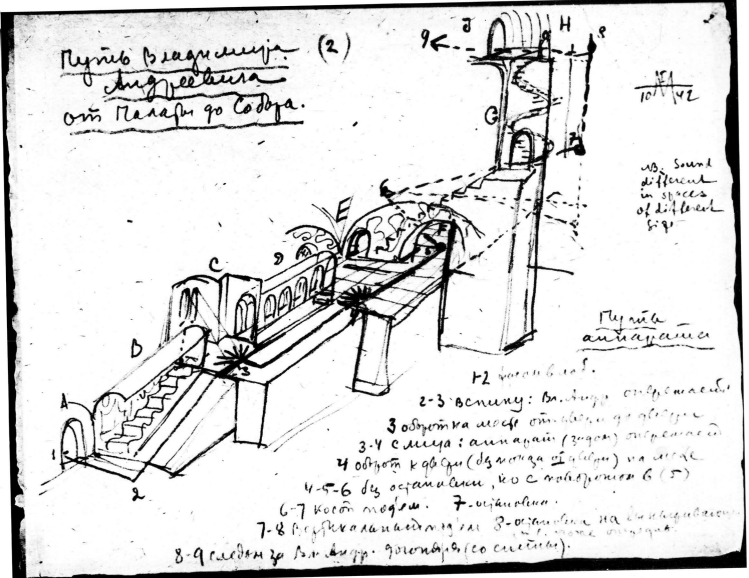

THE POSITIONS OF THE MOVING CAMERA.

Path of Vladimir Andreyevich from the Palace to the Cathedral (2).
10 Jan 1942
NB. Sound different in spaces of different size.
Path of the camera.
1-2   Centered on forehead
2-3   From behind: V.A. is ahead of camera
3   Turn in place from door to door
3-4   Facing camera: camera backs ahead
4   Turn to door (without looking <u>from</u> the door) on same spot.
4-5-6 Without pause, but with turn at 5
6-7   Oblique rise 7—pause
7-8   Vertical lift 8—pause and catching up (and perhaps even getting ahead)
8-9   Follows V.A. and catches up with him (from the back)

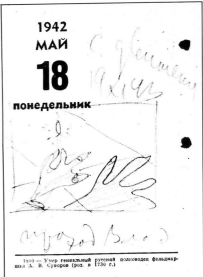

1942
МАЙ
18
понедельник

1800 — Умер гениальный русский полководец фельдмаршал А. В. Суворов (род. в 1730 г.)

TOP: FIRST SKETCH OF THE PASSAGE OF VLADIMIR, ON A CALENDAR PAGE.

Pale light <u>from</u> window (pale morning light). NB. Behind him moving lights from oprichniks' candles and their roaring song. [Translation of text (with drawing) not reproduced.]

ABOVE AND BELOW: DETAILS OF VLADIMIR, WITH A CANDLE AND IN THE TSAR'S ROBES, ENTERING THE CATHEDRAL.

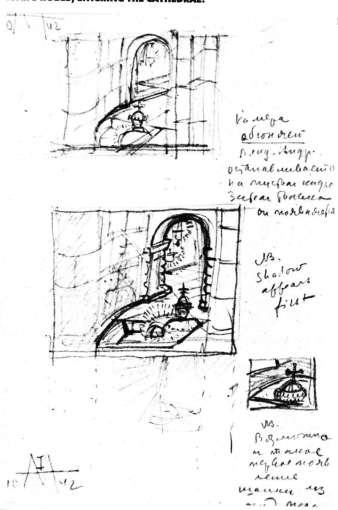

Camera overtakes Vlad. Andr., stops on a frame without figure, and then he appears. / NB. Shadow appears first / NB. Another possibility: to have the (crowned) hat appear first from beneath the floor. / 10 Jan 1942.

ABOVE: EISENSTEIN REHEARSING PAVEL KADOCHNIKOV AS VLADIMIR.

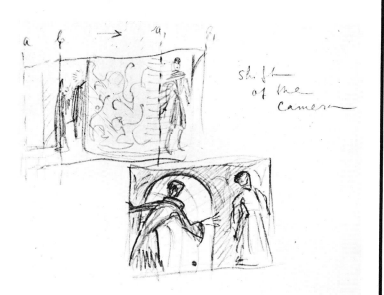

**THE ROBED OPRICHNIKI ON THE WINDING STEPS TO THE FLOOR OF
THE CATHEDRAL**

**EFROSINIA'S LAST SCENE, OVER THE BODY
OF HER DEAD SON, VLADIMIR.**

PART II:
The Boyars' Plot

From the memoirs of Serafima Birman

I do not remember rehearsing very much before Efrosinia's scenes in
the cathedral were shot. I do remember coming to an agreement
with Eisenstein as to how they were to be done. That, perhaps, was
the first time that Eisenstein and I talked on an even footing, without the distance of rank; the first time that we came to an agreement
before the filming instead of arguing while it was taking place. The
important thing is that these turned out to be Efrosinia's best scenes.
It was a stroke of luck that there was no time for prolonged rehearsing of my scenes in the cathedral. We received notice from Moscow
that on a certain day a commission from the Film Committee was
coming to see how work on *Ivan the Terrible* was progressing.

The commission was pressed for time and so on the day of their arrival Eisenstein scheduled the filming of my scenes (he knew that
one of the things they had come to investigate was how I was coping
with my role).

In other words, this visit was to prove who was right: the Committee
that opposed me, or the director who insisted on having me despite
their opposition.

Just before we began work, as I stood at the entrance to the sets, Eisenstein, outwardly calm, came up to me and made the sign of the
cross over me—he the skeptic, he the mocker.

And right he was. By so doing he transferred to me full responsibility
for the scenes.

I did not object.

I wanted to prove Eisenstein was right.

I did not want to be rejected as an actress.

At this moment I was in a state of creative inspiration that made me
forget everything vain, petty, and personal.

Silence! Lights on! Begin!

My very last scene was shot at night, since Eisenstein and Moskvin
were detained at a meeting.

I awaited them in costume and make-up, inwardly preparing myself.
Outside the brightly lit room night pressed darkly against the windowpane. The nights, I thought, were no different in Tsar Ivan's
time.

Time passed . . . voices. Here they come!

A whole crowd of people followed Eisenstein and Moskvin onto the
set. They arranged the lighting, moved me and Kadochnikov
about—now more to the left, now more to the right. Eisenstein and
Moskvin held a private conference. This light was taken out, that
one brought on. Preparations lasted about two hours.

Nobody, nothing, disturbed my deep concentration, not even Pavel
Kadochnikov who, taking advantage of our being posed with his
head on my knees, fell asleep and slept all through the experiments
with lighting effects.

The shooting began.

Eisenstein was not inspired. He seemed to be apathetic—the over-
wrought state he had been in for the last few days had sapped his
strength.

In a few days the commission returned to Moscow, gratified with
what they had seen.

Eisenstein later told me they had asked him: "What Birman is that?
Not the Moscow Birman, surely." When he assured them it was the
Moscow Birman they said: "Extraordinary!"

CLOCKWISE FROM UPPER LEFT: PAVEL KADOCHNIKOV AS STARITSKY, EUSTACE, KING SIGISMUND, AN EVIL CLOWN.

Pavel Kadochnikov's talent—not only as an actor but also for an unusually quick understanding of Eisenstein's principles and directorial wishes—brought him the role of Vladimir Staritsky, whose mother schemed to have him replace Ivan on the throne. Kadochnikov's memoirs reveal that Eisenstein wished to make fuller use of his talents:

When it was agreed that I was to play Vladimir Staritsky, Eisenstein suddenly remarked, "Perhaps you should also play Eustace," and the idea was dropped as suddenly as it had been broached. I thought he had forgotten the suggestion altogether; but when the time came to shoot Eustace's scenes [in Part III] I played the role. [There was no technical difficulty in his playing the two roles; Staritsky is murdered at the end of Part II and Eustace appears only in Part III.]

And that was not all. One day during the preparation for the "Fiery Furnace Play" (staged in the cathedral to intimidate Ivan) he suddenly asked me, "Can you do a cartwheel?" "I certainly can," and thus I was cast in my third role, a Chaldean, one of the evil clowns in the play.[*] It was not a large part, but it required acting skills totally distinct from the first two roles.

And finally, I was tested for a fourth role, King Sigismund of Poland—completely unlike my other roles. Eventually it was decided that Pavel Massalsky was to play the King.

---

[*]Most of this "morality play" was deleted from the roughly cut work copy of Part II, from which all the "objectionable" scenes were removed: this is the version we see today.

The color scenes of Part II were decided by a coincidence of several circumstances, described in a fragment of Eisenstein's memoirs:

There was the fact that Prokofiev left Alma-Ata before I did. But Ivan's feast and the dances of the *oprichniki* could not be filmed without the music being written and recorded in advance. And consequently this obliged us to transfer the filming of the feast and dance to Moscow.

But that wasn't all. Prokofiev became ill, and amidst his obligations to both *War and Peace* and *Cinderella* he could not find time that summer to give me the needed orchestrations. Autumn came and winter approached. The finished set had stood waiting since summer. The orchestration was delayed.

Just at that time, it happened that a conference on color was organized at the Dom Kino. Not so much on the desolate spectacle before us as it was an argument and discussion on something that none of us had yet had a chance to work on.  The emptiness of the discussion was irritating. Most irritating of all, though, was the free supplement to the discussion: screenings of examples of the color creations of the American and German industries, along with those few significant attempts of our own before the war to use two- and three-color negative systems—attempts vaunted and boasted. Now on our screens also could be shown a "miserable splendor of costume" and an "imitation" painted cheek. Irritation is an excellent creative stimulus.

Suddenly, amidst all this imported vulgarity, a film document in color appeared on the screen: *The Potsdam Conference.* Some parts of this film, as color, were horrible. But then came a series of interiors in the palace of Cecilienhof. In one room a blindingly red carpet covered the whole area of the screen. Cutting diagonally across it was a row of white armchairs upholstered in red. Color was functioning!

 Furthermore, the Chinese Pavilion at Sans Souci was shown in a few shots—and the gilded Chinese figures also came off well. Of even greater importance, we could also see on these figures high-lighted reflections from the surrounding greenery and from the white marble stairs.

So, the red works. The gold also looks right. And, of course, the black does, too. Blue might also work. Perhaps it's worth the risk of a trial.

The set for Ivan's feast had stood since the summer. The feast must burst like an explosion between the dark scene of the conspiracy against the Tsar and the gloomy scene of the attempt to kill him. Why couldn't this explosion be—in color? Color would participate in the explosion of the dance. And then, at the end of the feast, imperceptibly flowing back into black-and-white photography, the tragic tone of the accidental death of Prince Vladimir Andreyevich, killed by the murderer sent by his mother to kill the Tsar.

ABOVE: THE HEAD BODYGUARD, FYODOR BASMANOV, WITH AND WITHOUT HIS MASK AT IVAN'S FEAST.

In a letter of January 1946

> I was (and still am for about 3 weeks) busy like hell; just finishing to shoot and cut the second part of Ivan. This part includes two reels made in color. Color used in quite different a way than it is usually done—so that it gives a big additional chapter to what is nearly ready in book form. If everything is all right here with the picture I expect to take a vacation and finish the book—³/₄ of which is ready for print. Most of the stuff is unpublished (part of it even unwritten yet!) and is mostly concerned with the development of the principles started by *Potemkin* during these twenty years in different media (is that the way to say it?)—treatments of sound, music, color. The way of composing ecstatic scenes, etc. *Ivan* in connection with *Potemkin*. I will send you a detailed plan as soon as the film goes to the laboratory to be printed. Maybe it will be all right to include the script of Ivan as well into this book.

The awards and medals for Part I were celebrated with a dinner and dancing party in early February 1946. The people working on *Ivan* were also celebrating the completion of Part II. Eisenstein came directly from the cutting room to the party and collapsed on the dancing floor with a serious cardiac infarction. For several months he was kept hospitalized at the Kremlin Hospital and at Barvikha. During this time, and without his knowledge, Part II was reviewed by the authorities, harshly and publicly criticized, and banned.

After his recovery, he made two efforts to repair Part II and have the film brought back to life.

At Cherkasov's request, he and Eisenstein were given an appointment in March 1946 to discuss with Stalin alterations in Part II, and on the basis of this Eisenstein immediately made a roughly corrected cutting of Part II (it is this rough cut that survives), but he lacked the strength to make the new sequences that were needed for Part II. There was no talk of or plan for Part III: all materials for it, including four edited reels, had, by then, been destroyed.

But by March 21 there was changed news, in a cable:

JUST RECEIVED THROUGH IRSKY BRILLIANT SELECTION OF BOOKS THANKS IMMENSELY STOP AM LAYING SIXTH WEEK HOSPITAL AFTER HEART ATTACK THE DAY I MADE LAST CUT SECOND PART IVAN STOP LOOKING FORWARD LONG RECONVALESCENCE ENTIRELY DEVOTED WRITING BOOKS AWAITING CABLES LETTERS NEWS MUCH LOVE
                                              EISENSTEIN.

2 July 1946, to Ivor Montagu:

> I'm recovering very very slowly from my heart attack in February—and expect to return to my film activities sometime around October or November.

> Things were so drastic that even up to now I'm nearly out as to what might be labeled my writing activity—although I expected to give away most of the time of my reconvalescence to writing.

> (4¹/₂ months I had just to lay on my back—just waiting for my heart muscle to piece itself together, after it had split as a result of overworking. Now laying for months on one's back and not being exactly a harlot—is not much fun?)

PART III

The first sequence of *Ivan* that Eisenstein planned and wrote in 1941 was the confrontation of the Earthly Tsar with the Heavenly Tsar (in a fresco of the Last Judgment) while the roll of Ivan's victims is intoned, heard by Malyuta and the two Basmanovs. This sequence was filmed and destroyed with the rest of Part III, at the time that Part II was shelved. Eisenstein was then being treated in hospital for his heart condition, and was not told of the fates of Parts II and III. The following quotations from the published literary script are from the English translation, pages 225-47.

> The angry countenance of the Tsar of Heaven
> Sabaoth
> in a fresco of the Last Judgment.
> The Tsar of Heaven is holding the Last Judgment:
> He is calling the righteous to himself,
> casting sinners into fiery Gehenna . . .
> In the darkness below the fresco of the Last Judgment
> in a corner,
> where most insatiably of all
> the eternal fires devour sinners,
> lies prostrate
> Tsar Ivan.
> But more fearfully than hellfire, remorse tortures, scorches, gnaws
> at the soul of the Tsar of Earth—of Muscovy.

EISENSTEIN REHEARSING CHERKASOV FOR THE CONFRONTATION WITH THE HEAVENLY TSAR.

He accounts as his a fearful responsibility.
Sweat pours in streams from his forehead.
Scorching tears stream from his closed eyes.
The Tsar has grown thin, emaciated.
And seems yet older by a dozen years.

Malyuta tells the younger Basmanov:
In all were executed in Novgorod
one thousand five hundred and five souls . . .
And Ivan's lips whisper,
as though he were justifying the terrible deed:
Not from malice. Not from wrath. Not from savagery. For
treason.
For betrayal of the cause of the whole people.

Clearly sounds the obituary roll:
Anna. Irene. Alexis. Agatha. Xenia.
Her two sons. Isaac. Zachary's two daughters . . .
Malyuta tells the elder Basmanov:
Monasteries pillaged and destroyed number one hundred and
seventy . . .
And Ivan hastens to offer explanation of the bloody deed:
Not for self. Not for greed's sake. For the country. Not from
savagery.

But to safeguard the land.
And he gazes entreatingly into the eyes of the Dark
Countenance.
But the eyes do not gaze down.
Their painted gaze is set in the far distance.

Says Ivan in anguish:
Thou art silent? . . .
He waits. No answer.

Angrily, with defiance,
the Earthly Tsar to the Heavenly Tsar
has repeated threateningly:
Thou art silent, Tsar of Heaven?!
The Figure is silent.

Then flings, as a mighty gage,
the Earthly Tsar at the Heavenly Tsar
his jewel-studded staff.
The staff shatters on the smooth wall.
It smashes to splinters.
The scintillating stones fly through the air.
Scattered like Ivan's prayers, to Heaven addressed in
vain. . . .

And the Earthly Tsar sinks down,
crushed by the inexorability of the Tsar of Heaven.
Thou deignest no answer to the Tsar of Earth . . .
his strength forsaking him, beating himself against the
wall, whispers Tsar Ivan.
But the stern, painted Sabaoth on the wall is silent,
seated on His great throne above the stars.

He awaits an answer from Sabaoth.
But the wall is silent.

The Prayer for Forgiveness to start with.

Ivan against the background of the Last Judgment fresco.

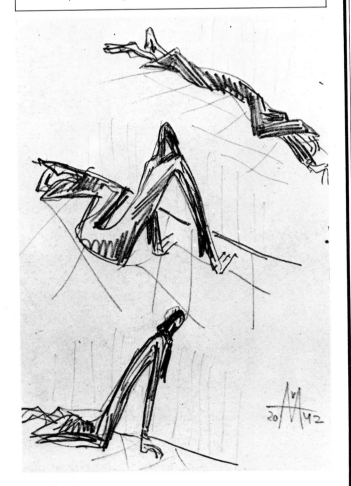

He sees God sitting high up above the flames. He sees the flames and realizes their meaning.

Ivan's plea.

<u>Above:</u> Proportions of Sabaoth correct / Scene of Grozny's plea (Garden of Gethsemane).
<u>Right:</u> "Not from malice. Not from wrath . . ."

Молчить небеснаго паль?..

Left: "Thou art silent, Tsar of Heaven?!"

The search for Ivan's make-up for Part III consumed much time. The chief make-up artist, Vasili Goryunov, had not previously worked with Eisenstein, and he recorded the surprises of his first encounters:

At our first work meeting Eisenstein brought a heap of books and a whole stack of his own drawings. What strange drawings! I had never seen anything like them. Our first conversation was about them:

G. These sketches can never be realized.
E. Where did you work before coming to films?
G. In the circus and operetta.
E. I should have guessed as much.
G. But these sketches are pure formalism.
E. I'll supply you with an idea for the image, and it will be up to you to realize it. But you must always work with the face of the player.

At a later meeting, while we were working together, he said quite casually: "I forgive you for calling me a 'formalist!' And now let us lengthen Cherkasov's head. You'll have to make a stiff wig, and think about his chin while you do it." And with that he made one of those "formalist" sketches, giving Ivan's head the shape of a cucumber.

Eisenstein had an extraordinary sensitivity for the proper proportions of the human body. In the appearance of each character he sought for the unity of the whole. Early in our work he asked me, "Have you noticed that Cherkasov's torso and arms do not harmonize with the shape of his head? It actually should have a shape like this"—and again he drew his "cucumber." In his memoirs he mentioned Alessandro Magnasco's paintings as also contributing to the figure of Ivan.

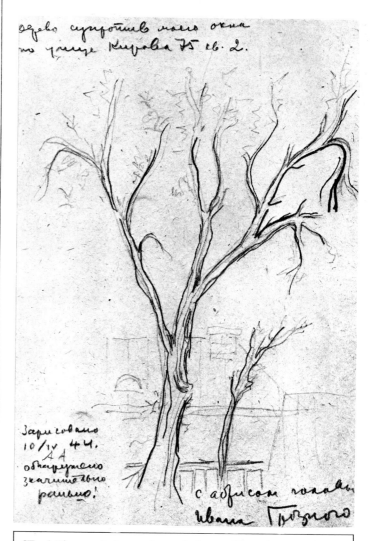

[Top] The tree in front of my window on Kirov Street N-75 apt. 2
[Left] Drawing made
    24 Oct 44
    Alma-Ata
    Observed much earlier
[Right] Outline of the head of Ivan the Terrible.

TWO OF THE MANY SOURCES EISENSTEIN DREW UPON FOR IVAN'S MAKE-UP FOR PART III.

ABOVE: THE SILHOUETTE OF BRANCHES SEEN FROM HIS APARTMENT WINDOW.

BELOW: JOHN BARRYMORE AS MR. HYDE (1920).

A COMPARISON OF THE MAKE-UP FOR PARTS II AND III.

<u>ABOVE AND RIGHT:</u> SEEKING THE RIGHT MAKE-UP FOR IVAN IN PART III.

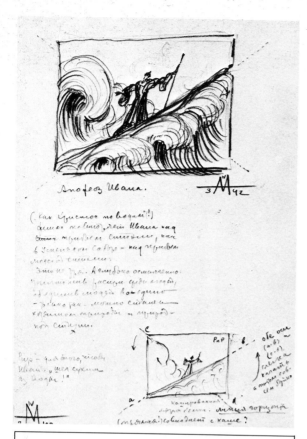

Apotheosis of Ivan ("Like Christ upon the Waters!") 3 Apr 1942
The finale in which Ivan subdues the onslaught of the waves echoes back to Uspensky Cathedral, where he triumphs over the onslaught of the human tide.
This is crucial. It has deep significance: putting an end to conflicts among the people, uniting the people into one whole is the only way to assume mastery over nature and nature's upheavals.
Rear projection so that Ivan "emerges dry from the waters"!
Rear / Both axes (a-b) and (c-d) are rolled lightly and then violently
Matte process for filming the sea—line of horizon (straight!) coincides with matte?

Finale   Bring to a complete meeting (before the total calm) 3 Apr 1942
Apotheosis of Ivan
(the moment of the highest swell of the axes)
NB.   The waves must be filmed with a stop-motion camera—in a furious tempo of waves rolling on top of one another.
     In this position the axes are made to stop—and slowly and symmetrically the axes are lowered.
The sky should be cloudless in order not to give away the trick of the rolling.
(but is it possible technically?)
Perhaps we'll have to print it on negative (before filming)
Section A is made with a roll, and the sky covered with a black screen!
(Difficulty is that the waves and the crest of the waves are higher than the horizon line)
The black screen coincides with the line of the horizon—
In front of it the camera is rolling.

Alone . . . ?

[PARENTHESIS: PROKOFIEV: WAR AND PEACE]

When Prokofiev came to Alma-Ata in 1942 to develop the musical ideas for his *Ivan Grozny* score, he brought along his opera of *War and Peace* to continue its orchestration. As the latter work progressed, the composer acquainted Eisenstein with the opera, scene by scene—until Eisenstein was making suggestions for its production. Samuil Samosud, conductor and artistic director of the Bolshoi Theater, concluded "that Eisenstein was the man to stage the opera. . . . Knowing how the completion of *Ivan* was his most urgent task, our theater offered him the position of consulting director."

By 1943 Prokofiev telegraphed Samosud:

EISENSTEIN CONSENTS TO WORK AS DIRECTOR, NOT CONSULTANT. REQUESTS URGENT ARRIVAL OF [PETER] WILLIAMS IN ALMA-ATA TO WORK OUT PLANS FOR SETS.

PROKOFIEV

But the Bolshoi Theater decided that a new production of such a large-scale work was unwise in wartime, and *War and Peace* was first heard by Moscow in a concert version in the summer of 1945. Eisenstein and Samosud met at that performance and agreed that only a full staging would do justice to the opera. Samosud arranged for its premiere to be at Leningrad's Maly Opera. After his heart failure, all Eisenstein's projects were halted. His surviving sketches for *War and Peace* bear the dates of his first enthusiastic discussions with Prokofiev.

The premiere of *War and Peace*, which was given in Leningrad June 12, 1946, used the final version in thirteen scenes:

Epigraph (including Overture and Prologue)
  1. Garden of the Rostovs
  2. Ball
  3. At Prince Bolkonsky's
  4. Dinner at Helene's
  5. Dolokhov's cabinet
  6. Room at Akhrosimova's
  7. Pierre's cabinet
  8. Borodinskoye before the battle
  9. Shevardinsky Redoubt during the battle
  10. Interior of izba
  11. A street in Moscow
  12. Dark interior of an izba
  13. Road to Smolensk

While all of Eisenstein's sketches cannot be linked positively to the scenes outlined, the official designer did base some of the sets on Eisenstein's ideas.

RIGHT AND OPPOSITE PAGE: SKETCHES FOR SCENES OF WAR AND PEACE.

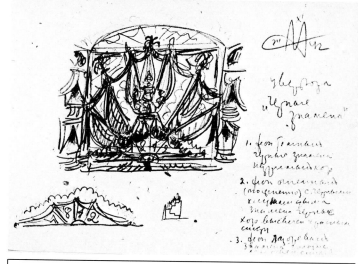

24 Oct 1942 / Overture / "Black Banners"
1. Dark background / black banners / invisible chorus
2. Flaming background with (gradually) black clouds of smoke / black banners / chorus is lighted red, from below
3. Azure background / golden banners / chorus is lighted blue

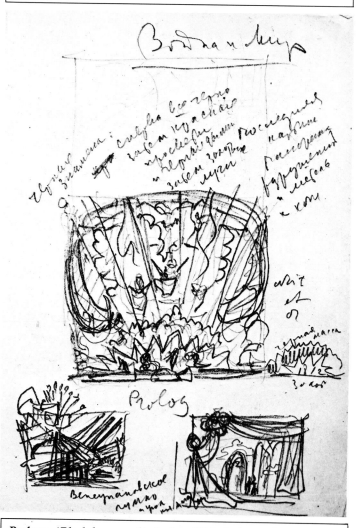

Prologue / Black banners: beginning <u>all</u> black then red points glimmer through the black smoke then golden rays / Last scene. A panorama of destruction and blizzard and horses / A Venetsianov threshing floor and the harvest of Prince B?

[Left] Military emblems of the past.
[Center] The moon shines through the trees diffused.
[Right] At the end, on the right, the sun shines through the banners on—KUTUZOV 17 Feb 1943.

Right. French banners are covered by waves of black crepe (impression of Napoleon's tomb, Paris 1907 [sic] / Golden domes of Moscow rise up (during the fire these domes disappear in the flames) / Out of the chaos of small banners a huge eagle emerges and Kutuzov steps on its head / 18 Feb 1943.

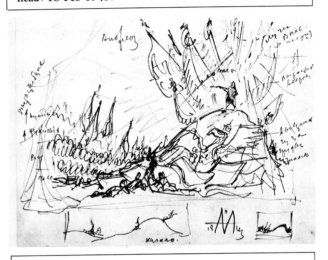

"Kaleidoscope" . . . lances . . . seen through transparent ceiling 18 Feb 1943.

Apotheosis / gold / (Walküre rays) / growing higher / wings wings / size / [battle]field / beginning [of scene 9?] / Fan out and grow larger / eagle comes out from behind the piled-up banners / 18 Feb 1943.

Left. If they don't come—bring them! / Execution of the Russians / Scene 11 / A street in Moscow 18 Feb 1943.

[Top right] Shadows move behind the transparent screen . . . and guardsmen of . . . but the movement is downward
[Bottom left] Emblems: Fallen shako, horse. Torn banner with sickle, scythe, pitchfork, and rake thrust through it 18 Feb 1943.

During the first half of 1945 Eisenstein's appointment book shows the beginning of trouble with Parts II and III of *Ivan Grozny*; also, the large number of foreign films that he saw or was invited to see (the number of Xs indicates his approval, the number of Gs [*govno*: crap] his disapproval).

Mar 27	*Memphis Belle* (Documentary)
28	5-7:30 Cherkasov with me.
29	Morning finish Gr[ozny?]. [an article?]
	1:30 Int[ernational] Lit[erature]. return books.
	2 Art Council of the Bolshoi. Bryants[ev pereulok?]
	4:30 Galoshes
	5 Kremlyovka Yu. 1. Phone [about] *Nitouche*
	6:30 Eiber. (teeth)
30	8 *Nitouche*
31	*Human Comedy* XXX
Apr 2	*Bathing Beauty*
3	*Laura*
4	*Stormy Weather* X *Wake Island*
5	*Chopin* [A Song to Remember?] G
6	*Bambi.* X
8	*Bathing Beauty.*
9	6:30 Reception at Holland Embassy.
10	*Gas Light*
11	2 Went to see [Natamad?]
12	10:30 Received "Life" (photos of *Ivan*)
	11 Screening of material for Part II of *Ivan Grozny*. Committee not full. Daumier for 325 rubles. Gold for teeth. Eiber. *Phantom of the Opera. Story of a Jeep.*
13	Gold for teeth. Phone Karakhan. Received in Academy.
	5 VOKS. American documentary film.
	7:30 judgment of films
14	*Hold Up the Dawn.* X
19	1-2 ring V. A. [Milman?] 5 VAK. [on doctoral dissertations]
20	*Random Harvest.* Greer Garson. Ronald Colman.
22	12:30 Send car for Soifertis. 1-5 Soifertis with me.
	A Guy Called Joe. Spencer Tracy. XXX
23	*It Started with Eve.* Toscanini.
26	5. VAK. *Hunchback of Notre Dame.* GGG
27	*Five Graves to Cairo.*
28	Tretyakov [Gallery?]
29	*Shadow of a Doubt.* Hitchcock & Th. Wilder.
May 4	*The Man from Half Moon Street.*
9	VOKS. Mrs Churchill
10	Birolain. M & Mme. Catrou
11	K.
12	*Private* [Hargrove]. G *Henry V.* GGG
17	*Star Spangled Rhythm.* XXX
27	*Kid from Spain.* G
28	*My Friend Flicka.* Horse in color.
30	*Counter attack* [?] GG *Tahiti Nights.* GG
June 2	[in Leningrad telephones] Cherkasov V.2.99.29. Kasheverova B.1.01.23. Orbelli Hermitage. *Great King* [play about Ivan Grozny by Solovyov] Alexandrinka.
3	*Sylvia.*
5	*Ballerina* Loretta Young.
7	Art Council of the Committee. *Moon over Miami.* Committee. *Stormy Weather.* [not the film]
9	Goskino Press. Dacha.
11	*War & Peace* by Prokofiev.

When he was immobilized at the Barvikha Sanitorium and his new dacha in 1946, he continued to see American films through the kindness of Miss Elizabeth Eagan of the U.S. Embassy, who brought or sent 16mm. copies to him, along with a steady flow of books. A letter sent to her reads:

> . . . let Arthur bring me the picture "Meet me in St. Louis": I'm terribly fond of Judy Garland! And don't you have by any chance a copy of "Forever Amber"? I'd like to read that very much.
>
> Is there no way to find Agatha Christie's "Murder of Roger Ackroyd" in Moscow? (the old detective story)

Detective novels were always in demand: one of the many books Eisenstein had planned was to be devoted to novels of detection and deduction.

EISENSTEIN'S LETTER THANKING ELIZABETH EAGAN FOR THE FILM *NATIONAL VELVET* (1944) AND LEWIS JACOBS'S HISTORY, *THE RISE OF THE AMERICAN FILM* (1939).

MOSCOW 800

On September 30, 1946, a film was proposed to Eisenstein to celebrate the 800th anniversary of the founding of the city of Moscow. In the few days before the project was set aside he sketched two aspects of it that particularly interested him: the function of color in films and the "montage of epochs" that he had been trying to realize since *Qué Viva México!*

". . . the spiral development of historical events, repeating and revealing new qualities and aspects in certain crucial moments of history." One possibility was "the three hordes, the Tatars, the attack of 1812, and the Germans"; from all of these Moscow had saved Europe.

Another continuity of epochs for *Moscow 800*:

0. Moscow of icons
1. Wooden Moscow
2. Moscow of white stone
3. Moscow of calico (the textile mills) *
4. Iron Moscow
5. Moscow of steel (planes, tanks—war)
6. Moscow of the rainbow (celebration of war's end a peaceful rebirth)
7. Moscow of growth and strength

*Notes were made here for a young heroine—a mill girl—who would represent Moscow just as the *soldadera* represented Mexico.

ABOVE AND RIGHT: THE BALL COSTUMES FOR <u>PIQUE DAME</u>.

PIQUE DAME

Eisenstein's last project for the stage was a ballet that Prokofiev had composed in 1936, based on Pushkin's story "The Queen of Spades," which had not been satisfactory to the ballet companies. He supplied a libretto and sketched a choreography for the entire ballet, but this last collaboration between Prokofiev and Eisenstein was to remain unrealized.

<u>ABOVE</u>: THE COUNTESS IN YOUTH, WITH THE MASK OF AGE.

THE WORLD UPSIDE DOWN

Although these three drawings were made the same day, May 26, 1945, their connection cannot be definitely established. Did the novel by Anatole France bring the difficultly transported souls to a heaven that was merely *The World Upside Down*? Or are these two half-serious suggestions for a production at the Music Hall? The "upside down" tricks and jokes seem designed for theater rather than the more flexible camera.

[Top] "DON'T ASK ME WHY" / The World Upside Down
/ Passing herds
[Bottom] Toward the end rain begins to fall—verticals. Drops in the fountain. Wind makes apples fall.

The City. In this scene the aviator jumps by parachute!

[Top] The Revolt of the Angels
[Bottom] 6 June 45 / Elevator Station to Heaven
/ The moment materialization occurs body and soul become indivisible—much trouble in transportation of souls.

MEMOIRS AND THE COLLECTED WRITINGS

Today I start to write my "Portrait of the Author as a Very Old Man."—December 24, 1946

When he wrote from the hospital that he was writing a "comic autobiography," his casual tone ought not to have deceived me: this was a project long precious to him. Joyce, of course, had had a hand in it: the experiment in 1928 of a "stream of consciousness à la Joyce" begins by his saying that if his art potency should disappoint him he will "write my very scrupulous autobiography in that super-exact manner of Joyce's description of Bloom."

In his often-consulted *Autobiography* of Mark Twain he found a comforting thought that matched his physical condition:

> I am writing from the grave. On these terms only can a man be approximately frank. He cannot be straitly and unqualifiedly frank either in the grave or out of it.

In the past he had often jotted down memories; now his system was to ignore chronological order, "putting all the associations that cluster around the sentence or idea I am writing." The combination of uninhibited truths and free association continues to make problems for his editors and censors.

The *Memoirs* filled the first volume of his posthumously published collected works.

1947, Eisenstein's last year, was filled with the impossible effort to complete his major books, even though nothing was being written for immediate publication. All Soviet publishing channels had been closed to him; they were not to reopen until after his death.

There was no happier prospect for his major unfinished films. Cherkasov and he made yet another appeal to Stalin to allow them to continue the repair and completion of *Ivan II*—but they received no encouragement even though Eisenstein had removed its most offending passages in his last day's work in the cutting room.

Ivan III was not discussed again. Its four completed reels and all uncut footage intended for it, including Prokofiev's manuscript and recorded score, were totally destroyed. Only the drawings and scenario survived.

Bezhin Meadow's cut negative and work-print were stored in the vault where the most valuable negatives from Mosfilm and Lenfilm had been placed when German forces began to bomb Moscow and Leningrad. A German bomb fell near the vault and its contents were subsequently destroyed by the firemen's hoses. There are, however, rumors that Eisenstein's personal copy of *Bezhin Meadow* was among the cans of film removed from his Potylikha apartment the morning after his death.

This last year Eisenstein finally saw the films made by others from his footage for *Qué Viva México!* In March he viewed prints of *Thunder Over Mexico* and *Time in the Sun*—a last blow to his continuing hopes that something still might be recovered from the Mexican tragedy. He wrote an angry introduction to the Mexican script for the (unpublished) French edition of his writings.

There had been a time when he spoke of following *Ivan Grozny* with *The Brothers Karamazov*, but he now knew there would be no more films for him to make.

Besides his constant writing and reading there was little to be done. In April he proposed a work outside the closed channels: a ballet of *Pique Dame* to a Prokofiev score that had been rejected earlier by the Bolshoi Theater. The Music Hall was another possibility still open to him: France's *Révolte des Anges?*

And there were cables planning a second volume for American publication: its contents and title, *Film Form*, had been approved by the authorities. Visitors came occasionally to the dacha. At the approach of winter, he was returned to the heated apartment near the studio.

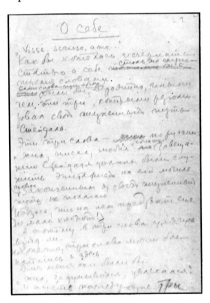

"Visse, scrisse, amo."

How I wish I could sum up my life with the same economy—in three words.

The words would probably not be those that Stendhal chose to sum up his life's path.

His three words, that mean "I lived, I wrote, I loved," were, according to his will, to be engraved on his tombstone.

True, I do not yet consider my life's path to be ended. (And I fear there are still some troubles ahead!) That is why three words are not quite enough.

But, of course, if I were pressed for a choice, three could be found: They would be, for me:

> I lived, I pondered, I thrilled.

And let this serve to express how I lived, and on what I pondered and thrilled.

A Chronological Outline of Sergei Eisenstein's Life and Work

1898 10 Jan. [new calendar, **22 Jan.**] Born in Riga to Julia Ivanovna (née Konetskaya) and Mikhail Osipovich Eisenstein, civil engineer and architect.

1906 Visits Paris and sees his first film (Méliès's *Les 400 Farces du Diable*).

1908 Enters the first class of the Riga city secondary school.

1909 His mother moves to St. Petersburg, leaving husband and son in Riga. On his first visit to St. Petersburg sees his first circus.

1912 Attends Riga performance of Nezlobin Theater's production of Gozzi's *Princess Turandot*, directed by Fyodor Komissarzhevsky.

1913 Edits school weekly, *Klassen Revue*, illustrated with his caricatures.

1914 Spends the summer with his mother in Staraya Russa. Meets the widow of Dostoyevsky.

1915 **May** Completes his secondary schooling in Riga.
Sept. Enters the Institute of Civil Engineering, Petrograd.

1916 Sees Meyerhold's production of Calderón's *Steadfast Prince* and visits Yevreinov's vaudeville theater.

1917 **Feb.** Takes examination in higher mathematics; transfers to the Ensigns' Engineering School and enrolls in the city militia. Witnesses February Revolution on streets of Petrograd. Sees Meyerhold's productions of Molière's *Don Juan* and Lermontov's *Masquerade*; sells political caricatures to the journal *Satirikon* and the *Petrograd Gazette*.
Mar. Is called up for military service.
Aug. His section of the Ensigns' school ordered to the front. Writes and designs *Dawn of the Red Alarm* and *Evolution of a Witch*.
Oct. October Revolution. Sells caricature to *Ogonyok*; designs sets and costumes for a group of unrealized productions.

1918 **Jan.** After the Engineering School closes, returns to the Institute.
Feb. Volunteers for Red Army construction of Petrograd defenses.
Sept. Leaves for the Northeast Front. Studies commedia dell' arte, Freud and Pavlov.

1919 **Mar.** His army group moves to Dvinsk.
June Studies stage problems intensively, reads theater literature, including medieval texts, and plans productions.
July Army group moves to Kholm, Pskov Province.
Nov.–Dec. In Veliki Luki, tries out plans in local cultural club, where he meets the artist Konstantin Yeliseyev.

1920 **Jan.–Feb.** Designs and plays principal role in Averchenko's *The Double*, and plays a clown in Sluchaini's *Mirror*.
Feb.–Mar. Designs and plays in Amnuel's *Marat*.
Mar.–June. Writes and designs *Authentic Comedy about the Lustful Witch*. . . .
July Transferred to front-line theater troupe as designer for theater and agit-trains.
Aug. Arrives in Minsk, where he and Yeliseyev work as a design team.
Sept. Demobilized to Moscow, receives permission to enter the General Staff Academy to study Japanese.
Oct. Appointed head of the design section of the Central Workers Theater of Proletcult. Begins designs for production of *The Mexican* (adapted from Jack London).
Nov. Leaves General Staff Academy.
Dec. Starts a workshop in direction; among his students: Strauch, Alexandrov, and Glizer.

1921 **Apr.** Becomes a member of the theatrical collegium at Proletcult. Designs a production of Mayakovsky's *Mysteria-Bouffe*.
Mar. First open rehearsals of *The Mexican*.
Sept. Enrolls as student in V. S. Meyerhold's workshop in direction.
Nov. Begins work on Ostrovsky's *Enough Simplicity in Every Sage*, as adapted by S. M. Tretyakov for Proletcult; designs, with Yutkevich, *Macbeth* for V. Tikhonovich, and *A Good Relation to Horses* for the Foregger Workshop.
Dec. Meyerhold assigns him the design of Ludwig Tieck's *Puss-in-Boots*.

1922 **Jan.** Begins designs for Shaw's *Heartbreak House* at Meyerhold Workshop.
Autumn Works as apprentice director on Meyerhold's production of *The Death of Tarelkin*, by Sukhovo-Kobylin. Leaves Meyerhold to become director in new permanent theater of Proletcult.
Winter Attends Kuleshov's film workshop for three months.

1923 **Mar.** First film, *Glumov's Diary*, as interlude in his Ostrovsky staging.
Apr.–May First performances of *Enough Simplicity in Every Sage*.
June No. 3 of *Lef* contains his first theoretical manifesto, "The Montage of Attractions."
Summer (?) With Tretyakov prepares a brochure on expressive movement.
Nov. Premiere of his production of Tretyakov's *Do You Hear, Moscow?*

1924 **Feb.** Premiere of his production of Tretyakov's *Gas-Masks* in the Moscow gas works.

Mar. Assists Esfir Shub in recutting Lang's *Dr. Mabuse* for Soviet distribution.

Apr. Proletcult proposes to Goskino a film cycle, *Towards Dictatorship [of the Proletariat]*; fifth in series, *Strike*, is chosen as first production, with assistance by Esfir Shub on shooting script; production begins, with Eduard Tisse as cameraman.

Oct. Writes "The Montage of Film Attractions" for Alexander Belenson's *Cinema Today* (published Feb. 1925 with Eisenstein's essay rewritten by Belenson).

Nov. Separates from Proletcult for future film production.

Dec. Begins research with Bliokh and Alexandrov for filming Isaac Babel's *First Cavalry Army* (unrealized) at Sevzapkino.

1925 **Mar.** Assigned to Goskino to make the anniversary film of the 1905 Revolution; to work with Nina Agadzhanova-Shutko on the scenario *The Year 1905*; first filming in Moscow.

Apr. Public release of *Strike*.

June–July Alongside work on the *1905* scenario, prepares with Babel a film plan for his *Benya Krik*, and with Alexandrov sells a pot-boiler scenario, *Bazaar of Desires*, to Proletkino.

Aug.–Dec. Concentrates on and completes one episode of *1905: Battleship Potemkin*; first public performance at the anniversary celebration in the Bolshoi Theater.

1926 **Jan.** Public release of *Battleship Potemkin*. Tretyakov prepares script for next film, on the Chinese Revolution, *Zhung-kuo*. First German showings of *Potemkin*.

Mar.–Apr. Sent with Tisse to inspect Berlin film studios, consults with Edmund Meisel on score for new release of *Potemkin* (censored version).

June Completes with Alexandrov a scenario for *The General Line*.

July After seeing *Potemkin* in Berlin, Fairbanks and Pickford visit Moscow and invite Eisenstein to work at United Artists.

Sept. Sovkino proposes a film for the tenth anniversary of the October Revolution.

Nov. Begins work with Alexandrov on plan for *October*. Filming for *The General Line* begins in Baku, Rostov-na-Don, the Mugan Steppe, and northern Caucasus.

1927 **Jan.** Returns to Moscow, halts work on *The General Line*, and resumes work with Alexandrov on scenario for *October*.

Feb. Screening for writers and critics of *General Line* fragments.

Mar.–Apr. To Leningrad with filming group, first shots for *October*.

June Films storming of the Winter Palace.

Sept. Returns to Moscow to begin montage of *October*, while Alexandrov and Tisse continue filming in Leningrad; Meisel comes to Moscow to begin work on *October* score. In cutting room, makes notes for two film projects: *Capital* and *The Glass House*.

Nov. First screening of *October* at Bolshoi anniversary celebration; revised montage begun.

1928 **Mar.** Public release of *October*. Takes *Ulysses* to study in Gagri (the Crimea).

May Appointed to direction course at State Technicum of Cinema (GTK). Revision of *The General Line* scenario with Alexandrov.

June Resumes filming of *The General Line*.

July Issues manifesto on use of sound, also signed by Alexandrov and Pudovkin.

Aug. Joseph Schenck in Moscow to discuss Eisenstein's work with United Artists. Moscow performances of the Kabuki theater.

Sept. Begins montage of *The General Line*. First lectures at GTK. First ideas for a satire, *"MM Is Making Deals"* (*"MM torguet"*), with Maxim Strauch as director.

1929 **Spring** Stalin summons Eisenstein and Alexandrov to discuss weaknesses of *The General Line*.

Apr.–May Additional filming for *The General Line*, now entitled *Old and New*; prepares sound plan for Meisel's work on *Old and New*, sound version to be financed and completed in Berlin or London.

Aug. Eisenstein, Tisse, and Alexandrov sent abroad, with copy of *Old and New*, first to Berlin.

Sept. Attends Congress of Independent Cinema at La Sarraz, Switzerland; visits and speaks in England and Belgium. Assists Tisse in a Swiss production for Lazar Wechsler.

Oct. Public release in Soviet Union of *Old and New*.

Nov. Gives a series of lectures for the Film Society in London. Considers *Man from Darkness*, about Sir Basil Zaharoff, for Paris production.

1930 **Jan.** Paris and tour of France with Moussinac; Netherlands and return to Berlin.

Feb. Gives address at the Sorbonne, but police forbid showing of *Old and New*.

Apr. Discussions and signed contract with Paramount representative Jesse Lasky.

May With Tisse, leaves France for the USA. Alexandrov is left behind to complete *Romance Sentimentale* (rejoins group in June.)

Aug. With Alexandrov and Ivor Montagu, begins preparations to film *Sutter's Gold* (cancelled).

Sept. The three begin work on scenario of Dreiser's *An American Tragedy*.

Oct. Paramount dissolves contract with Eisenstein.

Nov. Signs contract with Mrs. Upton Sinclair to make a film in Mexico.

Dec. Group arrives in Mexico; Mexican government approves film plan.

1931 **Jan.** Films earthquake damage in Oaxaca to add to funds for *Qué Viva México!*

Feb. Filming continues in Tehuantepec, location of the "Sandunga" novella.

Mar. Group inspects Yucatan (for the Prologue) and begins the bullfight episode in Mérida (for *Fiesta*); sketches for a Haitian film, *Black Majesty*, and a *Hamlet* staging.

1931 **Apr.** Group works in Chichén-Itzá and Izamal, Yucatan.

May Rain halts filming; Eisenstein works on his book *Direction*. Arrival at the Hacienda Tetlapayac, location of the "Maguey" novella.

Aug. Group films in Mexico City (for the Epilogue).

Dec. Completes "Maguey" and negotiates with General Calles and President Obregón to use Mexican army for the "Soldadera" novella.

1932 **Jan.** Sinclairs halt production of *Qué Viva México!*

Feb.–Mar. Group leaves Mexico and drives across America to New York.

Apr. Group returns separately to Moscow (Eisenstein on 9 May).

Aug. Begins scenario and casting for comedy MMM.

Oct. Confirmed as head of direction faculty at GIK. Exhibition of his Mexican drawings in New York. Consults on scenarios in Armenia and Georgia. Proposes Moscow staging of *Once in a Lifetime* with Strauch and Glizer. Also prepares staging of Zola's *Thérèse Raquin*.

1933 **Mar.** Begins work on program for teaching theory and practice of film direction at GIK. Writes vol. I of *Direction*.

May Breaking his promise to Eisenstein, Sinclair allows the Mexican footage to be cut and released (27 June 1934) as *Thunder Over Mexico*.

June Works on scenario of *Moscow*.

July In Kislovodsk Sanatorium in seriously depressed condition.

1934 **Mar.** Replies to Goebbels's praise of *Potemkin*.

Apr.–July Prepares to stage Natan Zarkhi's play, *Moscow the Second*.

Sept. Inspects studios at Yalta and Odessa. Discusses filming of *La Condition Humaine* with visiting André Malraux.

Oct. Marriage to Pera Attasheva.

Dec. Discusses with Paul Robeson his new project, a film of the Haitian revolution, *The Black Consul*. Completes draft of *Direction*.

1935 **Jan.** Speaks at First All-Union Conference of Film Workers; is awarded title of Honored Art Worker of the RSFSR.

Mar. Sees performances of Mei Lan-fang's company and films a scene from Mei's repertoire. Begins shooting script of Rzheshevsky's scenario, *Bezhin Meadow*.

May First shots for *Bezhin Meadow* (Prologue).

June To locations on state farm near Sea of Azov and outside Kharkov to film *Bezhin Meadow*.

July Death of Zarkhi ends *Moscow the Second* project.

Oct. Confinement with smallpox and month's quarantine halt shooting of *Bezhin Meadow*.

Dec. Shooting resumed near Mosfilm studios with night scenes.

1936 **Mar.(?)** Shumyatsky asks for revisions in *Bezhin Meadow* script, and Eisenstein works with Isaac Babel on new version.

Apr. Revised "Programme for Teaching the Theory and Practice of Film Direction" published in *Iskusstvo Kino*.

Aug.–Oct. Resumes filming of *Bezhin Meadow* in Crimea with new Babel version of script and new casting.

Nov. Editing of *Bezhin Meadow*.

Dec. Robeson offers to work in *The Black Consul* from July to October of

1937.

1937 **Jan.–Feb.** Shows Lion Feuchtwanger five hours of roughly cut *Bezhin Meadow*; sketches a staging for Feuchtwanger's *The False Nero*.

Mar. Order from Film Committee to cease further production of *Bezhin Meadow*.

Mar.–Apr. Three-day conference on banned film; Vsevolod Vishnevsky sends letter of praise to Eisenstein. Eisenstein publishes "Mistakes of *Bezhin Meadow*" and writes to Stalin; hears Vishnevsky's new scenario, *We, the Russian People*, written for him.

May Rest cure in Kislovodsk, where he is informed that Pyotr Pavlenko has drafted first version of *Rus* (later retitled *Alexander Nevsky*). Makes notes for production of Vishnevsky's untitled scenario on Spain.

Sept. Works with Pavlenko on *Rus*.

Dec. Their scenario published in *Znamya*; Prokofiev agrees to compose score.

1938 **Jan.** Shumyatsky removed as head of Film Committee, replaced by Dukelsky. Eisenstein works on shooting script of *Rus* with Dmitri Vasiliyev and Tisse; brings Konstantin Yeliseyev into its production.

Mar.–May Writes essay "Montage 1938" (later first chapter of *The Film Sense*). First work sessions with Prokofiev.

June Filming of *Alexander Nevsky* begins at Mosfilm and at Pereyeslavl-Zalessky.

July "Battle on the Ice" filmed near Mosfilm Studios.

Oct. Editing of *Alexander Nevsky*.

Nov. Completed film shown to film workers.

Nov.–Dec. Prepares to film *Frunze* (or *Perekop*) on scenario by Fadeyev and Nikulin; public release of *Alexander Nevsky*.

1939 **Feb.** Receives Order of Lenin.

Mar. Awarded title of Doctor of Art Research.

Apr. Organizes his lectures in final version of *Direction*, vol. I.

May Adapts Maupassant's "Mademoiselle Fifi" as *Daughter of France*. With Pavlenko, plans *The Great Ferghana Canal*.

June–July Visits Uzbekistan with Tisse and Pavlenko; invites Prokofiev to compose the *Ferghana* score.

Aug. Works on shooting script with Pavlenko. Signing of German-Soviet Non-Aggression Pact; *Alexander Nevsky* is withdrawn from circulation.

Oct. Plans book *Pushkin and Cinema*. *Ferghana Canal* film is cancelled.

Dec. Bolshoi Theater invites Eisenstein to stage Wagner's *Die Walküre*.

1940 **Feb.** Broadcasts on German program.

Mar. For a Pushkin film, tries a color treatment for one scene of Pushkin's play *Boris Godunov*. Sketches "A First Outline" for the Pushkin film *The Love of a Poet*.

Apr. Begins rehearsals of *Die Walküre* at the Bolshoi. Discusses with Film Committee several projects: *The Beilis Case* (play by Lev Sheinin), *Prestige of an Empire* (a color film on T. E. Lawrence), other subjects for color, the plague in the Middle Ages, and Giordano Bruno.

July–Aug. Writes essay "Vertical Montage" (later chap. 4 of *The Film Sense*). Draws up gloomy accounting of his career.

Oct. Premiere of *Die Walküre* at the Bolshoi. Appointed artistic director of Mosfilm.

1941 **Jan.–Feb.** First production notes for *Ivan Grozny*. Fifteenth anniversary of *Battleship Potemkin*.

Mar. Receives State Prize (1st Class) for the direction of *Alexander Nevsky*.

May Completes first treatment of *Ivan Grozny*.

June German invasion of Soviet Union. Discussion at Mosfilm on new forms for film in the defense effort; Eisenstein proposes short fictional films and offers models from American and English literature.

July Speaks on radio program to America, "To Brother Jews of All the World."

Aug. Joins editorial committee of the "Fighting Film Albums" and plans with Quentin Reynolds a compilation of war newsreels, *Moscow Strikes Back*. Offers essays for *The Film Sense* for American publication.

Oct. Freed from administrative duties at Mosfilm while working on *Ivan Grozny*. With Mosfilm staff, is evacuated to Alma-Ata in the Kazakh Republic.

Nov. Prepares a detailed plan for *Pushkin*.

Dec. Completes literary treatment (for publication in Dec. 1943) of *Ivan Grozny*, now in two parts; sends treatment to Prokofiev with request for his collaboration.

1942 **Jan.–July** Works on shooting script of *Ivan Grozny*.

Apr. Writes to Cherkasov's wife, to persuade him to play the role of Tsar Ivan.

Aug. Publication in New York and London of his first book, *The Film Sense*.

Sept.–Dec. Teaches at evacuated VGIK. Consents to direct Prokofiev's opera *War and Peace*.

1943 **Jan.** Notes his wish to follow *Ivan Grozny* with Dostoyevsky's *Brothers Karamazov*. Works on his book *Method*.

Apr. First filming of *Ivan Grozny* (the Reception Chamber for Parts I and II); the scenario has now been divided into three parts, against the advice of his closest friends; photography now divided between Tisse (exteriors) and Andrei Moskvin (interiors).

June Alexander Korda appeals to Eisenstein and Pudovkin for advice in filming *War and Peace*.

Sept. VGIK returns to Moscow and Eisenstein is temporarily separated from his classes. Completes essay "Charlie the Kid" for inclusion in collection on Chaplin, edited by Eisenstein and Yutkevich for publication in 1945.

1944 **Jan.(?)** Publication of vol. I in series *The World Cinema* on David Wark Griffith, containing essay by Eisenstein.

Jan.–June Filming continues in Alma-Ata on all three parts of *Ivan Grozny*. Continues work on the color experiments for the *Pushkin* film.

June Mosfilm and Eisenstein return to Moscow. Montage completed of *Ivan Grozny*, Part I.

Oct. Finished film submitted to Film Committee.

1945 **Jan.** Public release of Part I, with exhibition of its costumes; continues work on Parts II and III. Moscow conference on color film and his decision to film two reels in color for Part II. Writes "Non-Indifferent Nature" and essay "The Twelve Apostles" for unpublished collection on *Potemkin*.

Aug. Consents to postwar co-production with an American firm of *War and Peace*.

Sept. Receives copies of *Thunder Over Mexico* and *Time in the Sun*.

Oct. Returns to VGIK classes.

1946 **Jan.** Announcement that he has received State Prize (1st Class) for *Ivan Grozny*, Part I. Completes montage of Part II and makes a draft montage of four reels without music for Part III.

Feb. At celebration of prize, suffers severe cardiac infarction and enters Kremlin Hospital.

Feb.–July At Kremlin Hospital, at Barvikha Sanatorium, and at cottage outside Moscow, writes memoirs.

Aug. Publication of condemnation of *Ivan Grozny*, Part II, and destruction of unfinished Part III; works on writings for eventual publication.

Sept. Outlines film for 800th anniversary of city of Moscow.

Oct. Publishes self-criticism of *Ivan Grozny*, Part II.

Nov. Begins his book *Pathos*.

1947 **Jan.** For a proposed four-volume French edition of his writings sends selected typescripts to Armand Panigel.

Feb. Cherkasov and Eisenstein discuss with Stalin and officials the alterations that would make possible the release of *Ivan Grozny*, Part II.

Apr. Project for a ballet of Pushkin's "Pique Dame."

May Research for "Pushkin and Gogol"; decisions for second American book of essays (*Film Form*).

Oct. Initiation of a Cinema Section, to be headed by Eisenstein, within the Academy of Sciences.

Nov. Plans, with Luriya, a joint course at Moscow University on the psychology of art; continues book on direction.

1948 **22 Jan.** Eisenstein's fiftieth birthday.

10 Feb. Dies while writing foreword for a new edition of Kuleshov's textbook on direction.

12 Feb. In his will, Eisenstein leaves his brain to Alexander Luriya.

13 Feb. Buried at Novo-Devichi Cemetery.

This outline is based on a chronology prepared for the Oesterreichisches Filmmuseum's Eisenstein retrospective in 1964. Corrections and additions have been made according to Gosfilmofond's *Sergei Mikhailovich Eisenstein* (Moscow, 1966) and Werner Sudendorf's *Sergej M. Eisenstein: Materialen zu Leben und Werk* (Munich, 1975).

Sources of Documents

Abbreviations Used in Source Notes

Barr Alfred Barr Archive, New York

Berger Collection of Spencer Berger, Connecticut

BFI Collections of the British Film Institute, London

Birman Serafima Birman, *Life's Gift of Encounters*, Moscow, 1959; translated by Margaret Wettlin in *Soviet Literature*, no. 3, 1975

Bolshoi Collections of the Bolshoi Theater Museum, Moscow

Campos Ponce Collection of Lic Xavier Campos Ponce, Mexico; photographs given to Yon Barna

EA Eisenstein Archives at TsGALI (State Archives of Literature and Art) and Eisenstein Kabinet, Moscow

EM Eisenstein Collection, Museum of Modern Art, New York

Goryunov Vasili Goryunov, reminiscences in *Eisenstein in the Memories of His Contemporaries*, Moscow, 1973

Gosfilmofond State Film Archives, Moscow

IM Collection of Mr. and Mrs. Ivor Montagu, Garston, England

Leyda Collection of Jay Leyda, New York

Kadochnikov Pyotr Kadochnikov, reminiscences in *Eisenstein . . . Contemporaries*

Lilly Upton Sinclair Archive at the J. K. Lilly Library, Bloomington, Indiana

MA Meyerhold Archives at TsGALI

MMM Script published in *Iz Istorii Kino*, no. 10, 1977

MoMA Collections of the Museum of Modern Art, New York

Montagu Ivor Montagu, *With Eisenstein in Hollywood*, Berlin/New York, International Publishers Co., 1969

Mosfilm Museum of the Mosfilm Studio, Moscow

Moussinac Léon Moussinac, *Sergei Eisenstein*, translated by D. Sandy Petrey, New York, Crown Publishers, 1970

Nizhny Vladimir Nizhny, *Lessons with Eisenstein*, New York, Hill & Wang, 1962

Prokofiev Sergei Prokofiev, *Sovietskaya muzika*, no. 4, 1961; translated in *Cinema Journal*, fall 1973

SA Maxim Strauch Archives at TsGALI

Selznick *Memo from: David O. Selznick*, ed. Rudy Behlmer, New York, Viking Press, 1972

Seton Marie Seton, *Sergei M. Eisenstein*, New York, Grove Press, 1969

Sovfoto Sovfoto Agency, New York

Viertel Salka Viertel, *The Kindness of Strangers*, New York, Holt, Rinehart & Winston, 1961

Voynow Collection of Mrs. Zina Voynow, New York

Yutkevich Sergei Yutkevich, "Eisenstein, Scene-Painter," introduction to album of Eisenstein's theater designs, Moscow, n.d.

INDEX

ABOUT THE AUTHORS

Jay Leyda, Gottesman Professor of Cinema Studies at New York University, is the author of *KINO: A History of the Russian and Soviet Film*; *The Melville Log: A Documentary Life of Herman Melville*; and *The Years and Hours of Emily Dickinson*, among other books. He has also written countless articles on film and translated three collections of Eisenstein's essays on film theory: *The Film Sense*, *Film Form*, and *Film Essays*.

Zina Voynow, Eisenstein's sister-in-law, is a documentary filmmaker and free-lance film editor. Her documentaries include *My Hands Are the Tools of My Soul* (on American Indian art) and *Henry Moore* (on the British sculptor). She has also made feature films and films for television.

GRAPHICS

The text of this book was set in the film version of Goudy Oldstyle, a typeface designed by Frederic Goudy. The face was first shown in 1914, but was not made available for machine typesetting on the Monotype until 1930. The caption and display typeface is Kabel Ultra Bold, an adaptation to photosetting of the original Kabel created by German type designer Rudolph Koch. The first weight in metal was introduced by the Klingspor foundry in 1927.

This book was photocomposed by Clarinda Company, Clarinda, Iowa.

Printing and binding were done by The Murray Printing Company, Westford, Massachusetts.

Production and manufacturing coordination were directed by Kathy Grasso.

R. D. Scudellari designed the book and directed the graphics.

Book design and layout were styled by Gina Davis.